Beyond Competition

Beyond Competition

The Economics of Mergers and Monopoly Power

Thomas Karier

M.E. Sharpe
Armonk, New York
London, England

Copyright © 1993 by M.E. Sharpe, Inc.

Library of Congress Cataloging-in-Publication Data

Karier, Thomas Mark
Beyond competition: the economics of mergers and
monopoly power / Thomas Karier
p. cm.
Includes bibliographical references and index.
ISBN 1–56324–127–7 (c). — ISBN 1–56324–128–5 (p)
1. Consolidation and merger of corporations. 2. Monopolies.
3. Competition.
I. Title.
HD2746.5.K36 1993
338.8′3—dc20
93–4200
CIP

Printed in the United States of America

The paper used in this publication meets the minimum requirements
of American National Standard for Information Sciences—
Permanence of Paper for Printed Library Materials, ANSI Z39.48–1984

∞

BM (c) 10   9   8   7   6   5   4   3   2   1
BM (p) 10   9   8   7   6   5   4   3   2   1

For

Ester, Marco, Jose, Mirna, and Victor

Contents

Figures and Tables

Figures

Tables

Preface

As economics becomes increasingly fragmented into independent fields, there are at least two unifying concepts: supply and demand, and monopoly power. This is a book about power; one that supplements a strong microeconomic analysis with historical examples and empirical evidence.

Monopoly power is a reccurring theme in economics, forming a bridge between the early writings of Adam Smith and the modern empirical analyses of today. The concept is widely used in industrial relations, trade theory, urban and regional economics, money and banking, and macroeconomics, and it is nearly indispensable for industrial organization, economic history, and microeconomics.

This text offers a comprehensive examination of monopoly power in its many different dimensions. Beginning with its classical origins, the book traces its evolution through Marxist, neoclassical, and post-Keynesian schools. During its formative years, major contributions were made by Abba Lerner, Michal Kalecki, Nicholas Kaldor, Joan Robinson, Edward Chamberlin, Paul Sweezy, Joe Bain, and John Kenneth Galbraith. From there, the book goes on to define monopoly and economic power in relation to markups and profits, thus providing an essential microeconomic foundation.

Other chapters survey the empirical investigations that confirmed the existence of monopoly power and clarified its role in the economy. Firms with monopoly power distinguish themselves in a number of different ways. They tend to have higher markups and profit rates, they are more likely to collude, export, and make foreign investments, and they are less likely to practice prolonged price competition. This book draws heavily on actual corporate behavior to illustrate each of these topics.

One of the strengths of monopoly theory is that it continues to be relevant for understanding current issues. Several of these are described in the book, including the 1980s merger boom, government regulation, executive salaries, trade barriers, corporate PACs, and the issue of competitiveness.

No project like this can be undertaken without help and support.

The Jerome Levy Economics Institute provided generously for this work and I am especially indebted to the director, Dimitri Papadimitriou, for his encouragement and good counsel. The Economic Policy Institute and the Northwest Institute for Advanced Study supported other aspects of my research, essential for several chapters. As far as my own understanding of the issues described in the book, I have especially appreciated my conversations with James Brock, Dave Bunting, William Dickens, Richard Wiles, John Kenneth Galbraith, Lisa Brown, Larry Mishel, and colloquium participants at the Levy Institute, Vassar College, Washington State University, and Eastern Washington University.

Beyond Competition

An Introduction to Corporate Power

The fact is, we find the element of monopoly all about us. . . . "
—John Moody, 1904[1]

It is considerably easier to identify who has economic power than it is to explain exactly what it is. Exxon is obviously endowed with more of it than the local vegetable store; RJR Nabisco has more of it than any local restaurant; and IBM wields more of it than the corner bakery or hairdresser. Individually, most of us have very little of it but we are exposed to it every day through our consumptive habits. In fact it is virtually impossible to avoid firms with economic power if you want to make a telephone call, drive a car, watch television, fly in an airplane, buy gasoline, smoke a cigarette, use a computer, or purchase any number of consumer goods or services.

The names of powerful firms are widely known because of the products they sell. We may know nothing else about the company but we know who produces Coca Cola soft drinks, MacDonald's hamburgers, General Motors cars, Exxon gasoline, Goodyear tires, Kodak film, IBM computers, CBS programs, and Xerox photocopiers. As these companies flood every channel of modern communication with their advertisements, their names are indelibly recorded in the minds of millions of potential customers. The cumulative effect of decades of hard-hitting advertising is that firms with substantial economic power are seldom unknown.

Powerful firms also impress themselves on the public because they are newsworthy. Their mergers, takeovers, or joint ventures are regular features in the business pages of newspapers and magazines. Record profits or executive salaries are allotted time on the daily television or radio news. Considerable airtime is dedicated to giant corporations when they are in financial exigency, seeking concessions from creditors or a bailout from the government.

Even though corporate power may be easy to identify, it remains poorly understood. What is it exactly that these firms have that hundreds of thousands of small businesses do not? Size is obviously one difference but what are the others? How does power originate and for what purpose? How does the behavior of firms depend on their level of power? How does corporate power affect consumer prices, workers' wages, executive compensation, and returns to investors? And finally, what drives these companies and where are they headed? Neither the advertisements nor the news reports are intended to answer these questions. But the answers are essential for understanding the world in which we live.

The Theory of Monopoly and Economic Power

The word *power* is used in economic discourse to mean many different things, but in this text its meaning is precise. *Monopoly power* refers to the degree of practical control that firms have over their prices. For some firms, small changes in prices will result in large changes in the quantity of output that consumers will buy. For all practical purposes, the choice of prices for this firm is rather limited; it has little monopoly power. For other firms, small changes in prices make very little difference in the quantity demanded by consumers. These companies have a much greater practical range of prices to choose from, giving them greater monopoly power. All firms can be distinguished by the quantity of monopoly power they possess.

While monopoly power can improve the potential profitability of a company, it does not guarantee it. In order to discuss the relationship between monopoly power and profits, we need to introduce another concept, *economic power*. This term is defined as the maximum potential profit of a firm. Actual profit and economic power are equivalent only when the firm charges the particular price that maximizes short-run profits. At all other times, economic power merely describes the potential profitability of a firm. Economic power is measured in thousands of dollars for some firms and in billions of dollars for others and is yet another way to distinguish one business from the next.

While monopoly and economic power often coincide, they are not synonymous. It is possible for a smalltown newspaper and a remote gas station to have great monopoly power due to their considerable discretion over prices. But neither enterprise has the capacity to generate short-run profits on a scale necessary to be characterized as a truly great economic power. However, high monopoly and economic power coincide for enough firms that it is useful to refer to these firms as possessing corporate or business power.

Archetypal Firm

Any economic theory of business is based on an archetypal firm, one that serves as a point of reference. For example, in Adam Smith's theory of competition, the archetypal firm is assumed to be relatively small and to face many competitors producing exactly the same product. All decisions of the firm are derived from the strategy of maximizing short-run profits. As much as the firm would like to charge a higher price, it is prevented by the presence of many identical rivals, each charging low prices. The firm is compelled to maintain product quality and reduce production costs for the simple reason that it fears others are doing the same. Whoever falls behind will fail. Despite these intense fears, very little is expected to change over time as the firm remains relatively small and continues competing under remarkably constant conditions. Both its fear of failure and its hope for dominance seldom come to fruition.

The archetypal firm in the theory of monopoly power is considerably different. The firm that eventually attains power may have a humble origin, beginning with only a new invention. The firm obtains a patent for the product but nevertheless confronts rivals with similar products and similar ambitions. Although there are no perfect substitutes, there are initially too many producers of imperfect substitutes to be ignored. Taken together, the combination of substitute products constitutes a market.

Each of these rivals aspires to become the largest seller in the market. What follows is a period of competition with low prices and high expenditures for marketing and promotion. Each rival willingly forgoes current profits in order to achieve market dominance. Gradually, a firm emerges from the pack, increasing its market share while expanding into more and more geographically distinct markets. To accelerate the process it acquires a few of its competitors. As the firm expands, production and sales are concentrated in larger, more efficient factories, offices, and stores. Product promotion becomes more systematic and centralized, sales forces are trained and assigned to new markets, and advertising campaigns are tested and unleashed on a national scale.

Eventually the firm reaches a point where its desire for even greater market share in the national market begins to recede. Continued price competition or the acquisition of yet another rival runs the danger of stirring up antitrust regulators or inciting a backlash of public opinion. Consequently prices are allowed to gradually increase, gravitating toward the point that maximizes short-run profits. As the firm begins to abandon price competition, it also comes to rely more on advertising and R&D expenditures to compete for market share. Profits escalate and executives are rewarded with ever-increasing salaries and bonuses. The firm is also forced to share some of the surplus with workers, either involuntarily under a union contract or voluntarily as a way to avoid unions.

During this time, foreign markets become increasingly attractive to the firm. Expansion can continue in this arena without fear of spawning antitrust investigations or, at least initially, aggravating public hostilities against monopoly. Low prices and strong promotion efforts are combined to win greater shares of foreign markets. While much of this early growth is accomplished by means of exports, the firm eventually finds it necessary to meet further expansion with foreign production. This requires the firm to develop foreign operations or buy foreign enterprises.

While price competition is suppressed and short-run profits are at a maximum, the firm comes to appreciate the benefits of cooperative pricing. By either following the lead of a market leader or explicitly coordinating prices among rivals, the firm enhances its already substantial profits. In making the decision to price cooperatively, the firm has already weighed the probability of exposure against the expectation of greater profits.

Much of the economic surplus generated by the firm is distributed among investors, managers, and workers, but there is often enough left to finance additional research and development, real investments in plant and capacity, and additional acquisitions of direct rivals or even totally unrelated firms. By supporting these expenditures, the firm attempts to maintain its growth and market share.

Even during long periods of prosperity, there is always the danger of renewed competition. Patents may expire, new technologies may develop, consumer tastes may change, protective government regulation may be revoked, or late entrants may attain a size and level of efficiency necessary to challenge established leaders. Competition can break out among national or international rivals whenever aspirations for greater market shares can no longer be suppressed.

When competition reemerges, it is seldom in the exact same form as competition that originally gave rise to power. Competition in the age of monopoly is a battle of titans rather than a skirmish of ants. Rivals with substantial size and power have much better credit to sustain them during competition and they have more opportunities to gain support from national governments during battles with foreign rivals. But like the earlier competition, each contestant aspires to preserve and advance its national and international position.

Not all firms correspond to this archetype any more than all firms correspond to the archetype of perfect competition. But aspects of this description apply to a great number of firms that today dominate the economic landscape. What is it that makes these firms different from the small, local businesses, the ones lacking national and even regional significance? The answer is monopoly and economic power: the topic of this book.

Organization of the Book

The contents of this book describe the accumulation and exercise of power and are intended to provide the background necessary to understand corporate behavior. What follows is essentially a new theory, one that attempts to synthesize many of the contributions of earlier scholars and fill in the gaps wherever they occur. In order to give due credit to the originators of particular ideas, the next chapter is devoted entirely to describing the work of these early theorists. From Adam Smith to Karl Marx, from post-Keynesians to neoclassical economists, a wide range of thinkers have left their mark on what constitutes power and how it is exercised. As you will see, the theory of monopoly power is distilled from the ideas of many great and diverse economists. Because monopoly and economic power are so essential to understanding the behavior of large enterprises, Chapter 3 provides more detailed definitions and analyses of these terms. The fundamentals of monopoly theory described in that chapter constitute more than idle theory. A great number of statistical studies have attempted to identify the existence of monopoly power and some of these early studies are reviewed in Chapter 4.

Unions have long been understood to divert profits from powerful corporations to workers and a model of this behavior is presented in Chapter 5. But this topic raises the more general question of how firms respond to rising costs, which is explored in Chapter 6. The statistical evidence that unions actually do capture a share of the profits associated with economic power is reviewed in Chapter 7.

The next three chapters, 8, 9, and 10, analyze the role of power in various forms of corporate behavior. In order to maintain growth and profits, firms can choose among several different strategies including price and nonprice competition, cooperation, and mergers and acquisitions. But which choice a firm makes depends on power: its own and that of its rivals. Power is also important in foreign expansion, covered in Chapter 11, and in government functions, described in Chapter 12.

Finally, the present circumstances that determine the evolution of power also lay the foundation for the next economic order. Are we entering a permanent state of heightened international competition or is this merely the transition to a higher level of corporate power, one that is exercised on a global scale? This topic is left for the final chapter.

2

The History of Monopoly Theory

*We have only to take the word monopoly in its literal
sense, a single seller, and the analysis of monopoly
immediately swallows up the analysis of competition.*
—Joan Robinson, 1933[1]

Economic theories, like economies themselves, undergo their own
unique historical development. Many distinguished economists have
left their mark on monopoly theory as it progressed from the rough
outline sketched by Adam Smith to the precise formulations of modern
theorists. And like economic growth, the evolution of monopoly theory
can be characterized by periods of relative inactivity interspersed with
sudden and remarkable advances. In fact, the correspondence between
the real economy and economic theory is more than just an analogy.
Economists generally rework old theories or invent new ones in response to new developments or trends. It is hardly a coincidence that
monopoly theory experienced its most rapid development only after
the massive U.S. merger movement at the turn of the century and the
equally impressive round of mergers during the 1920s.

The concept of monopoly power runs through nearly all schools of
thought from the classical economists to the modern post-Keynesians,
playing a central role in some and amounting to nothing more than a
footnote in others. What follows is by no means an attempt to recount
all of these theories, which would undoubtedly fill volumes of unin-
spired reading. My more modest objective is to focus on the contributions of the relatively few scholars who had particular influence on the
modern theory of monopoly power.

The Classical Roots

A good portion of Adam Smith's *Wealth of Nations* was dedicated to attacking government-sanctioned monopoly. As early as 1776, when the book was first published, it was possible to discern certain negative attributes of firms granted the exclusive right to trade in a particular commodity or with a particular region. "The monopolists, by keeping the market constantly under-stocked, by never fully supplying the effectual demand, sell their commodities much above the natural prices, and raise their emoluments, whether they consist in wages or profit, greatly above their natural rate."[2] The monopoly villains in Smith's day were the trading companies, including the notorious East India Company. Smith concluded, "Such exclusive companies, therefore, are nuisances in every respect; always more or less inconvenient to the countries in which they are established, and destructive to those which have the misfortune to fall under their government."[3]

The *Wealth of Nations* owes much of its popularity to the fact that it is more of an archaeological treasure than a mere economic treatise. Generations of scholars have chipped away at its pages only to discover the rudiments of modern theories, and the case of monopoly profits is no exception. For example, a debate erupted in the 1980s over the question of whether unions receive a share of monopoly profits. Two hundred years earlier, Smith was convinced that wages tend to be higher under monopoly. He stated that monopolies "keep up the market price of particular commodities above the natural price, and maintain both the wages of the laborer and the profits of the stock employed about them somewhat above their natural rate."[4] With the aid of sophisticated statistical methods, modern research has generally arrived at the same conclusion: unionized employees benefit from monopoly power by capturing a share of monopoly profits.

While Smith's invective was principally reserved for monopolies created by mercantilist governments, he nevertheless paused long enough to acknowledge the tendency for collusion among individual private competitors. In a now famous quote that captures both his eloquence and his understatement, Smith claimed that "People of the same trade seldom meet together, even for merriment and diversion, but the conversation ends in a conspiracy against the public, or in some contrivance to raise prices."[5] As provocative as this statement is, Smith chose not to pursue the implications of it in the *Wealth of Nations*.

After all, if collusion or monopoly can arise spontaneously even without government sanctions, it could conceivably undermine the ideal of competitive efficiency that Smith labored so long to construct.

Where Adam Smith was the astute observer with a penchant for the entrepreneur, Karl Marx was the bellicose theoretician whose loyalties laid firmly with the working class. And as an observer of the evolving capitalist system, Marx was every bit a match for Smith. A fundamental characteristic of capitalism, according to Marx, is the overwhelming drive for capital accumulation. By means of reinvestment (which Marx called concentration) and mergers and acquisitions (which he referred to as centralization), private businesses in Marx's day were already expanding rapidly and controlling ever-increasing amounts of capital and labor. Marx left little doubt that he viewed this development as a natural component of the generally odious character of evolving capitalism. "Along with the constantly diminishing number of magnates of capital, who usurp and monopolize all advantages of this process of transformation, grows the mass of misery, oppression, slavery, degradation, exploitation. . . ."[6]

In addition to observing the natural tendency toward centralization, Marx recognized that this form of accumulation was not conducted by genteel means. He described the process as an "expropriation of many capitalists by few" and concluded that "one capitalist always kills many."[7] In a sense, he anticipated the methods of John D. Rockefeller, J. P. Morgan, Jay Gould, and other capitalists in their quest for economic power.

Like Smith, Marx devoted relatively little attention to analyzing the qualitative character of monopoly. This is hardly a fault since the process of centralization was just getting under way in Marx's day while competition still reigned supreme. However, in a particularly prescient passage, Marx observed that competition contained the seed of future centralization. "The smallest capitals, therefore, crowd into spheres of production which Modern Industry has only sporadically or incompletely got hold of. Here competition rages in direct proportion to the number, and in inverse proportion to the magnitudes, of the antagonistic capitals, whose capitals partly pass into the hand of their conquerors, partly vanish."[8] With this colorful prose Marx outlined the fundamental relationship between competition and the evolution of monopoly power. The presence of many small firms serves to heighten the level of competition that ultimately leads to their own demise.

Very few important contributions were made to the theory of monopoly following Smith and Marx until the resurgence of interest during the economic renaissance of the 1930s. With the notable exception of Thorstein Veblen, the intervening years were dominated by marginalist economists with an almost exclusive affinity for models of perfect competition. It is perhaps ironic that during the period from 1880 to 1930, when the theory of monopoly was suffering from such a period of drought, the real thing was flourishing in the form of trusts, holding companies, cartels, mergers, and consolidations.

The 1930s Renaissance

The 1930s ushered in a period of new ideas for economics in general and for monopoly theory in particular. Joan Robinson and Edward Chamberlin, in separate efforts, analyzed the behavior of monopolists under assumptions of profit maximization. By using marginalist tools and cleverly altering the assumptions of perfect competition they were able to show that monopolies maximize profits by reducing output and raising prices. At least this aspect of their work was anticipated by Smith more than 150 years earlier, but because they used marginal analysis, they received sufficient recognition to bring monopoly theory out of the eddies if not quite into the mainstream.

The real innovation in the Chamberlin/Robinson monopoly model was the idea that demand and marginal revenue curves for a monopolist slope downward. Firms can only sell more by reducing their price, which in turn reduces marginal revenue, the additional revenue of selling one more unit. Figure 2.1 presents the standard monopoly model. Firms maximize profits at output q^* where marginal revenue equals marginal costs, the additional cost of producing one more unit. Beyond this level of output, total profits decline because the cost of producing one more unit (marginal cost) exceeds the revenue from that unit (marginal revenue). Given that the profit-maximizing firm will produce q^*, the highest price that it can charge is p^*, the monopoly price.

While this simple model may not seem revolutionary, it managed to disturb a generation of economists who were taught to equate free markets with perfect competition. Few of the desirable properties attributed to the model of perfect competition—low costs, prices, and profits—applied to monopolies. Defenders of laissez-faire who had

Figure 2.1. **The Standard Monopoly Model**

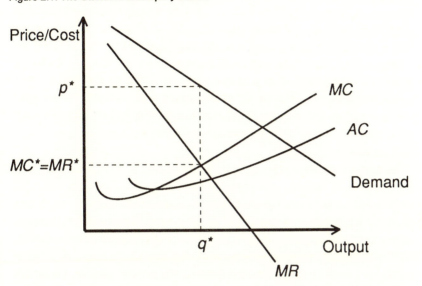

devoted themselves to demonstrating the theoretical efficiencies of perfect competition now faced a much more difficult task, to show that unregulated markets were in fact competitive.

Compared to Robinson, Chamberlin was clearly more cautious about breaking from the neoclassical tradition. In his theory of monopolistic competition, Chamberlin was willing to drop one unrealistic assumption, each firm competes against a multitude of identical producers, but was unwilling to part with an equally unrealistic one, free entry. Dropping the first assumption allowed firms to make monopoly profits but retaining the second assumption caused profits to gradually vanish. It was a familiar argument; other firms entered the market, attracted by monopoly profits, until these gains were eliminated.

Kaldor responded by showing how the simple assumption of "economies of scale" was sufficient to interrupt the free flow of competitors.[9] When economies of scale are high, a single new entrant contributes such a large increase in output as to cause a significant reduction in demand and profits for existing firms as well as the prospective entrant. An example would be a market that can accommodate nine producers profitably but not ten. Since the tenth firm does not enter the market, the first nine firms capture higher profits. From Kaldor's perspective the problem was one of "indivisibility," because half a firm cannot enter efficiently under economies of scale.[10] Today we would describe Kaldor's example as a barrier to entry associated with scale economies. Once the assumption of free entry was eliminated, firms were free to make profits indefinitely.

In a sense, one of Chamberlin's contributions was to shift the focus from price competition among firms already in the market to potential competition by outsiders. Also, by recognizing the existence of product differentiation, Chamberlin helped to break the logjam created by the assumption of many identical producers, one frequently violated in the real economy.

Robinson's work of the same period was similar in many respects to Chamberlin's, but she was perhaps more successful in describing the real world as it exists between pure monopoly on the one hand and perfect competition on the other. According to Robinson, the critical factor that determines a firm's place on a continuum between these two extremes is demand. Firms with flat demand curves of infinite elasticity are completely devoid of power since they have no discretion over prices.[11] Only those firms with downward sloping demand curves have any real choice about what price to charge. This particular relationship made demand a useful barometer of monopoly power; when demand elasticity was high, monopoly power was low and vice versa.

There is another reason why monopoly power should be defined in relation to demand elasticity. To claim that a firm has significant monopoly power implies that there are few good substitutes for the good or service that it sells. And as Robinson pointed out, "elasticity will depend upon many factors, of which the chief are the number of the other firms selling the same commodity and the degree to which substitution is possible."[12] In other words, it made little difference whether monopoly power was defined in relation to demand elasticity or the degree of substitution, because the two concepts were for all practical purposes interchangeable.

While Robinson never formally advocated defining monopoly power in terms of the demand elasticity, her work appeared headed in that direction. But before any concrete steps were taken, a direct proposal arose as to how monopoly power should be defined. Both Robinson and Chamberlin showed that prices exceed marginal costs under monopoly, which Abba Lerner transformed into a theoretical measure of monopoly power. The Lerner Index was defined as the relative difference between price and marginal cost.[13]

(2.1)
$$Lerner\ Index = \frac{Price - Marginal\ Cost}{Price}$$

Since price equals marginal cost under conditions of perfect competition and exceeds it under monopoly, Lerner proclaimed this index to be a promising measure of monopoly power.

The Lerner Index may have remained an appealing but impractical theoretical measure if it hadn't been rescued by Polish economist Michal Kalecki. The major shortcoming of the Lerner Index was a practical one: marginal cost, the additional cost of producing one more unit, is virtually never measured in the real world. Kalecki, however, argued that average variable cost was a close and practical approximation for marginal cost. It can be proven mathematically that marginal and average variable cost are exactly equal when excess capacity allows firms to increase production without any change in unit costs.[14] Chronic overcapacity, Kalecki argued, was characteristic of most modern industries and so it was reasonable to assume marginal and average variable costs were equal. This was the original justification for substituting average variable cost into the Lerner Index, although later Kalecki was able to cite empirical studies vindicating his position.[15]

The advantage of average variable cost is that the data necessary to calculate it are routinely available for most businesses and industries. Kalecki was able to collect some of this aggregated data to show how changes in his modified Lerner Index affected other macroeconomic variables such as the distribution of income.[16]

In retrospect, Kalecki's decision to adopt the Lerner Index rather than the inverse demand elasticity as the definition of monopoly power provoked considerable controversy. Although the inverse demand elasticity and the Lerner Index are equal under certain conditions, they are by no means interchangeable. The inverse demand elasticity determines the particular value of the Lerner Index that maximizes short-run or current profits. In practice, there are enough instances where the firm does not maximize short-run profits to justify treating the two as separate entities.

For example, firms do not maximize short-run profits when they are concerned about the effect of current prices on future demand and future profits. It is not uncommon for firms to cut current prices in order to force certain rivals into bankruptcy. This behavior reveals a clear preference for future profits as opposed to current ones. Lerner provided several other examples in his 1934 article of firms failing to maximize current profits, including the desire to "avoid political opposition or the entry of new competitors."[17]

Once it is clear that firms do not always maximize current profits then it should also be clear that the inverse demand elasticity and the Lerner Index are not equivalent. This leads to the question that faced Lerner in 1934: which one is a better measure of monopoly power? In weighing the choices, Lerner described his index as a measure of monopoly "in force" as compared to "potential monopoly" represented by the inverse demand elasticity. If a firm has a low demand elasticity but fails to exploit it by raising its price relative to costs, does it still have monopoly power? Lerner's answer was unambiguous: "The unused monopoly power will be there, but being unknown and unused it is, economically, as if it were not there."[18] Consequently, Lerner opted for the definition of monopoly power "in force."

The problem this created did not become apparent until Kalecki chose a variation of the Lerner Index as his measure of monopoly power. Kalecki defined monopoly power as the markup over average variable costs and demonstrated mathematically that it was related to an economy-wide profit rate. Critics and supporters alike complained that it was a tautology since the markup over average variable costs—Kalecki's degree of monopoly power—was by definition related to profits.[19]

This controversy illustrates the problem with the concept of monopoly power "in force." Advocates of monopoly theory were expected to demonstrate how monopoly power causes higher markups and profits. Lerner and Kalecki skipped this important step by simply defining monopoly power as a markup over marginal costs (Lerner) or average variable costs (Kalecki). Most critics and even many advocates of monopoly theory objected, forcing Kalecki to reconsider his position. In 1969, he conceded that the index merely "reflects" rather than defines the degree of monopoly.[20]

Additional research beginning in the 1950s resolved some but not all of these issues. First, Kalecki's version of the Lerner Index was treated as a simple markup and renamed the price–cost margin (PCM). While not exactly equivalent to either the Lerner Index or the profit rate, it is obviously a close relation. Second, industrial concentration and advertising were used to reflect monopoly power, a modification that appeared to placate many critics. Finally, empirical evidence supported Kalecki by demonstrating that concentration and advertising had positive effects on PCMs.

If concentration, advertising, and the Lerner Index all merely "reflect" monopoly power, then the question remains: what is monopoly power? To answer this, one must return to Lerner's choice in 1934. If he had chosen the alternate definition, the inverse demand elasticity, many of these debates could have been avoided. Monopoly power, as it is generally perceived, corresponds most closely to the inverse demand elasticity because both depend on the availability of substitutes. Furthermore, nothing would have prevented Kalecki from using price–cost margins to "reflect" monopoly power while defining monopoly power as the inverse elasticity.

Any criticism of Lerner and Kalecki for their definitions should be considered in the context of the important and lasting contributions made by these early pioneers. Lerner provided a valuable discussion of the relationship between the inverse demand elasticity and his index. Kalecki extended this line of thought by deriving the relationship between the Lerner Index and the prevailing profit rate in the economy. These were all important pieces to a puzzle that ultimately linked a micro-measure of monopoly power to the macro-distribution of income.

Market Behavior

Perhaps the most nagging question facing these early theorists was the question of interdependence or what is often referred to as oligopoly behavior. Robinson addressed this problem in 1934 when she wrote, "a certain difficulty arises from the fact that the individual demand curve for the product of each of the firms composing it will depend to some extent upon the price policy of the others."[21] Her solution at the time was to assert that the behavior of rivals could be incorporated into the firm's demand curve.[22] In her own retrospective published in 1978, Robinson confessed that "the reason oligopoly is neglected in the *Economics of Imperfect Competition* is not that I thought it unimportant, but that I could not solve it. I tried to fence it off by means of what unfortunately was a fudge in the definition of the individual demand curve."[23]

Kalecki's solution to the problem was to expand the determinants of the markup to include "a weighted average price of all firms," including the firm in question.[24] In this formulation, a firm's price is directly proportional to the average price of its potential rivals. But an average price is only meaningful if all firms produce identical products, which is a considerable retreat from the differentiated products of Chamberlin and Robinson. Kalecki's approach to oligopoly may have been less evasive than Robinson's, but it involved no less of a fudge.

The dilemma could be traced to the fact that the monopoly model produces unambiguous results only as long as the prices of other firms in the market are assumed to be constant. This was a reasonable first step but none of the early theorists were prepared to take the second step and include the actions of other firms in the market. There was, however, interest in the related question of what constitutes a market when conditions deviate from perfect competition. Markets are a simple matter when firms are assumed to produce identical products, but when they all produce different products it is not clear where a market begins or ends.

It was on this topic that Robinson and Kaldor made important contributions. Robinson began by defining a market as a "chain of substitutes" separated from other products by a "marked gap" in substitutability.[25] This is a pragmatic definition and describes the way most economists today think about markets for empirical studies. Since products are not identical, the best one can do is to group a "chain of substitutes" and hope that there is a "marked gap" between this group and the next.

As useful as this definition is, Kaldor rejected it for the sake of one that was more theoretically pure. In Robinson's version, the careful observer merely ropes off a group of related firms and calls it a market but for Kaldor a market only makes sense from the perspective of a particular firm.[26] Starting with any one firm, you can place all of its closest substitutes at a distance proportional to its degree of substitutability, but the resulting market is likely to depend on which firm you started with. Kaldor correctly pointed out that frame of reference becomes critical since each firm may perceive a slightly different market than its rivals. Once products are assumed to be "more or less different," the convenient fiction of absolute markets vanishes. Where Robinson offered a practical definition useful for empirical work, Kaldor provided a theoretically consistent one.

Oligopoly Theory

Following the rediscovery of monopoly in the 1930s, interest naturally gravitated back to the unanswered question of interdependent behavior. How will other firms in a market react when one changes its price? A major catalyst for answering this theoretical question was provided by Gardiner Means, who in 1935 observed an inconsistency in price changes during the depression.[27] It appeared that prices did not fall nearly as much in concentrated industries compared with un-concentrated ones. In a remarkable coincidence, a team of British economists, R. L. Hall and C. J. Hitch, and a lone American Marxist, Paul Sweezy, arrived nearly simultaneously at the same explanation in 1939.[28] According to their theories, rivals within an oligopoly will follow price cuts but not price increases. This type of behavior gives rise to the "kinked demand" curve and explains a good deal of price rigidity in markets with only a few producers, commonly referred to as *oligopoly*.

The kinked demand model is illustrated in Figure 2.2. Total output for this firm is q^*, which sells at price p^*. If price were raised above p^*, rivals would hold their prices constant, resulting in a large decrease in the quantity demanded. Output would fall below the profit-maximizing point because marginal revenue exceeds marginal cost. However, if the firm reduces its price below p^*, other firms automatically cut their prices, thus allowing the firm only a small increase in output. This time output exceeds the profit-maximizing point because marginal cost exceeds marginal revenue. Consequently, the firm is unlikely to change its price from p^* because a movement in either direction results in lower profits.

With the invention of the kinked demand curve price competition was no longer assumed to be a ubiquitous feature of all markets but rather a destabilizing condition most firms wished to avoid. In this respect, the model represented a substantial improvement over earlier models of perfect competition. But the simplicity of the kinked de-mand model, which accounts for its enduring popularity, is also the source of several deficiencies. One problem is that it tends to exagger-ate the risk of general price competition following a price cut by a single firm. Price cuts in this model automatically erupt into price competition, which certainly doesn't apply to all firms in all oligopoly markets. For example, the smallest firms within an oligopoly have a much greater chance of cutting prices without precipitating price com-petition than industry leaders.

The kinked demand model is perhaps least compelling when it comes to price increases. In this situation, firms that are uncompromis-ing in their opposition to price cuts are equally adamant in their refusal

Figure 2.2. **The Kinked Demand Model**

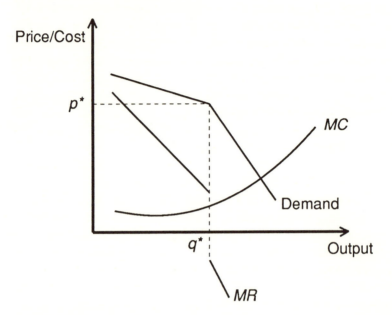

to follow price increases. This type of behavior is plausible when firms are currently maximizing their collective profits because then a price change in any direction must result in a loss. But short of this condition, there are numerous reasons why firms would want to and actually do follow price increases. These include upturns in the business cycle, outright collusion, and price leadership.

Although the kinked demand model made a significant contribution to the question of interdependent behavior, its subsequent development has been a disappointment. It only explained why prices are rigid but not how they are determined. Over the years it has seen few improvements, continuing to be reproduced in most introductory microeconomics texts in almost its original form. Countless students have been forced to memorize that price cuts are mimicked but price hikes are not as if it were some natural law of oligopoly.

For his part, Sweezy did correct some of these deficiencies by the 1960s when he published *Monopoly Capital* with Paul Baran. After discussing price leadership and tacit collusion, these authors concluded that there was less resistance to price increases than to price cuts. "Under oligopoly, in other words, prices tend to be stickier on the downside than on the upward side."[29] They further qualified their position on price competition by acknowledging that while it "is normally taboo in oligopolistic situations, this does not mean that it is totally excluded or that it never plays a role."[30] They went on to describe one of these conditions as the presence of an exceptionally low-cost producer with ambitions to gain market share. But these amendments, as sound as they were, never received the attention given the original, overly simplistic kinked demand curve.

Barriers to Entry

The theorists of the 1930s were careful to distinguish between competition among firms within a market and competition from new entrants. The number of good substitutes within a market determined monopoly power while the potential for new entrants determined barriers to entry. According to this distinction monopoly power could coincide with either low barriers as in Chamberlin's theory, or high barriers as in Robinson's. The lesson drawn from comparing the two was that monopoly power had lasting value only when accompanied by barriers to entry.

As early as 1934 Kaldor identified two entry barriers that could discourage potential entrants: scarce inputs and economies to scale. Kaldor successfully showed how these factors allowed firms with monopoly power to sustain long-run profitability. But many questions remained: what constitutes an entry barrier? How are barriers related to monopoly power? And what are the economic effects of barriers? Discussion of these questions could have rapidly degenerated into a quagmire of conflicting opinions if not for the exhaustive analysis provided in 1965 by Joe Bain in *Barriers to New Competition*.

In order to understand Bain's definition of barriers to entry, it helps to recall a proposition of perfect competition: firms will be inclined to enter a market with free entry until profits are eliminated and prices equal average costs. It was a logical step then to define barriers to entry as "the extent to which established sellers persistently raise their prices above a competitive level [minimum average cost] without attracting new firms to enter the industry."[31] One could quibble over numerous details but the basic premise is sound: barriers deter firms from entering an industry even when established firms are relatively profitable.

Bain assigned barriers to one of three major categories: absolute advantage, product differentiation, and economies to scale. Established firms have absolute advantages when they have unique access to some factors essential for production. These factors can be industry-specific, such as a rare material input or production techniques protected by patents or secrets. In other cases it may be something as common as credit, which established firms can sometimes obtain with lower interest charges. In general, barriers exist whenever access to these elements are better or cheaper for established firms than for new entrants.

Product differentiation also gives established firms an advantage for the simple reason that consumers traditionally prefer familiar brand names. As a result, new entrants are often compelled to charge lower prices than established firms even when products are virtually identical. New firms may find themselves at an additional disadvantage when product differentiation is enforced by patents, making it illegal to imitate certain product designs.

In some industries entry can be undertaken efficiently only on a very large scale. This may occur when large production runs are more efficient or when large firms wield more bargaining power in contracting with suppliers. Economies also arise in marketing because advertising and sales promotion are often more efficient on a large scale. Whatever their origin, economies to scale can constitute a barrier by reducing the field of prospective entrants. Also, when large-scale production is essential, the new entrant must consider the effect of entry on prices. A sharp increase in market production could depress demand and prices for each firm including the new entrant.

After describing each of these impediments to new competitors, Bain proceeded to estimate the relative height of barriers for twenty manufacturing industries. To no one's surprise, the results of his meticulous survey showed a close correspondence between barriers and concentration. For example, automobiles, cigarettes, and tractors had relatively high entry barriers and high concentration compared with shoes, cement, and canned fruits and vegetables, where both measures were either moderate or low. The implication was that barriers allowed firms to protect their monopoly power from potential entrants.

The correspondence between barriers and concentration was strong but not perfect, allowing Bain to compare the profit rates of industries with varying degrees of both. He concluded that either concentration or barriers could produce high profits—independently of the other—but the most profitable industries were consistently the ones with significant levels of both. Monopoly power was necessary to reduce competition within the market but barriers were necessary to prevent an influx of new competitors.

In order to appreciate the importance of barriers to entry it is important to remember that monopolists were able to generate profits, but without protection from new entrants, these profits were ephemeral. Only with barriers to entry did monopoly power have any reasonable chance of influencing prices and profits over a longer term.

Once again, innovations in monopoly theory were only responding to developments that had become increasingly apparent in the real economy. Barriers to entry were necessary to explain the apparent ability of large firms to exercise a high degree of control over prices and profits for long periods of time. General Motors, U.S. Steel, International Harvester, and Exxon were far from the temporary phenomena predicted by monopolistic competition. The recognition of barriers was thus an important breakthrough in the evolving theory of monopoly power.

Labor Unions

From the 1930s to the 1950s, monopoly theory made great progress; a mechanism was discovered for creating monopoly profits, measures of monopoly power were developed, more realistic definitions of markets were devised, the difficult question of interdependent behavior had been broached, and the concept of barriers to entry had been introduced. But events in the real economy were once again racing ahead of the accomplishments made in economic theory. This time it was the phenomenal growth of trade unions in the United States; no longer the courageous underdog of the depression era, trade unions had matured into formidable adversaries for many of the country's most powerful corporations. The steel industry now included U.S. Steel and the United Steel Workers of America just as the automobile industry included both General Motors and the United Automobile Workers.

These developments undoubtedly induced Kalecki to include unions in his pricing model by 1954. According to Kalecki, a firm could not continue to pass on union wage gains without eliciting "new demands for wage increases" and eventually settling on a "policy of lower profit margins."[32] But the most popular expression of these ideas came in 1952 from John Kenneth Galbraith's theory of countervailing power described in his book *American Capitalism*. By this time it was acceptable to assume monopolistic tendencies in big business and Galbraith firmly placed the contest between unions and business within this context. The excesses manifested by big business created both a need and motivation for trade unions, a countervailing power.

In Galbraith's theory, corporations had no one to blame but themselves for the fact that labor was organized and militant. Monopoly profits were like salt in the wounds of industrial labor, adding to the unrest that skillful union organizers translated into expanding membership. As evidence, one has to look no further than the campaigns of the Congress of Industrial Organizations in the 1930s, which exploited the vast difference between the fortunes of the owners and the extreme hardships endured by industrial labor.

Since the 1950s, countervailing power has had both a political and economic dimension. In the political arena, unions have generally been occupied with defending prior gains rather than pursuing any expansion of labor rights. The corporate side was more successful in rolling back these rights in the 1980s, primarily through pro-business appointees to the National Labor Relations Board and other antiunion policies of the executive branch. But the fact that both unions and corporations found it more difficult to pursue their own political agendas is exactly what is implied by the term *countervailing*.

In the economic sphere, however, the relationship between labor and management was both adversarial and synergistic. Unions were intent on ensuring that the monopoly surplus was distributed more equitably, which presupposed that corporations would continue to exercise control over their markets. The point of contention has been how to divide the surplus, not whether the surplus should exist. Consequently, there was little danger that the AFL-CIO would make antitrust a focus of its political agenda as long as it continued to receive a share of monopoly profits.

Like most economic concepts, the idea that unions capture a share of monopoly profits had become familiar in public discourse long before it was derived theoretically. One would expect union wage gains to push up marginal costs and squeeze monopoly profits, but what is the exact relationship?

A particularly simple solution was developed by Daniel McFadden and Melvyn Fuss (1978), a pair of mathematical economists whose major avocation consisted of translating competitive theories into mathematical formulas. As an offshoot of their work, however, they derived the effect of a wage increase on profits under monopoly conditions. The result showed that the decrease in profits ($\Delta\pi$) was proportional to the amount of labor (L) multiplied by the increase in the wage (Δw).[33] Or,

(2.2) $-\Delta\pi \simeq L\,\Delta w$

Although this equation is deceptively simple, it contains a very important implication. In response to slightly higher wages, a monopoly can reduce output, raise prices, and substitute other factors, and the decrease in profits is still proportional to the amount of labor times the wage increase.

The meaning of this equation is illustrated in relation to the monopolist's demand curve for labor in Figure 2.3. The area of the shaded rectangle in the figure is equal to the amount of labor (L) multiplied by the wage change (Δw) and according to (2.2) this must equal the decrease in monopoly profits. This area, defined as the change in employer surplus, is a direct measure of monopoly profits lost to unions.[34]

Conclusion

This concludes the long sweep of monopoly theory from the perceptive ramblings of Adam Smith to the esoteric precision of modern-day mathematical economists. This was by no means a comprehensive exploration but rather a search for the roots of monopoly theory as presented in this text. In some cases, ideas were discovered in isolation, disconnected from the larger context of monopoly theory. The kinked demand curve, for example, was never successfully incorporated into the broader theory of monopoly power. In other cases, debates pointed in a certain direction but stopped short of reaching a clear resolution. Much of the progress made in defining monopoly power and oligopoly markets served to eliminate alternatives rather than establish mutually agreed-upon conclusions. But in each case, these ideas and the debates they engendered provided the raw material for constructing a modern theory of monopoly power.

Perhaps one of the most remarkable aspects about monopoly theory is its eclectic origin. Although theorists later identified with the post-

Figure 2.3. **Loss of Monopoly Profits**

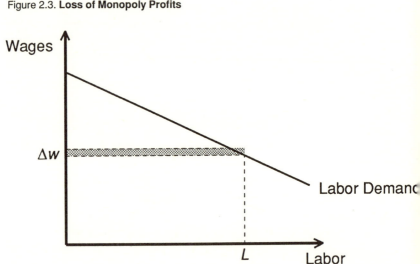

Keynesian tradition played a central role in the early development of this theory, important contributions were also made by economists associated with other leading schools of thought, including classical, Marxist, and neoclassical.

3

The Microeconomics of Power

"Competition" and "monopoly" are not polar opposites but integral parts of one competitive process that leads to concentration of power resources in a few hands. . . . competition weeds out many firms and leaves others in positions of greater leverage.
—Richard Du Boff, 1989[1]

During the 1930s, a number of distinguished economists attempted to inject the concept of monopoly power into the conventional theory of the firm. These pathbreaking efforts led by Chamberlin, Robinson, Lerner, Kaldor, and Kalecki provided valuable tools for economists investigating the behavior of particular firms and industries. But like many new ideas they also met with strong resistance, in this case from academics trained in the older theory of perfect competition. Monopoly theory not only contradicted many of the principal results of perfect competition but raised important objections about the efficiency of laissez-faire capitalism itself.

While the new theory had many detractors, it was also well protected from criticism. Since the original monopoly model was born from perfect competition, the two theories shared much in common, including profit maximization, marginal analysis, and mathematical rigor. It was difficult for proponents of perfect competition to attack the assumptions in Chamberlin and Robinson's monopoly model without denigrating their own. Given little hope of finding flaws in the theory, critics were inclined to simply ignore it or dismiss monopoly as nothing more than a rare phenomenon in the real economy.[2]

Despite such resistance, monopoly won a small niche within the larger body of economic thought. No contemporary text on microeconomics would be complete without a chapter on "pure monopoly" followed by one on oligopoly, making it almost impossible for even the most ardent believers in perfect competition to deny their students a basic familiarity with monopoly theory.

The Standard Monopoly Model

The version of monopoly theory that penetrated microeconomic textbooks, the standard monopoly model, is reproduced in Figure 3.1. It is based on the assumption that the monopolist maximizes short-run profits and other firms hold their prices and output constant. The profit maximizing output, q^*, is determined by the intersection of marginal cost (MC) and marginal revenue (MR). At this output, price is equal to p^* and average costs are equal to AC^*. Total profits are equivalent to the shaded area because both are equal to the product of average profit ($p^* - AC^*$) and total output, q^*.

The introduction of monopoly theory into mainstream economics was both a victory and a disappointment. It was a victory because it provided an alternative to the idealized theory of perfect competition. But it was also a disappointment because the conditions for the standard monopoly model were typically just as idealized and ambiguous as perfect competition. Where perfect competition required an infinite number of firms producing identical products, the monopoly model assumed a single producer in a market. A prominent microeconomics text claims that "the conditions of the model [pure monopoly] are exacting; and it is difficult, if not impossible, to pinpoint a pure monopolist in real-world markets."[3] The reason is that most markets do not have "one, and only one seller."

But this definition of monopoly is a vestige of the older theory of perfect competition in which the products of all market participants are assumed to be exactly identical. In the real economy of differentiated products, output varies from firm to firm and it is no longer obvious where markets begin or end. The authors of the textbook, John Gould and Edward Lazear, assume that markets should be broadly defined so that monopoly is indeed a rare phenomenon. But just as astute an observer could define markets very narrowly so as to decrease the number of rivals. Or in the extreme, Joan Robinson noted that firms have "monopolies over their own output," making all firms monopolists.

Figure 3.1. **The Standard Monopoly Model and Profits**

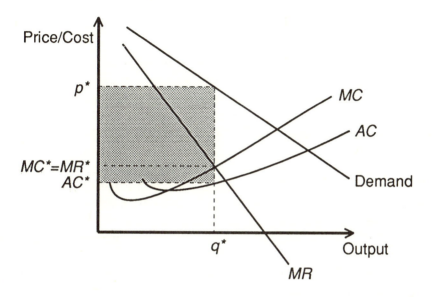

Monopoly Theory

The theory presented in this chapter demonstrates how the standard monopoly model can be adapted to describe markets with varying degrees of product differentiation. As a result it is not restricted to a few firms on the fringe of the economy but rather applies to all firms. In fact, it is so general that it even includes the case of a "perfectly competitive" firm, making the theory of perfect competition merely a special case of the more general theory of monopoly power.

There are three propositions that describe the general framework of monopoly theory. The first one specifies the role of the standard monopoly model.

PROPOSITION 1. *The standard monopoly model defines only "potential" values.*

These are potential values because they are based on two assumptions that are not always met in the real world. The first is that firms maximize short-run profits and the second is that other firms hold their prices constant. Only under these conditions will the firm actually set prices at the level determined in Figure 3.1. Since firms do not always maximize short-run profits, nor do other firms always hold their prices constant, actual values may differ from those in the model. In order to make this clear, it is necessary to distinguish between "potential" values determined by the standard monopoly model and actual values determined in practice.

The second proposition establishes the scope of monopoly theory.

PROPOSITION 2. *These "potential" values can be calculated for any firm.*

Since a short-run demand curve and cost curves can be constructed for any firm, the "potential" values can also be calculated. There is no reason why the calculation of potential values, illustrated in Figure 3.1, should be limited to single sellers or unusually large firms. The calculation can even be made for firms with flat demand curves, corresponding to the special case of "perfect competition."

The third proposition makes a connection between these theoretical values and real economic activity.

PROPOSITION 3. *These "potential" values influence actual behavior.*

This is the final and most important proposition. Monopoly theory would be of little value if it bore no resemblance to actual firm behavior. The fact that monopoly theory can describe and predict business behavior is what makes it a valuable theoretical tool.

The relationship between potential and actual values is not always an exact one. For various reasons, the potential values for a single firm may not always equal the actual values. Profits, for example, may fall short of their potential. But if we were to compare the actual profits of many firms we would expect them to be correlated with their potential profits. Statistical studies demonstrating this very relationship are reviewed in later chapters. The remainder of this chapter focuses on defining the potential values mentioned in the first two propositions.

One of the important potential values determined in Figure 3.1 is short-run profit. A firm may choose different strategies depending on whether its maximum potential profit is five thousand dollars or five billion dollars. The standard monopoly model provides just this type of information. It determines precisely the maximum potential short-run

profits, defined as *economic power*. A firm's capacity to generate current or short-run profits is equivalent to its economic
power.

Another way to illustrate the meaning of this concept is to calculate
the total profits for the firm in Figure 3.1 at each level of output. The
results, graphed in Figure 3.2, demonstrate that maximum short-run
profits, π^*, are generated at output q^*. These profits are, of course,
equal to economic power, E. This definition can be stated as,

(3.1) $$Economic\ Power = E = \pi^*$$

What is the relationship between economic power and actual profits? As previously mentioned, the two values are likely to be statistically correlated but they are not necessarily identical. Economic power
is by definition the highest point in Figure 3.2, and although actual
profits could attain this level, the two values will not always coincide.

The standard monopoly model determines another potential value
that needs to be defined. At the point that maximizes short-run profits,
the inverse elasticity of demand (η) is equal to the markup over marginal cost (m).[4] This result can be stated as,

(3.2) $$\frac{1}{\eta} = \frac{p - MC}{p} = m^*$$

It should be apparent that some firms have more discretion over
prices than others and that this is the essence of monopoly power.
Firms with flat demand curves have no real choice about their current
price since a higher price wipes out sales and a lower price is unnecessary. These firms have the least practical discretion about prices and
therefore have the least monopoly power. On the other hand, firms
have more discretion over prices, giving them more monopoly power,
when the demand curve is more inelastic.

It is logical that monopoly power should be inversely related to the
price elasticity of demand. Firms with a small elasticity have more
discretion over prices and therefore have more *monopoly power* (*M*).
This definition can be restated as,

Figure 3.2. **Economic Power**

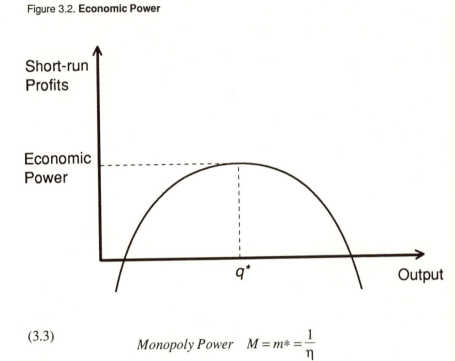

(3.3)   *Monopoly Power $M = m* = \dfrac{1}{\eta}$*

Notice that according to this definition monopoly power is not based on the current markup, but on the markup that maximizes current profits.[5] This is ensured by condition (3.3), which requires the markup to equal the inverse elasticity.

For all practical purposes the elasticity of demand is likely to lie between one and infinity. When the demand curve is flat, as in perfect competition, η is infinite and monopoly power takes its lowest value, zero. As the demand curve becomes relatively steeper, η decreases, and according to (3.3), monopoly power increases. Because it is assumed that η will always be greater than one at the point that maximizes short-run profits, monopoly power will always be less than one.[6]

This completes the basic definitions of economic and monopoly power. Economic power is equal to maximum short-run profits resulting from a markup equal to monopoly power. Both measures of power describe potential values of a firm derived from the standard monopoly model. In later chapters we will explore how these values affect actual profits and markups. But before turning to this issue, it is necessary to demonstrate two more relationships. The first one is between monopoly power and the availability of substitutes. One would expect that firms facing relatively few good substitutes would also have more monopoly power, a point that is demonstrated in the following section. And second, we need to specify the relationship between monopoly and economic power.

Substitution

A fundamental supposition in this theory is that monopoly power depends on the availability of substitutes, or more precisely, on the number and strength of those substitutes. To a certain extent this is captured in the inverse demand elasticity, because products without good substitutes have low demand elasticity and therefore high monopoly power. But it is also possible to show how individual substitutes affect monopoly power.

The traditional measure of substitution is the cross-price elasticity, which measures how the consumption of one commodity responds to changes in the price of another. If two goods are close substitutes, an increase in the price of one is expected to cause a large increase in the consumption of another. Specifically, this is calculated by dividing the percentage change in the consumption of one product (q_y) by the percentage change in the price of another (p_x). The cross-price elasticity between y and x is written as η_{yx}, and defined as,

(3.4)
$$\eta_{yx} = \frac{\Delta q_y / q_y}{\Delta p_x / p_x}$$

The cross-price elasticity may be the most familiar measure of substitution but for our purposes it is not the best. Instead, we will use a related measure defined as the substitution index. This index represents the percentage of x's revenue transferred to y as a result of an increase in the price of x. For example, if the price of x increases 10 percent and x loses 20 percent of its revenue to y then the substitution index is equal to 2, or 20 percent divided by 10 percent. When y is a good substitute, the substitution index will be particularly high as consumers transfer large amounts of expenditures from x to y. Formally, the substitution index (SI_{yx}) is defined as,

(3.5)
$$SI_{yx} = \frac{\Delta\,(p_y\,q_y)/p_x q_x}{\Delta p_x/p_x}$$

It differs from the cross-price elasticity primarily because it is based on changes in revenue rather than quantity. But another more subtle difference is that the cross-price elasticity measures substitution from the perspective of the substitute (y) while the substitution index measures it from the perspective of the initial good (x).

To illustrate this point, suppose that initially the revenue of x is one hundred dollars, compared to only one dollar for y. Furthermore, a 10 percent increase in the price of x causes 1 percent of x's revenue to be transferred to y. Assuming that the price of y remains constant, the consumption of y would increase approximately 100 percent. The two goods appear to be extremely good substitutes based on the cross-price elasticity, which is equal to 10 (100 percent divided by 10 percent) and y's producer is entirely justified in considering its product to be an excellent substitute for x. But the substitution index is only equal to .1 (1 percent divided by 10 percent), which means that the producer of x does not lose a significant proportion of its revenue to y and is unlikely to view y as an important substitute. Both producers are essentially correct based on their own particular frame of reference.

The substitution index therefore measures the relative strength of substitutes from the perspective of the firm that changes its price, in this case firm x. The index also provides a more meaningful basis for ranking substitutes. The strongest substitutes with the highest substitution indices will capture a relatively larger share of x's revenue when the price of x increases.

It should be noted that the substitution index, like the cross-price elasticity, is not symmetric and that SI_{yx} does not have to equal SI_{xy}. Although the two values could occasionally have similar magnitudes, they are not necessarily related. For this reason, the second subscript always identifies the variable with the price change.

Not surprisingly, the substitution index and the cross-price elasticity are closely related, assuming the price of y does not change. In this case, the substitution index is equal to the cross-price elasticity multiplied by the ratio of expenditures on y ($p_y q_y$) to expenditures on x ($p_x q_x$). This relationship can be specified as follows:[7]

(3.6)
$$SI_{yx} = \eta_{yx} \frac{p_y q_y}{p_x q_x}$$

It should be noted that when y is a substitute for x both the cross-price elasticity and the substitution index will be positive and when y is a complement, both measures will be negative. In the case of complements, SI_{yx} indicates the amount of revenue lost by y when the price of x increases.

We are now ready to show the relationship between substitution and monopoly power. This is an easy task since the own price elasticity of demand (η_x) is equal to one plus the sum of substitution indices for all commodities related to x. The derivation of this relationship can be found in the Appendix. Using this result and the fact that monopoly power (M) is equal to the inverse demand elasticity (η_x) we have the following relationship:

(3.7)
$$M = \frac{1}{\eta_x} = \frac{1}{1 + \sum_{i=1}^{n} SI_{ix}}$$

According to this equation, when there are many good substitutes for x, the sum of SI's in the denominator will be large, and monopoly power will be close to zero. As substitutes decrease in number or strength, the sum decreases and monopoly power rises. In the unlikely event that there are no substitutes whatsoever, monopoly power would equal one.

A firm can increase its monopoly power by decreasing the number or strength of its substitutes and the most direct way to accomplish this is to buy one or more competitors. In this way, the revenue that once dissipated to other firms can be reduced. The five major car divisions of General Motors serve as a useful example of this principle. If Chevrolet were an independent car company, an increase in its price alone would cause sales to spill over to all other substitutes, including other divisions of GM, such as Pontiac, Buick, Oldsmobile, and Cadillac. But as part of GM, a general price increase by Chevrolet and other GM divisions results in relatively smaller spillovers. There is no question here that Chevrolet exercises more monopoly power as part of GM than as an independent auto manufacturer.

Two Forms of Power

It is important to distinguish between monopoly and economic power because they represent different concepts. Two firms with identical levels of one may have widely varying amounts of the other. For example, Ede and Ravenscroft, the manufacturer of wigs for barristers in England, has significant monopoly power in the market for legal wigs. It controls 98 percent of the market but only employs six production workers.[8] It clearly exercises monopoly power but lacks the size to make it a world-class economic power. It is also possible for two firms to have exactly the same economic power but have very different levels of monopoly power. The firm with less monopoly power can make up for this deficiency through larger revenue.

The relationship between monopoly and economic power can be specified more precisely. Once again, it is necessary to state beforehand that all the price and cost variables in the following equations correspond to the particular point that maximizes short-run profits. In other words, all the values are determined at output q^* in Figure 3.1. With this in mind, economic power (E) can be specified as a function of three variables: monopoly power (M), total revenue (R), and a measure of capacity utilization (qD).[9]

(3.8) $E = RM + qD$ where $D = (MC - AC)$

Obviously, high monopoly power and high revenue will tend to increase economic power. The third term, qD, requires more of an explanation. It is based on the difference between marginal and average cost, which is graphed in Figure 3.3. The cost curves are drawn here as they are commonly believed to exist in the short run.

When the profit maximizing output reaches a relatively high level, identified by q_1, marginal cost will exceed average cost and qD will be positive, thus raising economic power. The actual amount, qD, is equivalent to the shaded area. If the profit-maximizing output were to decrease, to q_0, for example, marginal cost would equal average cost

Figure 3.3 **Capacity Utilization (qD)**

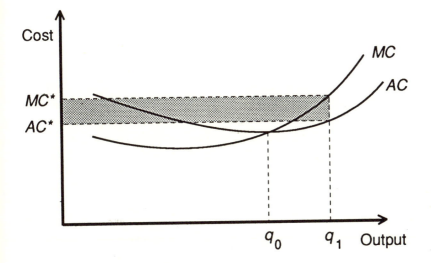

and the contribution to economic power would be zero. A further decrease in output would cause average cost to exceed marginal cost and qD would be negative, indicating a reduction in economic power.

The economic significance of qD is its relationship to capacity utilization. When a firm has little excess capacity the cost of additional production, marginal cost, is relatively high. The reason is that additional capital and equipment are not readily available. Therefore, marginal cost is greater than average cost, qD is positive, and economic power is higher. The effect of low capacity utilization is the opposite: marginal cost is relatively low, qD is negative, and economic power is reduced.

While total economic power obviously increases with revenue, it is sometimes useful to compare businesses on the basis of their relative economic power, independent of size. This can be accomplished by dividing through by revenue in (3.8).

(3.9)
$$\frac{E}{R} = M + qD/R$$

In this case, the ratio of economic power to revenue is determined by monopoly power and an index of capacity utilization. Firms with more monopoly power or higher relative capacity utilization will have more economic power per dollar of sales.

The importance of (3.9) is that it provides a bridge between monopoly theory and the real economy. Businesses and industries frequently calculate the ratio of profits to revenue as an indicator of economic performance. The claim of monopoly theory is that the ratio of economic power to revenue, defined by (3.9), is a primary determinant of the profit-to-sales ratio. Empirical support for this contention is the subject of the next chapter.

Also, at this point it should be acknowledged that many firms are composed of separate product lines or businesses. The total economic power of these firms can be written as the sum of economic power in n individual product lines.

(3.10)
$$E = E_1 + E_2 + E_3 + ... = \sum_{i=1}^{n} (M_i R_i + q_i D_i)$$

This suggests an additional way for a firm to increase its total economic power. It can increase the number of separate businesses under its control, which adds more potential profits to the total. By means of mergers, consolidations, takeovers, and new investment, firms pursue an expansion of economic power.

Summary

Economic power is defined in this chapter as the maximum "potential" profits of the firm in the short run, given the prevailing prices of rivals. Similarly, monopoly power is defined as the markup necessary to generate these profits. Furthermore, this profit-maximizing markup is exactly equal to the inverse elasticity of demand and is determined by the availability of good substitutes. Firms with many close substitutes have little monopoly power, because they cannot raise prices without a significant loss of sales. But as the number and strength of substitutes diminish, a firm gains more monopoly power and more discretion over its pricing.

This chapter also described the relationship between monopoly and economic power. Monopoly power is one of the determinants of economic power, along with revenue and an index of capacity utilization.

Firms with great economic power must have great monopoly power, large revenue, or high capacity utilization.

There is one final but important point about economic and monopoly power. Both terms describe intrinsic characteristics of all firms. Given accurate information about demand and costs, it should be possible to determine the economic and monopoly power of any firm. This chapter therefore completes the explanation of the first two propositions—the standard monopoly model defines "potential" values and these can be calculated for any firm.

The criticism leveled at Lerner and Kalecki is avoided in this chapter by defining a firm's monopoly power in relation to its current demand and cost curves, not by its current behavior. There is no tautology in the claim that monopoly power causes higher profit margins. This claim does, however, require empirical evidence. The early statistical investigations are reviewed in the next chapter.

Appendix

The specific relationship between the own price elasticity and the substitution index is derived here.[10] We begin with a budget constraint for all consumers such that the sum of their expenditures on n commodities must equal their income (I).

(3.11)
$$I = p_0 q_0 + p_1 q_1 + \ldots + p_n q_n = p_0 q_0 + \sum_{i=1}^{n} p_i q_i$$

Differentiating this with respect to p_0, we find,

(3.12)
$$\frac{\partial I}{\partial p_0} = 0 = \frac{\partial q_0}{\partial p_0} p_0 + q_0 + \sum_{i=1}^{n} \frac{\partial q_i}{\partial p_0} p_i$$

This can be simplified by multiplying through by $1/q_0$ and rearranging.

(3.13)
$$0 = \frac{p_0}{q_0} \frac{\partial q_0}{\partial p_0} + 1 + \sum_{i=1}^{n} \frac{p_0}{q_i} \frac{\partial q_i}{\partial p_0} \frac{p_i q_i}{p_0 q_0}$$

.

Using the definition of own price elasticity (η_0) and cross-price elasticity (η_{i0}) we have the following,

(3.14)

$$0 = -\eta_0 + 1 + \sum_{i=1}^{n} \eta_{i0} \frac{p_i q_i}{p_0 q_0}$$

And finally, using the relationship between the substitution index and the cross-price elasticity specified earlier in (3.6), we have the final result,

(3.15)

$$\eta_0 = 1 + \sum_{i=1}^{n} SI_{i0}$$

Therefore, one plus the sum of substitution indices for all commodities equals the own price elasticity. The substitution index will be positive for all substitutes and negative for all complements. When the substitution index is equal to zero the own price elasticity is unaffected since the commodities are unrelated. In addition, because income is spent on both consumption and savings, one of the n commodities should represent savings as a form of future consumption.

4

Early Statistical Evidence

> *To summarize, the theory of the dominant firm unequivocally*
> *points to high prices and suggests high profit rates for dominant*
> *firms. . . . By and large the relationship holds up for*
> *Britain, Canada, and Japan, as well as the United States.*
> —Leonard Weiss, 1974[1]

Measurement in economics is not yet, nor is it ever likely to be, an exact science. Between the lofty ideals of economic theory and the complex reality of economic activity lies the uncertain world of empirical economics. In this field, economic activity must be distilled to a set of numbers consistent with the demands of theory and yet reasonably representative of real-world behavior.

A successful test can usually reassure believers and at its best give critics reason to rethink their position. But what constitutes a successful test? A primary function of a statistical study is to demonstrate patterns or relationships consistent with the original theory. At the very least, proponents of any theory should be able to provide test results that correspond to theoretical predictions. Only the most vacuous theory fails to meet this minimum demand.

A second and often more stringent requirement for a successful test is that it should correspond closely to the theoretical framework. But where the ideal is unobtainable, compromise is inevitable. This is especially true in economics because theoretical values are seldom known. It becomes a matter of judgment as to how well the available data correspond to the illusive ideal. A strong familiarity with the data and a clear understanding of the theory can improve the quality of these judgments even if the subjective element can never be completely

41

erased. Therefore, much of this chapter is devoted to a discussion of theory and data.

The Hypothesis

The first empirical tests of monopoly power conducted in the 1950s were based on the simple hypothesis that profits should be higher in markets dominated by relatively few firms. It was expected that profits in these markets should lie somewhere between those of perfect competition and pure monopoly. It was also argued that the number of firms determine the feasibility of collusion. When only a few firms are involved, the prospects of negotiating and maintaining a collusive agreement are expected to be much stronger. These simple arguments provided the theoretical basis for many of the first empirical studies of monopoly power.

But as evidence accumulated, a coterie of critics began to challenge the findings.[2] There were many different ways to measure market power and even more ways to measure profits, and the actual relationship between the two seemed to depend on which methods were used. This was a difficult matter to resolve because the theory was initially not specific enough to provide standards for evaluating studies with contradictory conclusions. Without a theoretical standard, each test seemed just as valid as the next. Fortunately, both the theory and the method of analysis improved during the ensuing debate and the link between monopoly power and profitability became increasingly compelling.

The proposition was made in Chapter 3 that actual profits should be statistically related to potential profits as measured by economic power. The two will be exactly equal only when short-run profits are maximized and the prices of rivals are held constant. One way to state this proposition is that the ratio of actual profits to revenue is determined by the ratio of economic power to revenue and e, the random error.

(4.1)
$$d\frac{\pi}{R} = f\left(\frac{E}{R}, e\right)$$
where π = actual profits

E = economic power
R = revenue
e = random error

Unlike the equations in Chapter 3, which were either definitions, identities, or equilibrium conditions, (4.1) is a behavioral relationship. It claims that the profit rate (π/R) is determined by average economic power (E/R). Only when firms maximize short-run profits and other firms hold their prices constant will the two be equal, otherwise the error term will have some nonzero value.

Recall from Chapter 3 that average economic power was equal to the sum of monopoly power (M) and another term related to capacity utilization (qD/R).[3] Substituting this into (4.1) we have the following result.[4]

(4.2) $\pi = f(M, qD/R, e)$ where M = monopoly power
$$D = MC{-}AC$$
$$q = \text{output}$$
$$R = \text{revenue}$$

Ideally one would obtain the necessary data, calculate the variables in (4.2), and test for a statistical relationship. Unfortunately, few of these variables are actually available in the proper form. Even the most familiar, profits and revenue, present a problem. The average firm is involved in many different lines of business and may exercise different degrees of monopoly power in each. A thorough study would require separate profit and revenue data for each product line, something businesses do not normally report. In addition, monopoly power and marginal costs are rarely calculated for individual firms, much less individual lines of business. Obviously, some compromises must be introduced in order to test the relationship between the profit rate and monopoly power.

Measuring Monopoly Power

Before describing the indicators of monopoly power, it is useful to visualize what is being measured. Any group of firms producing substitutes can be illustrated in a scatter diagram, where each dot represents a firm and the size of the dot is proportional to sales. Furthermore, the distance between dots is related to substitutability so that good substitutes are relatively close together.[5] A group of close substitutes are defined as a market and identified by constructing a boundary around them. This type of market diagram is illustrated in Figure 4.1.

44

Figure 4.1. **Market Diagram**

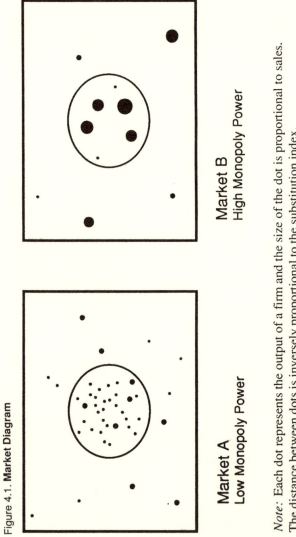

Market A
Low Monopoly Power

Market B
High Monopoly Power

Note: Each dot represents the output of a firm and the size of the dot is proportional to sales. The distance between dots is inversely proportional to the substitution index.

The monopoly power of each individual firm depends on the distance between itself and all others.[6] Monopoly power is generally low in market A, where most firms are close to a great number of other firms, but higher in market B, where firms are more spread out. This diagram illustrates an important point: the more firms there are in a single market, the less monopoly power any one of them will have.

It is also reasonable to expect relatively large firms to have more monopoly power than others. Recall from the previous chapter that the substitution index, which determines monopoly power, depends on the proportion of revenue lost due to a price increase. Everything else being the same, a large firm is likely to lose a smaller proportion of revenue than a relatively small firm. Therefore, monopoly power depends on the relative size of a firm as well as the number of other firms in the market.

Both of these attributes are captured by market share, defined as the ratio of a firm's revenue to that of the industry.

(4.3)
$$Market\ Share = MS = \frac{Firm\ Revenue}{Industry\ Revenue}$$

How is market share related to a firm's relative size and the number of rivals? It is easier to see this for a firm whose revenue is equal to the industry average (R^*). If there are n firms then the firm's market share is equal to R^*/nR^* or simply, $1/n$. Market share falls as the number of rivals increases. But if the firm's revenue is s percent larger than the average, its market share is equal to $(1+s)R^*/nR^*$ or simply, $(1+s)/n$. As the firm's size increases in relation to the industry average, its market share also increases. The fact that market share is determined by relative firm size and the number of rivals makes it a useful approximation of monopoly power.

In many cases we are interested in the average monopoly power of an industry. The two most common measures are calculated using market shares. The first is the concentration ratio, equal to the sum of market shares for the largest firms, usually the top four.

(4.4)
$$Concentration\ Ratio\ (4\ firm\ )= CR = \sum_{i=1}^{4} MS_i$$

Although concentration is not a precise measure of monopoly power, it is capable of distinguishing between wide variations. In most cases where mergers significantly reduce the number of large rivals in an industry, concentration will increase. And like market share, concentration depends on the number of firms in an industry and the relative size of the largest ones.[7]

Another approximation of monopoly power is the *Hirschman–Herfindahl Index* (*HHI*), which equals the sum of market shares squared for all *n* firms in a market. This is calculated as follows:

(4.5)
$$Hirschman–Herfindahl\ Index = HHI = \sum_{i=1}^{n} (MS_i)^2$$

This measure is frequently employed by antitrust investigators. The consolidation of leading firms in an industry will often cause a relatively large increase in the *HHI* compared to the concentration ratio. For instance, the *HHI* could nearly double if two firms, each controlling 30 percent of an industry, were to merge. The four-firm concentration ratio, on the other hand, would only increase incrementally by adding the market share of what was, prior to the merger, the fifth largest firm. Other than this difference the two measures are relatively similar. Both are calculated using market shares and both give greater weight to leading firms.

While these approximations of monopoly power are useful, they are not complete. Market share, concentration, and the *HHI* are positively related to firm size and inversely related to the number of substitutes, but they do not capture the prevailing substitutability between products. While this is difficult to measure directly, it is often closely related to the level of product promotion. Substitution is likely to be lower and monopoly power higher where firms or industries engage in considerable advertising.

Advertising is most effective for products with some physically distinguishing feature, at the very least a unique brand name or an appealing package. Where no distinguishing feature exists, the potential gain from advertising is nil and expenditures on advertising are typically low. An individual wheat farmer has the unfortunate distinction of producing a physically undifferentiated product, a fact that even the best advertiser cannot easily remedy.[8] For those industries where products are so undifferentiated that even advertising will not make a difference, substitution is likely to be high. This is one of the reasons advertising is a useful indicator of monopoly power.

But advertising doesn't merely indicate monopoly power; it also changes it. The immediate goal of advertising is to stimulate the demand for a specific product, but in the short run this can only be accomplished at the expense of other firms, generally those in the same market. Consequently, a primary objective of advertisers in altering consumer desires is to distinguish one product from another. If Chevrolet merely promotes the benefits of owning a new car, consumers may buy a Ford or a Chrysler. But if they extol the unique virtues of a Chevrolet, they stand to receive most of the benefits. One of the primary purposes of advertising is to heighten consumers' perception of product differences. When successful, the outcome of this effort is to reduce substitutability and increase monopoly power.

The relationship between monopoly power and advertising applies even when firms are involved in counteradvertising, where each proclaims the virtues of its product and denigrates those of its rivals. Some observers suspect that this type of advertising essentially balances out, resulting in no real change. But in fact, the cumulative effect of years of counteradvertising can greatly reduce substitution within a market, thus contributing to higher levels of monopoly power. Neither Pepsi nor Coke can claim that its extensive advertising campaigns defeated the other. But as a result of years of advertising, consumer loyalty to both beverages is remarkably high. Advertising expenditures, even in this case, continue to enhance monopoly power.

Capacity Utilization

The profit function (4.2), contains another term, based on the relative difference between marginal and average costs. As pointed out in Chapter 3, the sign of this term is largely related to the level of capacity utilization. When a firm operates at full capacity, the term is positive and tends to increase the level of economic power. At lower levels of capacity utilization, the term is negative, and so is its contribution to economic power. A good approximation for this term is the actual level of capacity utilization. And when this is not available, an alternative measure is growth. Firms or industries experiencing high growth rates are also more likely to be operating at or near full capacity. On the other extreme, those experiencing a decline in sales are more prone to suffer excess capacity. Therefore, growth, as measured with respect to output, sales, or capital, is likely to reflect the same underlying condition as capacity utilization.

Price–Cost Margins

The dependent variable in (4.2) is the ratio of profits to revenue. Revenue is easy to calculate whereas profits are not. The accounting rules defining profits are notoriously out of synch with its proper economic definition. One of the most significant shortcomings is the way capital costs are calculated. Production reduces the value of fixed capital, which is taken as a depreciation cost. But in an effort to reduce corporate tax liabilities, accounting practices and definitions have been altered to greatly accelerate depreciation. An artificially high depreciation rate will reduce profits with the greatest impact felt by those firms with high capital intensity.

An alternative approach is to substitute the price–cost margin for the profit-to-sales ratio and estimate the depreciation rate directly.[9] This can be illustrated by defining profits (π) as the difference between revenue and costs, including both variable (VC) and fixed costs (FC). The latter is equal to the product of capital (K) and the depreciation rate (d).

(4.6)
$$\frac{\pi}{R} = \frac{R - VC - FC}{R} = \frac{R - VC - dK}{R} = \frac{R - VC}{R} - d\left(\frac{K}{R}\right) = PCM - d\left(\frac{K}{R}\right)$$

Substituting this into (4.2), we have,

(4.7) $$PCM = f(M, D/p, d(K/R), e)$$

The advantage of (4.7) is that it uses price–cost margins and other available variables. And the depreciation rate can be estimated as the coefficient on the capital-to-revenue ratio term, thus eliminating another source of error.

Although the relationship between price–cost margins and monopoly power described in (4.7) was derived for firms, it also applies to industries.[10] Ideally an industry should be defined so that it includes only substitutes. But in practice, one usually relies on the Standard Industrial Classification (SIC), which is usually grouped by common production methods rather than substitution.[11] This can have the anomalous effect of placing rubber footwear (SIC 3021) and leather footwear (SIC 3149) in separate industries but shaving cream and toothpaste in the same one (SIC 2844). There is also the problem of including products that are merely inputs to the primary product as illustrated by the fact that motorcycle and bicycle parts are included in the motorcycle and bicycle industry (SIC 3751). Fortunately, the value of extraneous commodities is in most cases relatively small and therefore causes only a small departure from the ideal.

The early studies using industry data had two distinct advantages over those relying on firm samples. First, concentration ratios for industries were widely available while market shares for firms were not. Firm studies often resorted to using concentration ratios for the firm's primary industry. The results of these studies were often inconclusive.

Another significant problem with these early firm studies was the idiosyncrasies of tax data. As a consequence of this deficiency, any existing relationship between monopoly power and profits could have been obscured or even wiped out. In addition, company data were generally limited to a relatively small number of large firms. Using a biased sample like this makes it very difficult to generalize the results to all businesses.

The Evidence

Given that ideal data were not available, a good alternative was to test the following model:

(4.8) $PCM = a_0 + a_1\, Concentration + a_2\, Advertising\, /Revenue$
$+ a_3\, Growth\, (or\, Capacity\, Utilization)$
$+ a_4\, Capital/Revenue + error$

where $a_0 \ldots a_4$ are coefficients

All coefficients are expected to be positive including a_1 and a_2, which represent the effect of monopoly power on profitability. The model is completed by including a term for growth (or capacity utilization) and the ratio of capital to revenue.

Joe Bain is widely credited with initiating the empirical investigation of the relationship between profit rates and concentration. In his pioneering 1951 study, Bain concluded that profit rates for 335 firms from 1936 to 1940 appeared to be higher when industry concentration exceeded 70 percent. But his study, and many others that immediately followed, were plagued with problems. In some cases, the studies were based on different theoretical models, only remotely related to monopoly theory. In other cases, the combination of firm financial data and industry concentration produced volatile and often contradictory results. Bain's actual findings are not as important today as the fact that he launched a generation of empirical analysis.

It was not until the late 1960s when Collins and Preston introduced the use of price–cost margins that many of these obstacles were overcome. A distinct advantage of their study was that all of the key variables were derived from the same data source, the Survey of Manufacturers (SOM). This eliminated the questionable practice of assigning firms to industries based only on their primary commodity. The SOM avoids this questionable practice by subdividing the revenue and cost data from firms into appropriate industries. Furthermore, the revenue and cost data obtained from the SOM is less influenced by arbitrary tax laws than IRS profit data. And finally, the SOM includes a large percentage of all manufacturing firms in contrast to the small samples used in earlier research.

In one of their initial studies, Collins and Preston estimated the effect of the four-firm concentration ratio, the capital-to-sales ratio, and an index measuring the degree of geographic dispersion on price–cost margins (PCM). Geographic dispersion was intended to correct the concentration data for understating monopoly power when markets were local rather than national. The data for this study covered 243 manufacturing industries in 1958 and 1963.

Collins and Preston concluded that "a difference of ten percentage points in four-firm concentration is likely to be associated with a difference of almost one percentage point in price cost-margins."[12] They conducted additional tests using different concentration measures and distinguishing between consumer and producer goods, but the results were essentially unchanged. Higher concentration resulted in significantly higher margins in both types of industries, although the impact was stronger for consumer goods.

In almost all of these tests, the capital–sales ratio was positive as expected and usually highly significant. Margins also appeared to be higher when industries were regional or local, especially for producer goods. This provided evidence that concentration ratios tend to understate monopoly power when markets are less than national in scope. Although certain important variables, such as advertising and growth, were missing from this early specification, the quality of the data alone constituted a vast improvement over previous work. Following this pathbreaking research, other studies employed price–cost margins but included more variables and incorporated more current data.

The results of several prominent studies using industry price–cost margins are summarized in Table 4.1. The results invariably confirmed Collins and Preston's finding that concentration, as a measure of monopoly power, has a positive effect on price–cost margins. The estimated effects of concentration on margins summarized in the table were statistically significant and ranged from .04 to .17. What this means is that margins rose somewhere between .02 and .085 in response to an increase in concentration from zero to fifty. Since the average price–cost margin in manufacturing was approximately .25, it was fair to conclude that concentration had a sizable impact on margins.

Each of these studies made its own unique contribution to understanding the factors that determine margins. The studies of both Shirazi and of Weiss, tested the effect of advertising.[13] In both cases, monopoly power appeared to be significantly higher in industries with high expenditures on advertising. Rhoades and Kwoka found significantly higher margins in expanding industries which Weiss also found but only in his larger sample of 339 industries. Higher growth evidently led to higher capacity utilization and higher margins. In general, the empirical results were consistent with the specification in (4.8), providing strong support for monopoly theory.[14]

But even in these studies, not all problems were eliminated. Many included a variable designed to measure the entry barrier associated with large-scale production. It was typically based on the relative size of an efficient production unit, defined as the median plant or the average of the largest 50 percent of all plants in the industry. The ratio of this plant size to industry size was defined as minimum efficient scale (MES) and used to approximate barriers to entry. Margins were expected to be higher where the MES was larger.

While MES is a reasonable approximation of a scale barrier, it is

Table 4.1

Early Studies Relating Price–Cost Margins to Monopoly Power

Study	Estimated Impact of Concentration[a]	Results	Primary Data Source
1.		Higher returns in industries where eight-firm concentration exceeded 70 percent	333 firms and 42 industries, 1936–40
2.	.08 to .13	Positive return to concentration in consumer and producer goods	243 manufacturing industries in 1958 and 1963
3.	.11 to .17	Industry returns are positively related to concentration	241 manufacturing industries in 1963
4.	.10	Industry returns are positively related to advertising and scale in multiple regressions and concentration in simple regression	41 to 61 manufacturing industries in the U.K., 1963
5.	.07 to .10	Positive return to concentration and advertising	227 and 339 manufacturing industries in 1963
6.	.09 to .14	The positive return to concentration is reduced when estimated for logarithms of PCMs	102 and 393 manufacturing industries in 1963 and 367 industries in 1967
7.	.04 to .08	Industry returns are positively related to the market share of the two largest firms	314 manufacturing industries in 1972

a. This represents the increase in PCM when the four firm concentration increases from 0 to 100.
Notes:
1. Bain, 1951.
2. Collins and Preston, 1969
3. Rhoades, 1973. Table 1. Significant at the 1 percent level.
4. Shirazi, 1974. Equation, p. 73. Significant at the 1 percent level in the simple regression.
5. Weiss, 1974. Tables 12 and 13. Significant at the 1 percent level.
6. Orenstein, 1972. Table I, linear specifications, and Table II.
7. Kwoka, 1979. Specification 1 in Table 1. Significant at the 1 percent level when scale variable is adjusted for entry costs.

also one of the determinants of monopoly power and capacity utilization. When minimum efficient scale is high, it is easier for firms to
eliminate their rivals and discourage new entrants, yielding greater
control over prices and hence more monopoly power. It is not surprising that MES is highly correlated with concentration.[15] As a result,
when both concentration and MES are included in the same equation,
one runs a risk of multicolinearity reducing the statistical significance
of one or both variables.

The only study that attempted to measure the independent effect of
barriers on profitability was by Bain (1965). He restricted his sample
to firms with high concentration and observed a strong positive relationship between profitability and his index of barriers. He cited this as
evidence that barriers had a direct effect on profitability in addition to
the indirect effect through concentration.[16]

Critics and the Efficiency View

Table 4.1 includes only a small subset of all the studies investigating
the relationship between concentration and profit rates or margins. In
fact, as early as 1974, Weiss was able to identify forty-six studies on
this topic. While most of these found a positive effect of concentration
on profits and margins, none of them corresponded as closely to the
theory as those represented in the table. Many of them, for example,
relied on firm data. Nevertheless, some of the dissenting arguments
deserve special attention.

In 1972 Ornstein criticized the tests of monopoly theory, claiming
they were flawed because they should have been based on a nonlinear
equation rather than a linear one like (4.8). But this was a specious
argument because monopoly theory only makes the claim that actual
profitability and economic power are statistically related. The question
of what form this relationship takes is an empirical question, not a
theoretical one. When Ornstein's nonlinear model performed more
poorly than a comparable linear one, he attributed it to a failure of
monopoly theory. But what he actually did was to demonstrate the
superiority of the linear equation adopted by most analysts. Consequently only Ornstein's baseline results using a linear equation are
reported in Table 4.1.

Many of the early studies of monopoly power did not use price–cost
margins but relied on other measures of profitability. One of these, the

return on equity (profits divided by the total value of outstanding stock), is particularly irrelevant to monopoly theory. Stocks are bought and sold in a more or less competitive environment and one would expect an increase in monopoly or economic power to also stimulate demand for the stock. When economic power increases, so does the stock value. The fact that the return on equity is no higher for concentrated industries merely indicates that stocks have appreciated in proportion to economic power. It is equally erroneous to assume that the returns to power somehow dissipate as stocks appreciate. This process merely distributes the benefits of economic power among stockholders.

Another critic of these studies, Harold Demsetz (1973), suggested that highly concentrated industries were more profitable merely because they were more efficient. He reasoned that in any industry where large-scale production is relatively cheaper, large firms will naturally arise, resulting in both high profits and high concentration. This particular example requires economies to scale but the argument applies to any firm that produces a better product or provides a better service at a lower cost. Successful firms are rewarded for their greater efficiency with higher profits and fewer rivals. Therefore, Demsetz argued, high concentration merely reflected superior efficiency and competency.

Demsetz did not deny the existence of monopoly power; he merely defended it as the outcome of efficient and astute production. "[T]he reward for their entrepreneurial efforts is likely to be some (short-term) monopoly power and this may be associated with increased industrial concentration."[17] He went on to explain that the efficiencies being rewarded are derived from business acumen (a desirable product at a low price), large-scale production, and luck.

Are these in fact the primary sources of monopoly power? Historically, many concentrated industries became that way from extensive mergers and combinations. A surprising number can be traced back to the phenomenal merger wave that swept the country at the turn of the century. The modern corporate giant often grew slowly from internal expansion but rapidly from mergers and acquisitions. Demsetz argues that concentration exists in those industries where firms have been "fortunate enough to have made the correct decisions."[18] But this gross simplification ignores the critical role of mergers and consolidations.

Demsetz's view also fails to explain why concentration has been so stable over periods of many decades.[19] What prevents firms with a little luck and wise decisions from supplanting industry leaders like Exxon, General Electric, and Du Pont? Obviously there is much more inertia in monopoly power than the efficiency view allows.

Even where key decisions did lead to monopoly power they cannot always be construed as efficient. John D. Rockefeller decided to take many unethical steps in his quest to control petroleum refining. Does the fact that he succeeded make this decision "correct"? At least in this case, an argument could be made that overall efficiency was impaired by such practices.

Demsetz is correct that scale economies can contribute to the rise of monopoly power. But even here one should be careful about exaggerating their importance. The expansion of monopoly power appears to have grown far beyond the minimum level necessary for economic efficiency. Blair (1972) was one of the first to provide evidence of this phenomenon by pointing out the discrepancy between plant concentration and firm concentration.[20] If all firms operated a single plant on a scale commensurate with economic efficiency, few manufacturing industries would have concentration ratios exceeding 25 percent. High concentration is not so much a result of large plants as the fact that single firms operate many of them.

Economies to scale can also create a barrier to entry. Would-be entrants are more easily deterred where minimum efficient production requires an extremely large investment. This explains the reluctance of small chemical companies to take on Du Pont. It is difficult to unseat a powerful incumbent, especially without provoking retaliation. Economies to scale boost short-run profits by reducing costs and protect long-run profits by deterring entry. Because most large firms operate in several markets, an appropriate test of monopoly theory would compare economic power and profitability at each line-of-business (LB). One would expect LBs with greater power to also have higher profitability. But for many years neither variable was available at the line-of-business level. Firms typically aggregate key financial variables in financial reports and do not separate them for each LB.

The Federal Trade Commission attempted to resolve this problem by conducting a survey of 250 large companies, asking them to report profits, sales, and other financial data for each LB. Responses to the survey were compiled and used by Ravenscraft (1983) to study the relationship between monopoly power and profitability. The unique feature of this study was that profit margins could be matched directly to market shares for a large sample of 3,186 LBs. Although the sample was not representative of all businesses—it included only *Fortune* 500 firms—it nevertheless represented a significant advance over other firm-level studies.

As one would expect from monopoly theory, LBs with high market shares had considerably higher profit margins. An increase in market share from zero to fifty caused a significant increase in margins of approximately seven to nine percentage points. Other results showed that advertising had a positive effect on margins when market share exceeded the average. Growth also increased margins but the effect of R&D was unexpectedly negative. Ravenscraft explained the anomalous results for R&D by suggesting that 1975 was an exceptional year; perhaps because of the recession the return to R&D was less evident.

The results of this study confirmed the advantage of using LB market share rather than industry concentration to represent a firm's monopoly power. When Ravenscraft included concentration in the equation, it had the wrong sign while the coefficient on market share remained positive and highly significant. Market share proved to be the superior measure of monopoly power at the line-of-business.

Ravenscraft, however, was not prepared to reject the notion of "perfect competition" based on these results. Although his study demonstrated a strong positive relationship between profitability and market share, he was unwilling to part with the "view of the world that sees the economy as predominantly competitive."[21] Instead he claimed, like Demsetz, that market share reflected greater efficiency. But at the same time, Ravenscraft puzzled over the persistence of high market shares and profits. He wondered why units of suboptimal size did not "cut price to gain market share and the advantage of scale economies?" Where were the competitive forces that were suppose to undermine market power and eliminate excess profits?

Ravenscraft, like Demsetz, confused the issue of the existence of monopoly power with its origin. The fact that firms with high market shares have higher profit margins is strong evidence that monopoly power exists. Its origin is another matter. In some cases it may arise from efficiencies, luck, astute marketing, superior products, or economies of scale. In other cases, mergers and acquisitions, patents, or predatory pricing may be the source. But in every case, the end result is monopoly power.

Conclusion

The theory of monopoly power received strong support from empirical studies employing appropriate tests and utilizing comprehensive data. For several decades, studies found a positive effect of concentration and advertising on margins in manufacturing. Of those studies that used inferior data or strayed farthest from the theoretical standard, the results have been less consistent. Many of these were based on small biased samples of firms using unreliable data assembled for tax purposes. But even a simple tabulation of these studies would show a majority supporting monopoly theory.

The leading objection to these studies came from the efficiency hypothesis. While accepting the conclusion that market share and concentration were associated with higher profits, the efficiency view claimed that both were justifiable rewards for innovation, risk-taking, business acumen, and simple scale economies. But efficiency is only one route to monopoly power. The other shortcoming of the efficiency hypothesis is that it fails to account for the persistence of high concentration and profitability over time.

Even with the abundance of solid evidence in support of monopoly theory, there are limitations. Because data are not as comprehensive for nonmanufacturing, most of these studies are entirely limited to manufacturing. And now that this sector represents less than one-fourth of the total economy, it could be questioned whether the average manufacturing firm is representative of overall business behavior.

But a particularly important omission of these early studies is that they failed to include the effect of unions and international trade. This should not be ignored because unions can conceivably capture part or all of the returns to monopoly power. And imports can have a similar effect. The next generation of studies beginning in the 1980s corrected for these omissions, but before reviewing them it is first necessary to clarify the effect of unions and international trade on monopoly and economic power.

5

Unions and the Contest over Economic Power

> *Thus the trial of strength between union and management*
> *associated with collective bargaining is, essentially although*
> *not exclusively, over the division of profits.*
> —John Kenneth Galbraith, 1952[1]

Economic power creates the capacity to generate great profits but there is no guarantee that these profits will be entirely captured by the firm. As we will see in later chapters, existing and potential rivals can challenge and reduce a firm's economic power, especially in the absence of adequate barriers to entry. But challenges to economic power are not always external. As soon as a firm attains a certain degree of profitability, claims on its earnings are likely to arise from within the company. Each constituency, investors, top executives, and unions, would like to increase their relative shares of corporate profits. But the gain for one is a loss for another.

In the stylized version of the firm celebrated in the theory of perfect competition, there is no contest for profit shares because there are no profits. External competition is expected to dissipate profits before internal competition among owners, managers, and workers can even begin. But in the real world, where firms have economic power and barriers exist, it is impossible to ignore the fight for profit shares. While this important process is entirely neglected by the theory of perfect competition, it plays a central role in monopoly theory.

Economic power is defined as the maximum potential profits available to investors. To the extent that some percentage of these potential profits are committed to executive salaries and bonuses or union wages and benefits, economic power declines. When unions win particularly high wage gains or executives receive especially high compensation, the magnitude of economic power diminishes proportionately.

The primary purpose of this chapter is to describe how unions reduce monopoly and economic power. In order to explain this relationship it is necessary to develop two new tools. The first is a graphical model used to demonstrate how higher union wages reduce monopoly power. The second graph, representing employer surplus, is used to illustrate the division of potential profits between firms and unions. Together these two models are also useful for analyzing a number of other issues, including imports and executive compensation, which are taken up at the end of the chapter.

A Graphical Model of Monopoly Power

Monopoly power is defined as the markup over marginal cost that maximizes current profits. At this particular point the markup (m) is equal to the inverse of the price elasticity of demand (η).

(5.1) $\qquad m = 1/\eta \qquad$ where $m = (P-MC)/P$

It is possible to graph the markup and inverse elasticity because both are typically related to output. The intersection of the two curves is the condition described in (5.1) and only there will the markup equal monopoly power.

The first step is to graph the markup as a function of output. The shape of this curve is easier to understand if we rewrite the markup as, $1-(MC/p)$. As output increases, prices generally fall and marginal costs rise, causing MC/p to rise. This in turn causes the markup to fall. A higher output is associated with a lower markup.[2] For this reason, the markup is represented by a downward sloping curve in the lower section of Figure 5.1. Its relationship to the standard monopoly model is highlighted in this figure. At output q_1, price and marginal cost are equal and the markup is zero.

Before graphing the second term in (5.1) it is necessary to specify the relationship between output and demand elasticity. While there is again no fixed rule, it is often the case that the elasticity will fall with

Figure 5.1. **Graphical Determination of Monopoly Power (*M*)**

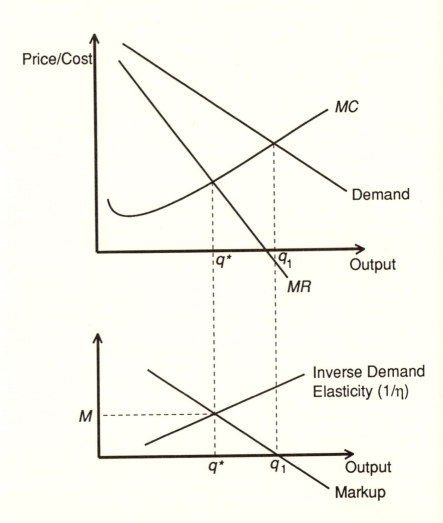

output, as Figure 5.2 illustrates.[3] There are two reasons for this. The first is simply related to the nature of percentage changes. When output is high the percentage change in output tends to be small. And at this level of output prices are generally low, which means the percentage change in prices will be large. The combination of a small percentage change in output and large percentage change in price leads to a relatively small elasticity at high output.

Figure 5.2. **Demand Elasticity and Output**

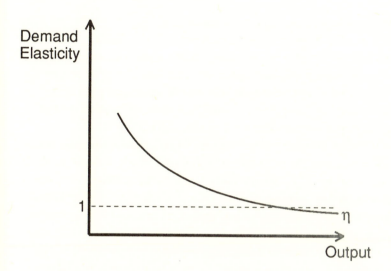

The other reason elasticities and output tend to move in the opposite direction is due to substitution. There are many instances where substitutes are stronger and more plentiful when prices are relatively higher. Consumers have a strong motivation to seek out other options and even accept inferior alternatives when prices are relatively high. At relatively low prices the opposite occurs. For instance, substitutes for a local newspaper may look relatively poor when the paper is priced at ten cents a copy but significantly better when it is priced at a dollar. Therefore, at low prices and high output, substitutes are relatively weaker, reflected in a low elasticity.

When the elasticity curve is downward sloping, the inverse elasticity curve in Figure 5.1 will be upward sloping. With both the markup curve and the inverse elasticity curve, we are now ready to determine monopoly power. At the point where the two curves cross, the markup equals the inverse demand elasticity, which is simply the maximization condition in (5.1). The markup at this point is equal to monopoly power (M) and output q_* is the same as the standard monopoly model.

The lower graph in Figure 5.1 provides a direct way of determining monopoly power. Once the markup and inverse demand elasticities are determined, the level of monopoly power and profit maximizing output are both determined by the point of intersection. This is the model of monopoly power.

The Role of Labor Unions

The effect of higher union compensation can easily be illustrated with this new model. Higher wages and benefits increase marginal costs, causing the *MC* curve to increase in the upper graph of Figure 5.3. This will affect the markup curve in the lower graph, but not the inverse elasticity, which depends only on the shape and position of the demand curve. Because demand does not shift, the entire change in monopoly power is caused by a shift in the markup curve.

The increase in union compensation, which causes marginal cost to rise, will also cause the markup curve to fall. Again it is easier to think about the markup as, $1-(MC/p)$. At any given output, price will remain the same as before because demand has not changed. Marginal cost, however, will rise. Consequently at any given output, the ratio of marginal cost to price *(MC/p)* will rise and the markup will fall. This translates into a decrease in the markup curve.

As a result of the falling markup curve, a new intersection is determined at a lower level of output. In other words, at higher marginal costs, the firm maximizes short-run profits at a lower level of production. The new intersection also occurs at a lower markup, resulting in a new, lower level of monopoly power. The ultimate effect of unions raising wages and compensation is to decrease monopoly power from M_0 to M_1.

If unions reduce monopoly power, they are also likely to reduce average economic power. This can be explained in reference to the following equation, originally derived in Chapter 3.

(5.2) $$\frac{E}{R} = M + \frac{qD}{R} \quad \text{where} \quad D = MC - AC$$

Since unions reduce monopoly power *(M)*, the effect is likely to show up as a decline in average economic power *(E/R)*. An exception would occur in the unlikely event that unions caused an offsetting increase in capacity utilization.

This is an important result because all of the early statistical tests failed to consider the possibility that unions reduce monopoly power and average economic power. None of the original measures devised to represent monopoly power—concentration, market shares, or adver-

Figure 5.3. **Rising Costs and Monopoly Power**

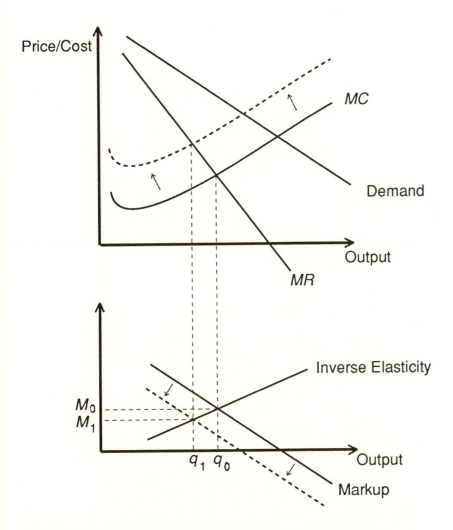

tising—could capture the effect of unions. Two similar industries with identical concentration and advertising could have very different levels of monopoly power depending on the bargaining strength of their labor force. The theoretical results presented in this chapter provide a strong justification for including unions in any statistical test.

Up to this point we have seen how unions can reduce monopoly power and the ratio of economic power to revenue. When unions raise worker compensation, they are also likely to reduce potential profitability, defined as economic power. A simple logical argument explains why. As we saw in the monopoly power model, profit-maximizing output will fall in response to higher wages. At this lower output, profits must be lower because it is different from the original output that maximized profits, and besides, wages are higher. Only in the most extraordinary circumstances would higher wages fail to depress potential profitability.

Firms with low economic power are often barely profitable and any further reduction could drive them into bankruptcy. Not surprisingly, unions naturally gravitate toward firms with substantial levels of economic power. In these firms, unions can increase the wages of their members and still leave enough economic power to generate adequate profits. In effect, investors are forced to share part of the returns from economic power with their workers.

Employer Surplus

We know that firms lose economic power when unions increase wages. But in order to specify the precise magnitude of the loss, it is necessary to introduce the concept of employer surplus. The explanation of this term begins with the labor demand curve, which shows the amount of labor a firm will purchase at any given wage. It is assumed in the following example that wages represent total hourly compensation including fringe benefits. This is important since unions are known to increase benefits in percentage terms at least as much as hourly wages.

According to Figure 5.4 the firm will hire L_0 units of labor at wage w_0. When labor is the only variable factor, its demand curve is equivalent to the amount of revenue generated from each additional unit of labor, defined as marginal revenue product (MRP).[4] Every unit of labor contributes some increment in output and MRP is simply the value of that output.[5]

Why is the MRP curve equal to labor demand? A firm maximizing short-run profits will hire a unit of labor if it adds more to revenue than costs. Another way to state this condition is that marginal revenue product must exceed the wage for the unit of labor to be profitable. Otherwise the firm would be paying more for labor than it receives in additional revenue. By this criterion, all of the units of labor in Figure

Figure 5.4. **Labor Demand**

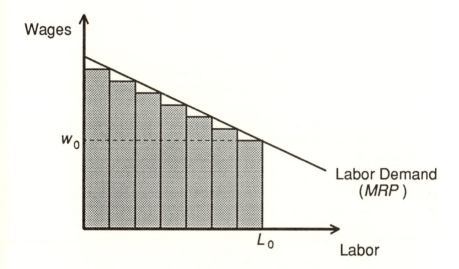

5.4 to the left of L_0 are profitable and all those to the right are not. Therefore we can assume that when the firm maximizes short-run profits, employment will equal L_0. Given any wage, we can find the profit-maximizing level of employment from the *MRP* curve. Labor demand and the *MRP* curve are equivalent because they both show the relationship between wages and the optimum level of employment.

The fact that the *MRP* curve slopes down implies that each additional worker contributes less in revenue than the one before. Why does this happen? It could be because each additional worker contributes less in output when other factors are held constant, a principle referred to as the law of diminishing returns. Or the value of each additional output diminishes because it must be sold at a lower price, a characteristic of all firms with monopoly power. Therefore, the negative slope for labor demand can be attributed to either diminishing returns or monopoly power.

The labor demand curve has several other important features. For example, the area below the curve, up to employment L_0, is equal to total revenue. This is illustrated in Figure 5.4 by constructing a rectangle whose width is equal to one unit of labor and height is equal to *MRP*. The area of the first rectangle (the largest) is simply equal to the *MRP* or the revenue derived from the first unit of labor. Each consecutive labor unit contributes less to revenue, as indicated by progressively smaller rectangles. The last rectangle coincides with actual employment, L_0. The sum of the areas for all rectangles is equal to the total revenue of the firm.

Furthermore, by defining the unit of labor as arbitrarily small, the width of each rectangle shrinks. As a result, the sum of the rectangles will approximate the area under the labor demand curve, illustrated in panel A of Figure 5.5.

Another important area in the figure is the large rectangle below the wage, w_0. The area of this rectangle, highlighted in panel B, is determined by the product of its height (w_0) and width (L_0), which makes it equivalent to total wage income, $w_0 L_0$. The third area, illustrated in panel C, is bounded by the labor demand curve and the wage and is defined as employer surplus. From all three graphs it should be apparent that the sum of employer surplus (S) and wage income ($w_0 L_0$) will exactly equal total revenue (R).

What is the significance of employer surplus? Because we have assumed that labor is the only variable factor, the maximum short-run profits of the firm (π^*) depend only on revenue (R), labor costs, and capital costs (dK).

$$(5.3) \qquad \pi^* = R - w_0 L_0 - dK$$

This can be simplified because the difference between revenue (R) and wage income ($w_0 L_0$) is equivalent to employer surplus (S). And maximum short-run profits (π^*) are by definition equal to economic power (E). Making these two substitutions and rearranging we have this important result:

$$(5.4) \qquad S = E + dK$$

Employer surplus (S) is equal to the sum of economic power (E) and capital costs (dK). Given any particular capital cost, employer surplus will be proportional to the firm's economic power, that is, its maximum potential short-run profits.

An earlier version of this concept was developed by J. B. Clark in 1899. Because Clark dealt exclusively with perfect competition, economic power was set equal to zero. Furthermore, the fixed factor in Clark's model was land rather than capital. Under these assumptions,

67

Figure 5.5. **Revenue, Wage Income, and Employer Surplus**

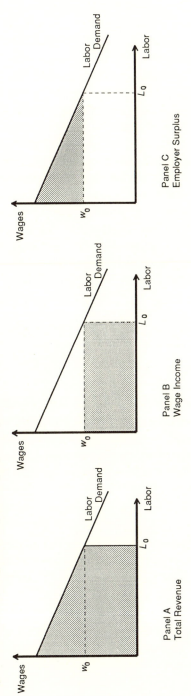

employer surplus is exactly equal to the return on land, or rents. Clark used this model to illustrate the distribution of income in a perfectly competitive market but in its general form, employer surplus includes the income from economic power.

This model is particularly useful for illustrating how unions affect economic power. If unions raise the wage rate from w_0 to w_u, the change in employer surplus is equal to the shaded area in Figure 5.6. The amount of the change will depend on three factors: the size of the wage increase, the initial level of employment, and the slope of the labor demand curve. More surplus will be lost when the wage increase is large, the initial level of employment is large, and the labor demand curve is relatively inelastic.

There is an important relationship between changes in employer surplus and changes in economic power. Because firms are unable to alter capital costs (dK) in the short-run, any immediate change in surplus must equal the change in economic power. This fact, derived from (5.4), can be written in the following form:

(5.5) $$\Delta S = \Delta E$$

where ΔS = change in employer surplus
ΔE = change in economic power

Therefore, the shaded area in Figure 5.6, the change in employer surplus, is also equivalent to the change in economic power.[6] This is a particularly simple way to demonstrate the effect of higher union wages on potential profits.

Employer surplus is also useful for illustrating how unions can alter the distribution of income. In the absence of unions, wages equal w_0 in Figure 5.7, employment equals L_0, and total surplus equals area, $A + B + C + D$. Some part of this total surplus is equal to economic power and the rest is equal to capital costs (dK). One way to separate the two is based on the fact that at a sufficiently high wage, defined as W_m, economic power will equal zero, causing employer surplus to exactly equal capital costs (dK). Therefore, in Figure 5.7, area A is defined as capital costs, and the remainder of the surplus, $B + C + D$, is equal to economic power.

When unions raise their wages from w_0 to w_u, employment declines from L_0 to L_u. Capital costs remain unchanged but economic power

Figure 5.6. **Change in Employer Surplus from Union Wages**

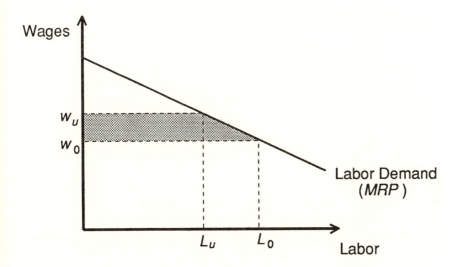

shrinks to area B. The loss of economic power can be divided into two parts, one gained by union workers and the other a net loss. Area C represents the union gain because it equals the product of the wage increase $(w_u - w_0)$ and union employment (L_u). Area D, because it is lost to both the firm and union workers, is defined as a net loss.

For some purposes it is useful to define the income of unions and firms relative to the original economic power. These shares can be calculated using the areas in Figure 5.7.

(5.6)   *Original Economic Power* $= E_0 = B + C + D$

Firm's Share $= B/E_0$
Union's Share $= C/E_0$
Net Loss $= D/E_0$

The sum of the firm's share, union's share, and net loss will be exactly equal to one. In the trade-off between union wage gains and economic power, it is impossible for either party to gain without imposing a loss on the other.

Figure 5.7. **Distribution of Employer Surplus: Firms and Unions**

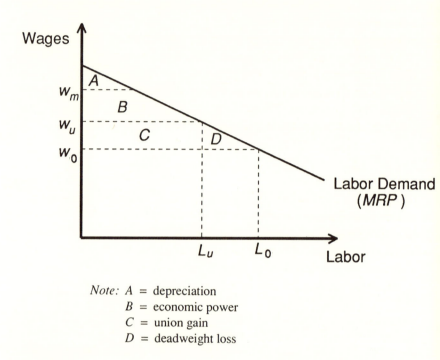

Note: A = depreciation
         B = economic power
         C = union gain
         D = deadweight loss

Imports and Power

By increasing the number of available substitutes, imports can have a negative effect on both monopoly and economic power. The monopoly power of domestic producers falls off in proportion to the number and strength of the new substitutes. Another immediate effect of imports is to reduce the level of demand for domestic producers, leaving them with more productive capacity than they need. In fact, the degree of excess capacity can become severe whenever imports grow faster than total domestic demand. With lower monopoly power (M) and lower capacity utilization (D/p), it is inevitable that average economic power (E/R) will decline.

The specific effect of imports on economic power can be illustrated with employer surplus. In the presence of imports, domestic firms are likely to experience lower demand and because of substitution, higher demand elasticity. These changes have a parallel effect on the demand for labor, causing it to fall and become more elastic.[7] A shift in labor demand from D_0 to D_1 in Figure 5.8 illustrates the effect of imports on a domestic firm.

In response to imports, employment falls from L_0 to L_1 and employer surplus decreases an amount equal to the shaded area. Again, since capital costs do not change in the short run, this change in surplus is exactly equivalent to the change in economic power. A large decline in labor demand, especially one accompanied by a large increase in elasticity, translates into a large loss of economic power.

Executive Compensation

In reality, the contest over profit shares is not limited to firms, unions, and imports. In many businesses, corporate executives, managers, and other nonproduction workers may command greatly inflated incomes by virtue of the economic power of their enterprise.

When union workers raise their compensation, some of the returns to economic power are diverted into higher wages and benefits. The firm, as a result, is likely to realize lower profits than it would if it were nonunion. Whether executives are responsible for a similar reduction in profits depends on the form of compensation. In some profit-sharing plans, profits are distributed to executives only after they have first been declared as profits. In other cases, profits are distributed before they are declared, causing reported profits to decline. Regardless of the form of compensation, it is safe to say that executives reap some of the profits associated with economic power. But how much of this reward shows up as a reduction in reported profits depends on the method of compensation.

Executives are also unlikely to suffer a loss of employment as a penalty for capturing a share of economic power. This is in contrast to union workers, where wage gains can lead to job loss. Top-level management is in a position to strategically adjust their shares of economic power without reducing the number of available positions. This is a distinct advantage they hold over union workers.

This does not mean that executives can plunder a company's surplus without limits. First they are constrained by the amount of economic power available. Firms with small domestic market shares, strong unions, or numerous foreign competitors will have less of a surplus to draw on. Furthermore, enough economic power must remain to pro-

Figure 5.8. **Change in Employer Surplus from Imports**

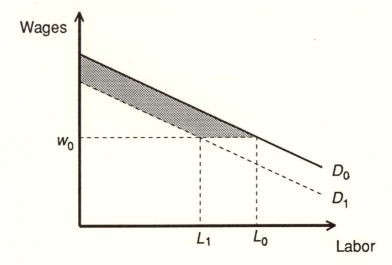

vide sufficient dividends and retained profits to placate investors. If executives fail to limit their acquisitiveness sufficiently they run the risk of inciting a mutiny by disgruntled shareholders. More than one hostile takeover in the 1980s was attributed to the self-serving policies of upper management.

Another important contestant for a share of economic power is the government. Through the corporate profit tax the government sector can capture a significant share of the returns to economic power. The role of the government is discussed in Chapter 12.

6

Do Firms Pay for Higher Costs?

An occasional strike is an indication that . . . the costs of any
wage increase cannot be passed along to someone else.
—John Kenneth Galbraith, 1952[1]

One of the fundamental questions confronting economic theory is to explain who pays for higher costs. This seemingly simple question actually underlies many heated debates in economics. Who, for example, pays for higher union wages or, for that matter, higher petroleum prices? Who bears the burden of the corporate profit tax? Do corporations ultimately pay the punitive damages leveled in a product liability suit or do consumers pick up the tab in the form of higher prices? In each case the burden could fall on consumers if firms raise prices or on employees if jobs are eliminated. But the focus on this chapter is on businesses, and what happens to their economic power when costs increase.

Chapter 5 introduced this question for the specific case of union wages. The analysis demonstrated how higher labor costs for a single firm reduce monopoly and economic power. But in the actual economy, the effect of rising costs is not always so simple. It will depend on many factors including the particular type of cost as well as characteristics of the firm. The purpose of this chapter is to extend the previous analysis so that it applies to a wider variety of situations.

Types of Costs

Traditionally, a distinction is made between costs as either variable or fixed. As indicated by the name, variable costs change immediately with the level of production but fixed costs do not. Most of the examples considered here pertain to variable costs, which are directly related to output. However, fixed costs are only fixed temporarily and can always be changed eventually. Therefore, many of the principles derived in this chapter apply to either type of cost.

Probably the most important characteristic of a cost increase pertains to its coverage. Is it confined to a single firm, a group of firms, or the entire economy? As one can imagine, the effect of a cost increase will be very different if it is universal and applies to the entire economy as opposed to a single firm. A firm would probably be much less concerned about an increase in energy prices that affected the entire economy than one that affected only its operations. However, even when cost increases are universal, they may not be uniform. A cost increase that has a different impact on each firm in a market is not the same as one that has a uniform effect.

Another important characteristic of costs is whether or not they depend on profits. Charges for raw materials like cotton, gold, or lumber are unlikely to respond to changes in the profits of textile plants, jewelers, or builders. In each of these examples costs are typically independent. In contrast, labor costs may not be, especially where unions adjust their wage demands to the prevailing profit level of an industry. Unions often fight for sizable increases during boom times when profits are high only to scale back their demands when profits plummet.

Each of these characteristics of costs plays an important role in determining the effect on business. Is the cost variable or fixed? How extensively does it impact other firms? Is it independent? Understanding these characteristics is essential for economic analysis.

An Individual Firm

The focus in this chapter is on the effect of cost increases on economic power. If there is no change in economic power it is reasonable to conclude that someone other than the firm is paying for the higher cost. But if economic power is significantly reduced, then the firm is carrying at least part of the burden. These results are related to the firm's performance since a loss of economic power is frequently accompanied by a loss of profits.

The analysis of a cost increase is divided into two steps. The first considers the change in monopoly and economic power of a firm in isolation from its rivals. If the cost increase is limited to this single firm, then this completes the analysis. But when rivals are also affected, we need to take a second step, and look at their probable responses.

How does a cost increase affect the monopoly and economic power of a single firm? This question was answered in Chapter 5. Higher marginal costs cause the markup curve to shift to the left in Figure 5.3, resulting in lower output and monopoly power. Monopoly power falls from M_0 to M_1.

Another important question is what happens to economic power when costs increase. According to the results in the previous chapter, an increase in a factor price, like wages, causes a decrease in employer surplus equivalent to the loss of economic power. As a result of factor prices rising from w_0 to w_u in Figure 5.6, economic power equivalent to the shaded area is lost.

If the cost increase is limited to a single firm, then this is the end of the analysis. The firm pays for some of the cost increase in the form of a reduction in economic power. And because output is lower, prices must be higher and consumers will also pay for some part of the cost increase.

Whether or not the company survives depends on its initial level of economic power. Firms with an abundance can afford to lose some of their surplus before their survival is threatened. But for other firms the loss of economic power will exceed their initial level. They cannot survive very long when their maximum potential profits are negative. These firms are destined to fail, if not immediately, at least when their credit is exhausted.

An important application occurs when a corporation loses a lawsuit and is forced to pay damages.[2] Only if economic power exceeds the damage settlement is the firm spared from imminent failure. Judges and juries are likely to weigh these facts before placing a final figure on damages. A settlement that bankrupts the business may not be in anyone's interest.

If this were the only type of cost increase the analysis would be relatively simple. But most cost increases are not restricted to a single firm. They can just as easily affect more than one firm, ranging from a small group to the entire economy. While the primary effect described here for a single firm still applies, it must now be amended to include the secondary effect determined by rival responses.

Economywide Cost Increases

On one extreme are cost increases that affect a single firm and on the other are cost increases that have a uniform effect on the entire economy. How does this alter the analysis?

The difference is that it is now no longer appropriate to assume that demand curves remain constant. As higher costs strike increasing numbers of firms, the general tendency for price increases becomes pervasive. For most firms, the optimum output, the one that maximizes short-run profits, decreases. As firms reduce output they simultaneously raise prices.

What happens to our single firm in the previous example? It will experience an increase in demand as its rivals raise their prices. And this higher demand tends to offset the loss from the higher cost. In fact, with a sufficiently large increase in demand the loss of economic power could be completely offset. It is even possible for employment to remain at its original level as illustrated in Figure 6.1.

Once again, the initial effect of an increase in factor price from w_0 to w_1 is a loss of employment from L_0, where it intersects the original demand curve, to L_1. This causes a decrease in economic power equivalent to shaded area A. But this time rivals increase their prices, causing an expansion in the demand for the product, and with it, the factors necessary to produce it. As factor demand rises, the optimum employment at wage w_1 shifts again, this time from L_1 back to L_0. It is only to simplify the illustration that the level of employment returns precisely to its original level.

The net change in economic surplus is equal to area B less area A. If the effect of rival price increases is weak, then the gain represented by area B will be relatively small. But if the effect is strong, then B may actually offset the entire loss in area A. It is the response of rivals that reduces the loss of economic power due to an economywide cost increase.[3]

The neoclassical model of perfect competition can be used to illustrate the case of an economywide cost increase. In perfect competition it is generally assumed that individual firms have a minimum level of economic power, just sufficient to ensure continued production.[4] It is also assumed that a cost increase uniformly affects every rival. In the first step, economic power drops below the minimum required level. But a counterbalancing response is also set into motion. Firms reduce

Figure 6.1. **Economywide Cost Increase and Employer Surplus**

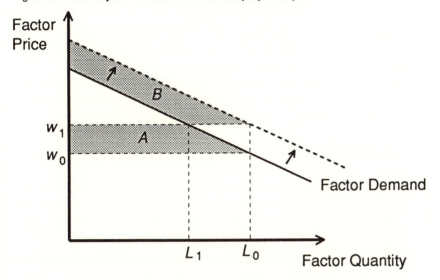

Note: A = Loss in economic surplus from higher costs
B = Gain in economic surplus from higher demand

production, causing a general increase in prices, thus lifting individual demand curves. If the increase in demand is sufficient to recover the initial loss of economic power, the firms will regain economic viability. But if it is insufficient, then some firms must fail. Each failure provides a small boost in demand for the survivors. The exodus continues until individual economic power returns to its original level. At this point, area B will exactly equal area A. In perfect competition economic power always returns to its original low level.

Another example, this one historical, occurred in the 1970s as a result of two sudden increases in oil prices. The first, in late 1973, was related to the Arab-Israeli war and the second, in 1979, to the fall of the Shah in Iran. Both of these cost increases were relatively unique because they impacted large segments of the economy. As a result, firms responded with widespread price increases, which probably attenuated individual profit losses.

One of the obvious repercussions of such a general cost increase is inflation. With so many firms raising prices, inflation begins and often develops a momentum that can be very difficult to arrest. Expectations of rising prices, cost-of-living-adjustments (COLAs), indexing, and collective bargaining can all contribute to a protracted inflation. What happens to economic power during this period depends entirely on the rate of increase in demand relative to costs. If costs rise faster than demand, monopoly and economic power as well as profits are likely to fall, but if demand rises faster the opposite occurs. Some firms win while others lose but for many, demand and costs rise proportionately resulting in no effective change in economic power.

A Group of Rivals

Somewhere between the case of a single firm and the entire economy are cost increases that affect a group of businesses. As in the case of a single firm, rising costs initially cause a reduction in monopoly and economic power. But as in the economywide case, there is also a secondary effect on demand. A firm's demand will rise as long as the cost increase also affects the prices of its rivals. How large an impact depends on how many rivals are affected and the strength of substitution between their products. If only one distant rival is affected, the increase will be relatively small. But if a large number of rivals are impacted, demand will increase and the loss of economic power will be proportionately smaller. In the special situation that all rivals are affected equally, the results are the same as in the economywide case.

There is also the possibility that all rivals will be affected, but not equally. Some may be highly exposed to these particular costs while others are not. The increase in interest rates in the early 1980s raised the costs of production for most farmers but the ones that were most heavily in debt suffered disproportionately. Not all cost increases have a uniform impact.

The analysis of a cost increase for a group of rivals is also represented by Figure 6.1. The net change in economic power is again equal to the difference between area B, gained from the price increase of rivals, and area A, the direct loss. The primary difference in this case is that the gain, area B, is not as large as it would be if all rivals were uniformly affected.

Of particular interest in this case is what happens to rivals that are not directly affected by the cost increase. These firms do not suffer an initial loss of economic power but they do benefit as their less-fortunate rivals increase their prices. They gain in economic power with no offsetting loss. There is, therefore, a redistribution of power away from those who have the most exposure to those particular costs in favor of those with the least exposure. When costs do not affect all rivals uniformly, it is inevitable that some will prosper at the expense of others.

Dependent Costs

In the normal course of discussion, costs are assumed to be independent of prevailing profit levels. Suppose, for example, that an unexpected frost in Florida caused the price of oranges to rise. This would constitute a cost increase for the juice producer who buys oranges from individual farmers. The cost is also independent because its magnitude is not determined by the profits of the juice producer.

A similar claim for independence would be more difficult to sustain in regard to union wages. Many factors enter into the process of collective bargaining including the profitability of the enterprise. When profits are high, unions are much more likely to press for higher wages and firms may be less likely to resist.

When costs explicitly depend on profit levels, the analysis is significantly altered. If rivals respond uniformly with price increases, their power and profits may continue largely intact. But by preserving high profits they effectively invite yet another round of cost increases. Common sense tells us that this cannot continue indefinitely. Eventually the firm or market will exhaust the capacity to pass on costs. With a little foresight a firm may manage to avoid this trap, but only by accepting lower profits in the first place.

Where cost increases are not independent, as in the case of union compensation, firms must eventually face the fact that any immediate success in protecting current profits may only be short-lived. The catch is that it is impossible to permanently avoid a loss of power without inviting renewed demands for higher wages.[5]

An exception occurs where union labor is more costly but also more productive. These union workers may have better training, lower turnover, higher-quality equipment, or simply better management.[6] In this case, unit labor costs do not differ between union and nonunion firms and there is, no reason to expect a difference in economic power.

Profit taxes are not typically described as a cost of production but they are often perceived as such by firms. They are not a variable cost because they do not depend directly on output. But they do vary directly with profits, which makes them a dependent cost. The first effect of a profit tax, like any cost, is to decrease the level of economic power. But the ultimate effect depends on the secondary effect, the response of rivals. Will all rivals increase their prices in response to the tax, thus offsetting the initial loss of economic power? One reason to believe that rivals would respond is because the profit tax is economy-wide. But there are a number of reasons to suspect that the response could be weak.

First, unlike an increase in wages or energy prices, the profit tax does not alter the profit-maximizing level of output for the firm in the short run. The output that maximizes profits under a 30 percent profit tax is the same level that maximizes profits in the absence of the tax. There is, therefore, no clear signal for firms to reduce output and raise prices. A uniform price response by rivals is by no means assured.

Another difficulty is that the profit tax does not uniformly affect all firms. The reason that profit taxes are not uniform is because profits themselves are often determined by random and firm-specific events. Profits can be positive one year and negative the next. In addition, profits vary because firms practice a wide range of different strategies, some more successful than others. The combination of these factors means that profit taxes per dollar of sales can vary widely, even within industries.[7] As a result, a uniform price response by rivals is unlikely to offset the direct loss of economic power caused by a profit tax.

Conclusion

While most cost increases are likely to lead to price increases, a more difficult question is what effect they have on economic power and profits. The answer depends on both the nature of the cost increase as well as firm characteristics. The simplest possibility is that the cost increase is limited to a single firm. In this case both monopoly and economic power will fall, creating pressure on markups and profits to fall as well. Because firms without economic power typically have few profits they risk going out of business while firms with ample power may survive but under conditions of reduced profitability.

It is important to remember that cost increases are not necessarily limited to a single firm. As they become more widespread, the loss of potential profits diminishes. Economic power is less vulnerable to cost increases that affect part or all of a market than those that impact a single firm. In the special case that cost increases are economywide, a general rise in prices can go a long way toward mitigating any direct loss of economic power and profits.

All of these observations apply to unions in a rather complex way. Where the extent of unionization is limited to a single firm or even a small subset of rival firms, a loss of economic power is almost inevitable. Firms can still survive as long as higher union costs do not exceed the firm's original level of economic power.

Where unions cover a high percentage of rivals, the response may be quite different. In a market characterized by low economic power, there is little possibility of a firm absorbing higher union wages without reducing output and raising prices. Any union gain in this case cannot be extracted from existing economic power since there is so little to begin with. It is conceivable in this instance that higher union wages could be paid for entirely from higher prices. Historical examples of this can be seen in trucking and mining, where for many years unionization rates were relatively high. Higher prices could be maintained because entry of nonunion firms was impeded in trucking by regulation and in mining by the limited number of production sites. Consequently higher union wages could be paid for by higher prices.

The situation is qualitatively different for firms with great economic power. It is not essential for these firms to pass on all of the higher labor costs to consumers because they can often pay for them out of profits. But more importantly, it may not be in the long-run interest of these firms to protect short-run profits. Although economic power may initially be preserved, it cannot be protected indefinitely from ever-increasing wage demands. At some point, economic power is likely to suffer.

This completes the broader discussion of the relationship between costs and power. In the next chapter we turn to the second generation of empirical studies of monopoly power. The unifying characteristic of this work is that it tested the effect of unions on monopoly and economic power.

The Second Wave of Statistical Evidence

Thus, the degree of monopoly power will be kept down
to some extent by the activity of trade unions. . . .
—Michal Kalecki, 1971[1]

The first wave of monopoly studies, beginning with Bain in 1951, established monopoly power as a key determinant of business behavior. The most compelling evidence was based on a positive statistical relationship between various measures of monopoly power and actual profits, approximated by price–cost margins. A broad variety of studies covering many time periods arrived at the same general conclusion: markups were higher in concentrated industries. But each of these shared one common deficiency—they failed to consider the effect of unions. A strong union in a concentrated industry is in an ideal position to reduce monopoly power and capture some fraction of excess profits. Ravenscraft's study in 1983 marked the end of its generation of research because it was one of the last to ignore unions.

The second generation of monopoly studies, beginning in the 1980s, took unions into account. These newer studies also contributed other interesting innovations. For example, some of them tested the effects of imports and R&D on margins and monopoly power. Imports can reduce monopoly power by expanding the number of substitutes. And like advertising, R&D can raise monopoly power by increasing the degree of product differentiation and deterring prospective rivals from entering the market.

In many other respects, the new research took advantage of empirical methods pioneered in the earlier work. Nearly all the studies used industrial concentration or market share as the primary measure of monopoly power. Growth was frequently used to control for capacity utilization while some measure of scale was used to account for barriers to entry.[2] Advertising was often included because of its contribution to monopoly power and capacity utilization. And once again, the most comprehensive studies took advantage of industry data and used price-cost margins.

Specifying a New Test

In order to test the effect of unions and imports on margins, it must first be expressed in mathematical terms. The easiest way to proceed is to begin with (4.8) from Chapter 4. In this equation, the price-cost margin is expected to be positively related to concentration and advertising as approximations of monopoly power. This is confirmed when coefficients a_1 and a_2 are positive and statistically significant.

$$(7.1) \quad PCM = a_0 + a_1\, Concentration + a_2\, Advertising/Revenue$$
$$+ a_3\, Growth\ (or\ Capacity\ Utilization)$$
$$+ a_4\, Capital/Revenue + error$$

The problem with this specification is that it does not allow the possibility that unions reduce monopoly power. In its current form, an increase in concentration will cause margins to increase in proportion to a_1, regardless of whether unions are present or not. A more realistic presumption is that the return to concentration should be lower in a firm or industry exposed to strong unions. This possibility can be introduced by defining a new variable, *Union*, as the percentage of workers unionized and substituting $(b_1+b_2\, Union)$ for a_1 in (7.1). Making this change we find the following expanded equation:

$$(7.2) \quad PCM = a_0 + b_1\, Concentration + b_2\, Union \times Concentration$$
$$+ a_2\, Advertising/Revenue$$
$$+ a_3\, Growth\ (or\ Capacity\ Utilization)$$
$$+ a_4\, Capital/Revenue + error$$

The difference between (7.2) and (7.1) is primarily the new term, the product of unions and concentration. This is referred to as an interaction term because it captures the interactive effects between the two variables. When unionization is zero, the new term vanishes and the effect of concentration is determined exclusively by b_1. What we want to test, however, is whether margins of concentrated industries are lower when unionization is high. If this is true, then b_2 estimated in (7.2) will be negative.[3]

As in the earlier studies, we expect margins to be higher in concentrated industries so b_1 should be positive. In fact, now that we have separated the effects of concentration and unions, the coefficient on concentration is likely to be even larger. To illustrate this, suppose that concentration raises margins by .10 at the same time that they are reduced .06 by unions. Estimates based on (7.2) should produce the correct values while estimates based on (7.1) may show concentration raising margins by only .04 (or .10 minus .06). Therefore, estimates of the return to concentration may be higher as well as more accurate once the proper specification is used.

There are a number of ways to expand (7.2) to make it even more compatible with monopoly theory. For example, if unions reduce the return to monopoly power then they could reduce the coefficients on advertising and R&D as well. This would require two more interaction terms between these variables and unions. There is also the fact that imports can reduce monopoly power, thus requiring additional interaction terms between imports and concentration as well as advertising and R&D.[4]

While the first few studies focused on the interaction term between unions and concentration, later studies included some of these additional interaction terms. There are limits, however, since adding a complete set of interaction terms is likely to create serious problems for statistical estimation.[5] As a compromise between this practical difficulty and the theoretical ideal, many of the studies included some limited number of interaction terms. The results have been illuminating.

Empirical Evidence

In a pathbreaking test of these relationships, Richard Freeman (1983) estimated a model for PCMs using two separate data sets; the first contained 139 industries from 1958 to 1976 and the second covered 68 industries from 1965 to 1976.[6] Consistent with earlier studies, Freeman found generally higher price–cost margins in industries with high levels of concentration and advertising.[7] The capital-to-shipments ratio was also included as required by (7.2) and showed a consistently positive effect on margins.

What was unique about Freeman's study was that he included both a union variable and an interaction term between unions and concentration. His results led him to the conclusion that unions significantly reduce the effect of concentration on margins, constituting the first comprehensive evidence that unions reduce monopoly power. Specifically, Freeman found that the coefficient on the interaction term between unions and concentration was negative and highly significant so that unions appeared to have their largest negative effect on margins in concentrated industries.

Equally provocative was the finding that unions appeared to have virtually no effect on margins where concentration was low. This was tested by including an individual term for unions in the regression equation. The coefficient on this term measures the effect of unions when concentration is zero and this value was not statistically significant.

There was another more subtle result in Freeman's study that provided additional evidence of monopoly power. The return to concentration increased once the negative effect of unions was accounted for. With a slight adjustment for the fact that Freeman used logarithms, it is possible to show that the coefficients on concentration increased between .04 and .13 percentage points when union interaction terms were included.[8] In other words, the effect of concentration on margins was larger once unions were properly accounted for. Freeman's results also show that unions reduced margins between 21 percent and 65 percent. The hypothesis that unions reduce monopoly power received strong support from this study.

This original work marked the beginning of a new generation of monopoly research that incorporated the effects of unions. A subset of these new studies using industry data and PCMs is summarized in Table 7.1. In every case, unions caused a significant reduction in margins and, with the exception of Domowitz et al. (1986), the reduction was confined to concentrated industries. The incongruous results in the Domowitz study seem to be related to problems of statistical estimation.[9] In general, the evidence provides overwhelming support for the belief that unions cause a significant reduction in monopoly power.

86

Table 7.1

Contemporary Studies on the Return to Monopoly Power

Study	Measures of Monopoly Power	Important Results	Profit Measure	Primary Data Source
1.	Concentration* Advertising*	Unions reduced the effect of concentration on margins	PCM and return to capital	139 manufacturing industries, 1958–76
2.	Concentration* Advertising*	Unions reduced the effect of concentration on margins	PCM and return to capital	68 industries, 1965–76
3.	Concentration* Advertising*	Unions reduced the effect of concentration on margins	PCM	341 state by industry observations in 1972
4.	Concentration* Advertising*	Unions reduced margins	PCM	139 manufacturing industries, 1968, 70, 72
5.	Concentration* Advertising*	Unions reduced margins in both concentrated and unconcentrated industries	PCM	284 manufacturing industries, 1958–81
6.	Concentration* Advertising	Unions and imports reduced the effect of concentration on margins	PCM	107 manufacturing industries, 1965–80
7.	Concentration*	Unions reduce margins	PCM	125 manufacturing industries, 1968–72

Sources: 1. Freeman (1983); 2. Freeman (1983); 3. Karier (1985); 4. Voos and Mishel (1986a); 5. Domowitz, Hubbard, and Peterson (1986); 6. Karier (1988); 7. Ghosal (1989).
Note: * signifies that the variable had a significant effect on profits (5 percent level).

My own study in 1985 was based on a unique sample where each observation corresponded to a specific industry and state in 1972. Because unionization rates vary widely across states even within the same industry this data provided a useful test of the effect of unionization on monopoly power. If firms in industries and states with high unionization have less monopoly power, then their margins should reflect this fact. This is precisely what I found. Unions reduced margins by approximately 68 percent where concentration was especially high.[10] In moderately concentrated industries unions still caused a reduction of 55 percent, and in the least concentrated industries, where average margins tended to be considerably lower, the effect of unions was essentially zero.

As part of my analysis, I also calculated the effects of unions on the margins of eight highly concentrated industries in 1972. The results presented in Table 7.2 show that virtually all of the monopoly power arising from concentration in the automobile and steel industries was eliminated by unions. More fortunate were the manufacturers of instruments, chemicals, petroleum and coal, and electrical equipment where firms managed to retain approximately half of their original monopoly power.

The results of one of these studies suggest that monopoly power fluctuates over the business cycle. Domowitz, Hubbard, and Peterson used a sample of 284 industries to measure changes in the effects of concentration and unions on margins from 1958 to 1981. As in other studies, they found a strong positive effect of concentration and advertising on price–cost margins. But the effect of concentration appeared to fall significantly during periods of high unemployment. One reason suggested for this, although the evidence was rather weak, was that unions take a larger share of monopoly profits during recessions. This is possible since union wages are often locked in by long-term contracts even when demand falls. As a result, unions may tend to squeeze monopoly power during recessions, resulting in relatively lower margins.

In my 1988 study included in Table 7.1, I measured the effect of both unions and imports on monopoly power. As described earlier, this required the use of an interaction term between import intensity and concentration. The negative coefficient found for this term implied that imports also reduce monopoly power. The total reduction in margins was 61 percent of which 47 percent was attributed to unions and 14

Table 7.2

Effect of Unions on Monopoly Power: Specific Industries in 1972

	Percentage Unionized	Percentage Reduction in Monopoly Power
Primary Metal Industries	.64	106
Transportation Equipment	.58	96
Stone, Clay, and Glass Products	.51	85
Tobacco Manufacturers	.39	65
Chemicals and Allied Products	.28	46
Petroleum and Coal Products	.33	55
Electrical and Electronic Equipment	.33	55
Instruments and Related Products	.22	36

Source: Calculated from Karier (1985), Table 3.

percent to imports.[11] Another way to interpret these results is in terms of employer surplus. Unions captured approximately 47 percent of the surplus through higher wages while imports captured 14 percent by reducing domestic demand, leaving 39 percent for firms.

One should be reminded that these results were based on average values over a fifteen-year period from 1965 to 1980 and cannot be expected to accurately represent the distribution for any single year. Also, developments since 1980 could have significantly altered the distribution. For example, the recent U.S. experience with declining unionization rates and rising imports would tend to shift the surplus accordingly. Although it was not possible to measure changes in the distribution over time, the study did provide evidence that the return to concentration advanced significantly during this period. This meant that the surplus was expanding, providing a larger pie to divide among the various claimants.

Confirmation of several of these results was provided by Voos and Mishel (1986a) who analyzed price–cost margins for 139 manufacturing industries in 1970.[12] Consistent with previous research, concentration and advertising significantly raised margins but unions reduced them. No attempt was made in this study, however, to determine whether the union effect was related to concentration. But the authors did point out the possibility that unions may be more likely to establish themselves in the first place in more profitable industries. Unions appeared to take the above-average profits of some industries and reduce them to below average. To the extent that this is true, estimates in the other studies understate the actual union profit effect.

In all of these studies, with the exception of Domowitz et al., unions had only a weak and insignificant effect on margins in unconcentrated industries. Part of the reason may be that unions have been less successful raising wages in these industries. It is also more difficult to force margins down if they are already at low levels due to competitive pressures. And finally, where unions did succeed in organizing a high percentage of the industry such as in trucking or coal mining, higher wage costs could be paid for by a general price increase rather than lower profits or margins.

Profit Losses Compared with Wage Gains

Nearly all of the studies in Table 7.1 corroborated two important aspects of monopoly theory: concentration tends to raise monopoly power whereas unions and imports tend to lower it. But there is another aspect to the theory; the profits lost by firms should be equal to the sum of union compensation gains and a deadweight loss. How do estimates of the total profits transferred from firms to unions compare with estimates of union compensation gains?

The results of two different studies measuring both these effects are summarized in Table 7.3. Voos and Mishel estimated a union profit loss for the early 1970s between $8.2 billion and $13.8 billion based on their sample for all manufacturing.[13] This range is lower than my own estimate of $21.7 billion for 1972 based on union effects in concentrated industries. Estimates of union gains in wages and benefits, presented in the second column, were relatively closer. Voos and Mishel found union workers making $10.3 billion more than comparable nonunion workers compared with the range of $11.2 to $15.9 billion that I estimated.

To summarize these findings, the profits lost because of unions appear to equal or exceed the additional compensation won by unions. The fact that firms may lose more than unions actually gain is really not as puzzling as it first appears. According to the theory, this is exactly what one should expect, because the profit loss is equal to the union compensation gains plus a deadweight loss. The deadweight loss

Table 7.3

Comparison of Union Profit Effects and Compensation Gains

Study	Union Profit Effects (Billions $ 1972)	Union Compensation Gains (Billions $ 1972)
Voos and Mishel (1986a)	−8.2 to −13.8	10.3
Karier (1984)	−21.7	11.2 to 15.9

is essentially the reduction in the total surplus available to both firms and unions, which results from an adjustment to higher wages. This reduction, or deadweight loss, in combination with union wage gains should exactly equal the profit loss.

Another reason why profit losses could exceed union gains is related to the "spillover" effect. According to this view, management increases nonunion compensation in an attempt to discourage further unionizing or in order to preserve the wage differentials of the firm's original wage structure. In the presence of spillovers, unions can cause an additional decline in profits by increasing compensation of nonunion workers in the firm. In general, the gap between profit losses and union gains can be explained by deadweight losses, spillovers, or some combination of the two.

How important is the union profit effect relative to total reported profits? Officially reported profits of $41 billion in 1972 would have been 20 percent to 53 percent larger without unions.[14] Obviously the union share of monopoly profits is too large to be ignored. But it should again be pointed out that the sharp decrease in unionization rates since 1972 must have significantly reduced the union share.

Firm Studies

Ideally one would like to test the theory of monopoly power using a sample that includes individual lines of business for all firms but because of practical difficulties in obtaining data, this is currently impossible. It should be pointed out that all of the studies cited up to this point were based on a comparison of margins for samples of manufacturing industries. In addition to this research, several studies have tested similar relationships using samples of individual firms or their lines of business. In many respects, these firm studies showed considerable progress from their counterparts in the first generation of monopoly research.

The most consistent result of the studies listed in Table 7.4 is that every one of them found that unions reduce profitability. This result is unusually consistent across both firm and industry studies. Furthermore, all three of the studies that included R&D (2,3,5) found this variable to have a positive effect on profitability. Almost as consistent was the finding that market share had a positive effect on profits, demonstrated in four (1,4,5,6) of the five studies that included this variable.

Beyond these basic results, there are few other areas of agreement. Two of the studies (4,6) found that concentration had a significant positive effect on profits while another (5) found a significant negative effect. Differences were even more pronounced in regard to the interaction of unions with market share or concentration. Three of the studies (2,4,6) found unions reduced profits primarily among firms with high market share or in highly concentrated industries. The author of one of these studies (2) concluded that "the most interesting result in this article is that unionized workers are the primary beneficiaries of monopoly power."[15] However, two studies (1,6) found that unions reduced profits most for firms with low market share. How can these contradictory findings be explained?

Although the quality of recent firm studies is generally better than the first generation's, they have not managed to overcome all of the problems. Two of them (3,5) used the union coverage of the industry rather than the firm because appropriate data was lacking. How well industry unionization rates apply to any single firm is anyone's guess. And many of the studies (3,4,5,6) included both concentration and market share in every regression. This can create problems, because concentration is functionally related to market share and including them in the same equation creates a bias that reduces the statistical significance of both. Furthermore, some of the studies used experimental measures of long-run profitability, like Tobin's q, which are only remotely related to monopoly and economic power.

But the most important characteristic of many of these studies (1,2,3,5,6) is that they relied on small samples of very large firms. In several cases, the firms studied were all included in the *Fortune* 500, an elite subcategory of the largest U.S. industrial corporations ranked

Table 7.4

Firm Studies of Monopoly Power

Study	Measures of Economic Power	Important Results	Profit Measure	Primary Data Source
1.	Industry concentration Market Share*	Unions reduce returns for firms with low market share Imports reduce returns	Return on sales	Lines of businesses for 250 large companies, 1970–80
2.	Concentration Advertising* R&D*	Unions reduce the return to concentration by 77 percent	Return on capital and Tobin's q	252 firms in 1976 (some industry data for some)
3.	Concentration Market Share Advertising* R&D Patents*	Unions reduce the return to R&D but increase the return to advertising	Excess value	367 firms from the *Fortune* 500, 1977
4.	Concentration* Relative market share*	Unions reduce the return to concentration	Pretax profits per sales	71 firms by SMSA observations in grocery retailing, 1972
5.	Concentration* (wrong sign) Market Share* R&D*	Unions reduce the return to market share and R&D Imports reduce the return to concentration	Return on capital and Tobin's q	367 firms from the *Fortune* 500, 1977
6.	Concentration* Market share*	Unions reduce returns primarily in unconcentrated industries	Return on capital and Tobin's q	247 firms from the *Fortune* 500, 1976 & 77.

Sources: 1. Clark (1984); 2. Salinger (1984); 3. Connolly, Hirsch, and Hirschey(1986); 4. Voos and Mishel (1986b); 5. Hirsch and Connolly (1987); 6. Hirsch (1990).

Note: *signifies that the variable had a significant effect on profits (5 percent level).

by annual revenue. The *Fortune* 500, however, constitute less than one-fifth of one percent of all industrial corporations. The samples are relevant because large firms are more likely to have high levels of monopoly and economic power.

With this understanding, it is possible to reinterpret the results of firm studies. Unions reduce the profitability of large firms, which typically have high levels of monopoly and economic power. Whether this effect is stronger in firms with high or low market share is difficult to measure when firms with very low shares are systematically excluded from the sample. We find conflicting results only because the sample is not broad enough to include both ends of the spectrum.

In some studies, the use of lines of business can introduce a wider range of monopoly power. The primary industry of the enterprise may have a high market share and its smaller subsidiaries, a low share. But do subsidiaries accurately represent the large number of smaller independent firms? In some cases, subsidiaries sell their output directly to the parent company at prices determined by the accounting department of the central office rather than the market. Even costs can be arbitrarily assigned to subsidiaries when they involve central office operations that benefit both parent and subsidiary in some uncertain proportion. These relationships can become more complicated if the firm attempts to exploit the subsidiary to solve a problem of cash flow in the parent corporation.[16] Or some parents have been known to load their subsidiaries with valuable assets just prior to declaring bankruptcy.[17] These are just some of the reasons why small subsidiaries are not equivalent to small independent firms.

Despite these limitations, there are a few original results in these studies. For example, two of them (3,5) found that unions reduced the return to R&D. It appears that unions can capture a share of employer surplus regardless of its source. Another firm study (5) showed that imports can reduce the return to concentration, much like in the industry studies.

The only study in Table 7.4 that did not explicitly focus on large firms was conducted by Voos and Mishel. They compared the profit to sales ratio for a sample of grocery firms in a variety of geographic markets and found results that were very similar to the industry studies. Concentration and market share appeared to raise profitability while unions reduced it. They also found the familiar result that the negative union effect was confined to concentrated industries. By choosing a specific industry as their sample, the authors avoided the problem of dealing exclusively with large firms.

The Pass-On Theory of Union Costs

Even among those who recognize the existence of monopoly power, there has always been a certain resistance to the idea that unions capture a share of profits. According to Baran and Sweezy, "... under monopoly capitalism employers can and do pass on higher labor costs in the form of higher prices. They are, in other words, able to protect their profit margins in the face of higher wages (and fringe benefits)."[18]

While this argument is theoretically plausible, it contradicts the results of almost every empirical study reviewed in this chapter. Not only is the union profit effect consistently negative, it is almost exclusively confined to large firms or concentrated industries. Union compensation is not as easy for firms to pass on without affecting profits as some analysts once believed.

In addition to this statistical evidence, there is another reason to suspect that unions have had a negative effect on monopoly profits. The intense hostility that corporations have historically demonstrated in their battles with unions is inconsistent with the theory that union costs are effortlessly passed on. Labor history is replete with examples of intense struggles between labor and management over union recognition. After incurring great costs to avoid unionization, it would be more than a little astounding to find corporations turning around and passing on union costs without any injury to themselves. Even today, the opposition continues, although the form of that resistance has changed dramatically. Businesses now appear willing to relocate entire plants, subcontract out work, and engage high-priced consultants merely to avoid unions. It seems reasonable to assume that such hostile and costly opposition would not be undertaken if the elimination of unions did not promise some pecuniary benefit.

Wage–Price Spiral

The fact that unions share in the returns to economic power does not preclude the possibility that unions and firms may occasionally clash over the prevailing distribution. Especially during inflationary periods, unions and firms may attempt to increase their own shares of the surplus giving rise to what is often referred to as the wage–price spiral. The critical issue in such a situation is whether wages or prices rise faster. When wages rise faster than prices, the union share rises relative to the firm's but when prices rise relatively faster, firms are the winners. In the event that wages and prices rise proportionately, neither side achieves any real gain but the impasse fuels the inflationary spiral.

During these periods it is likely to appear as if firms effortlessly pass on wage gains into higher prices, especially when wages and prices rise proportionately. But the most that one can conclude from this experience is that whatever distribution existed before the inflationary period is likely to persist. It is only when wages and prices increase at different rates that the distribution of monopoly profits is affected, and this depends on the relative bargaining strength of unions and firms. The fact that firms can pass on union wage increases during inflation does not mean that unions have not already taken hold of some fraction of the returns to economic power.

Conclusion

A frequent objection to monopoly theory has been the contention that the magnitude of reported profits is hardly large enough to warrant much concern. But in this chapter it was shown that monopoly power would be far greater if not for the "countervailing" effects of unions and imports. Research during the first wave of monopoly studies overlooked this important fact.

There is no reason to expect that the distribution of monopoly profits is limited to firms, unions, and imports. Executives, managers, and other nonproduction workers represent another constituency in a position to claim a share of profits. Research in this area has been slow due to a lack of comprehensive data but what evidence exists suggests that some profits are diverted to executive compensation. All this means is that we have yet to fully account for all shares of economic power.

Price Competition

The achievement of market power is a major proximate goal of firms.
—Hyman Minsky, 1986[1]

One of the propositions of monopoly theory is that the potential values, monopoly and economic power, are statistically related to actual measures of business performance, price–cost margins, and profits. In order to test this claim, numerous studies investigated the statistical correspondence between actual profitability and variables approximating average economic power. The fact that the two were statistically related provided strong support for monopoly theory.

This raises another question. Why don't profits always equal economic power? Why are the potential values only statistically related to the actual values? The reason is that firms do not always maximize short-run profits and other firms do not always hold their prices constant. One important example of this is price competition. A firm might come to the conclusion that it could increase its future profitability if it kept its current price relatively low. While future profits may end up higher, current profits will fall below the level of economic power. Similarly, if rivals cut prices for basically the same reason, the firm's profits would again fall below its economic power.

A divergence between potential and actual profitability can also occur when firms cooperate, and raise prices together. They may do it in deference to a powerful market leader or as part of a contractual, albeit possibly illegal, agreement. Whatever the motivation, the participating firms stand to increase their actual profits above and beyond the benchmark determined by economic power. Cooperation is potentially more profitable than independent action.

These relationships are summarized in Figure 8.1. The dotted line represents equality between average economic power (E/R) and the ratio of profits to revenue (π/R). Firms land on the line only if they and their rivals maximize short-run profits. In the event that firms cut prices now in hopes of expanding future profits, they fall below the dotted line in the region identified as price competition. But if firms raise actual profitability above average economic power by means of collective action, then they are placed in the region of cooperation.

If we were to plot the points for all firms on this graph, some would fall on the line, others above or below it, but in general this plot should reveal a positive correlation between average economic power and the return on revenue. This was the point of dozens of empirical studies reviewed in previous chapters.

A positive correlation between potential and actual profitability provides an important insight into general business behavior. But in order to understand any particular firm, we must explore why actual profits sometimes diverge from their potential, in other words, why some firms compete while others cooperate. Are there certain characteristics of firms that propel them in favor of one strategy over another? The purpose of this chapter is to investigate the characteristics that motivate price competition, leaving other forms of competition and cooperation for Chapter 9.

A Definition

The term *price competition* is used frequently by economists but not always with the same meaning. Some refer to it as the act of setting prices below the prevailing market level. But when firms produce differentiated products there is no single market price and price competition loses its meaning. This is unsatisfactory because we know that firms producing different but related products will occasionally use prices as a means of competing and eliminating rivals. What is needed is a definition of price competition that does not apply exclusively to markets with identical products.

One possibility is based on the difference between actual price (p_0) and the price that maximizes short-run profits (p^*). The degree of price competition is defined as the percentage deviation between these two prices.

(8.1)
$$Degree\ of\ Price\ Competition = \frac{p^* - p_0}{p^*}$$

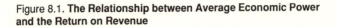

Figure 8.1. **The Relationship between Average Economic Power and the Return on Revenue**

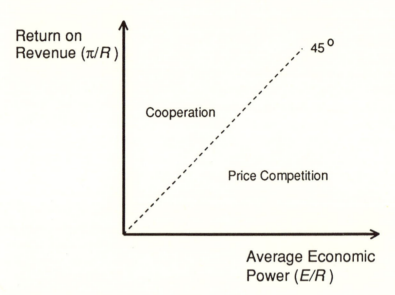

Whenever the current price falls below the level that maximizes current profits, the firm is engaged in price competition.[2] It is understood that a firm practices price competition with the intention of boosting future demand.

The advantage of this definition is that it applies readily to all kinds of markets regardless of whether products are homogeneous or not. In the special case of perfect competition where all products are effectively identical, the optimum price (p^*) is expected to prevail in the market. To the extent that any firm breaks from the pack and sells below the market price, it engages in price competition.

Future Demand and Expectations

An essential element in price competition is the relationship between current prices and future demand. To see this, suppose current prices have absolutely no effect on future demand. Price competition becomes entirely unnecessary because there is no reason to reduce current price below p^*. Why sacrifice current profits if nothing is to be gained? Obviously price competition is only a viable strategy when it holds the prospect of raising future demand.

It is often expected that a high current price will reduce future sales. One reason for this is that substitution does not always take place immediately. It may take time for consumers to find adequate substitutes or to make the purchases necessary to alter consumption patterns. As a result of these delayed substitutions, current prices can affect future demand.[3]

Another reason for this relationship is related to entry. If barriers are relatively low, a high current price may increase the influx of potential rivals, thus reducing the future demand of the firm. The magnitude of barriers is critical because highly protected firms will face significantly less potential competition. A firm with patent rights or secret production methods, for instance, can set higher prices without fear of losing its sales to newcomers.

We can now be more specific about the reasons for price competition. It is useful either to deter entry or to reduce future substitution. Consequently, price competition is most likely to appeal to firms facing easy entry and strong long-run substitution.

It must be emphasized that it is not always as important how firms respond as how they are expected to respond. When a firm decides not to cut its price for fear of retaliation by other firms it is acting on expectations. In practice, the actual outcome of current strategies is typically too late to affect current decisions. Firms are left to rely entirely on their expectations, which are, of course, informed by past experience. One can readily see that in order to understand the behavior of firms it is necessary to focus on expectations, what they are and how they are formed.

In the following analysis we assume that firms formulate expectations of future profits based on all available information. Any factor that has any bearing whatsoever on future demand and costs is assumed to be incorporated into these expectations. These include: consumer behavior and income, rival responses, general business conditions, union demands, and government intervention.

Expectations of future profits also typically depend on current decisions. Whether a firm decides to maximize current profits or practice price competition is likely to send it on very different paths. Only by comparing the expected profits associated with each path is it possible to assess the relative desirability of each strategy.

A Model of Price Competition

One strategy available to a firm is to maximize current profits at every point in time. Of all the possible pricing strategies, this one is the least likely to invite a response because prices are neither particularly low nor high. If other firms follow the same course, the firm's profits will equal its economic power. Future demand may rise or fall, but prices and markups in each period always maximize short-run profits. When a firm proceeds in this way, its profits trace out a certain pattern over time defined as its *neutral* path. In the three possible neutral paths illustrated in Figure 8.2, profits either expand (path N_A), contract (N_C), or remain constant (N_B). Obviously the firm expects only one of these to actually represent its neutral path.

How would the path change if the firm practiced price competition? It would probably expect lower profits in the current period and, if the strategy has any possibility at all of being adopted, higher profits in the future. Figure 8.3 compares a path of price competition (A) to a neutral path with constant profits. Although many more possibilities exist, associated with different degrees of price competition, this example illustrates the basic choices confronting a firm.

How would a firm choose between these two strategies? It may decide that current profits are much more important and stick to the neutral path. Or it could follow path A if the prospect of large future profits outweighs the current loss. But a much more systematic way to make the decision is to compare the sum of profits generated from each strategy, properly discounting all future values.[4] The firm is most likely to select the strategy with the highest value. For example, suppose π_t represents the expected profits of a particular path at any time, t. Defining d as the discount rate, the present value of expected profits, $PV(\pi)$, can be calculated from the following equation:

$$(8.2) \qquad PV(\pi) = \pi_0 + \frac{\pi_1}{(1+d)^1} + \frac{\pi_2}{(1+d)^2} + \cdots \frac{\pi_\infty}{(1+d)^\infty}$$

The present value of profits for every path can be calculated using (8.2) and then compared. The strategy with the highest present value is the one most likely to be chosen by the firm.

The choice of strategies can also be illustrated graphically. From the

Figure 8.2. **Three Possibilities for a Neutral Path**

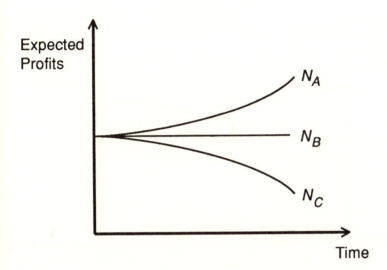

expected profit paths in Figure 8.3 we can calculate their present value by discounting profits at every point in time. Expected profits in the first year are not affected, but those in the future are reduced at an increasing rate. The new values are likely to look like those in Figure 8.4. This adjustment is useful because the sum of discounted profits for each strategy is equal to the area under each curve.[5] The best strategy, the one with the greatest sum of discounted expected profits, has the largest area under its curve.

A firm would consider price competition only if the area under the curve for this strategy exceeds the area under the curve for the neutral path. By using this criterion, the firm is no longer necessarily maximizing short-run profits. But it is maximizing profits in a much broader sense, one that includes both the present and the future. A firm is willing to sacrifice current profits only if future gains, properly discounted, more than compensate for the current loss.

When firms engage in price competition and succeed they can gain an expansion of future demand, usually at the expense of their immediate rivals. Higher demand translates into greater future economic power, which is ultimately the goal of price competition. Losers are forced to accept lower future demand or, in some circumstances, are extinguished through bankruptcy, merger, or takeover.

Figure 8.3. **Two Strategies: Neutral Path *(N)* and Price Competition *(A)***

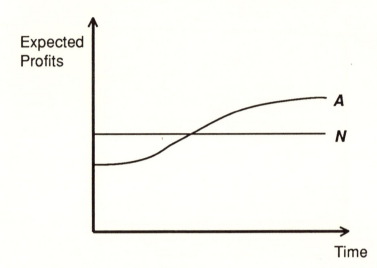

While the duration of price competition will vary from case to case, it will generally be proportional to the degree of price competition. The greater the sacrifice in current profits the sooner one can expect a resolution. The duration may be even shorter for firms starting off with low economic power because they are ill-equipped to endure prolonged losses.

When a firm reduces its price, it drains revenue from its rivals. In terms of our model, it reduces the neutral paths of rivals, raising the likelihood that they will also engage in price competition. Whether or not rivals decide to retaliate will have a large impact on the expected profits of the original firm. Therefore, any firm contemplating the use of price competition must carefully assess the likely response of rivals.

When is retaliation likely? A firm with a great number of relatively large rivals can hardly expect its own insignificant price reduction to become a catalyst for widespread price competition. The gain in revenue may be relatively great for the small firm while the corresponding losses are relatively minor for large firms. The same reasoning applies when there are a multitude of rivals, even of comparable size. Why would any one firm want to retaliate if it bore only a small part of the total loss? Assuming that the original competitor correctly assesses the situation, its fear of retaliation would be relatively low.

Figure 8.4. **The Present Value of Two Profit Paths**

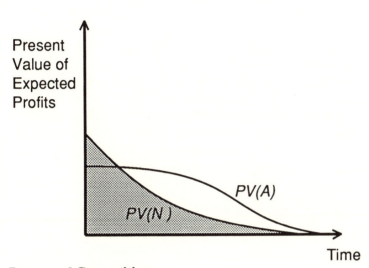

Power and Competition

In either of these cases, where rivals are relatively large or relatively numerous, the expected probability of retaliation decreases. Both of these characteristics are likely to coincide for firms with low monopoly power, leading to the unsurprising conclusion that these firms may be more inclined to practice price competition. Underlying this behavior is their strong sense of anonymity.

The likelihood of price competition is related to monopoly power in other ways. One of the goals of this strategy is to increase revenue relative to rivals but this could be perceived as predatory, deemed illegal under Section 2 of the Robinson Patman Act.[6] Relatively large firms may be more susceptible to these charges because they are less likely to escape detection and because the permissible range of pricing practices is more restrictive for market leaders. Firms may be legitimately concerned about the cost of an adverse settlement under a Section 2 complaint as well as the considerable amount of time and legal resources required. Before being settled, charges against three major companies, IBM, Xerox, and AT&T, dragged on for years, involving significant costs and uncertainties.[7]

Additional problems arise for large firms if the ultimate goal of price competition is to buy out one or more rivals. Even though anti-trust enforcement declined after 1982 it can still be invoked to tame the acquisitive instincts of firms with sizable amounts of monopoly power. In order to emphasize this fact, the Justice Department rewrote its guidelines in 1982, making clear that mergers were more likely to be challenged when they involved firms with high market shares or caused large increases in market share.[8]

Since regulatory decree circumscribes the right of firms with sub-stantial power to drive their competitors into bankruptcy court or into their own fold, they are understandably more reluctant to engage in price competition. An important function of antitrust regulation is to prevent excessive growth in monopoly power by suppressing price competition among firms with significant market shares.

It is always possible that a firm with substantial power will choose price competition despite the danger of government intervention and retaliation by rivals. Even market leaders may find this strategy the most profitable alternative when confronted by price-cutting rivals. In fact, while market leaders seldom initiate price competition, they may be inclined to respond to challenges posed by smaller rivals.

For example, the long stability of U.S. cigarette prices was disrupted by the smallest of the six tobacco companies, Liggett Group. In 1980, Liggett introduced price competition by selling generic cigarettes at prices as much as 35 percent below the major brands. The cigarettes themselves were actually the same as Liggett's name brand although the packaging was less exciting. For a time the strategy worked and Liggett captured an increasing share of the market. The third largest tobacco company, Brown and Williamson Tobacco (B.A.T. Indus-tries), was unwilling to let this attack go unanswered. It countered with price competition by introducing a low-priced generic of its own. Fur-thermore, B&W stated in its own documents that it was willing to lose money on generics in order to reduce the losses suffered by its name brands and put an end to Liggett's challenge. The outcome of this episode was an antitrust case in which Brown and Williamson was convicted in 1990 of predatory pricing and fined $148 million based on treble damages.[9]

Another example is the Utah Pie Company, which attempted to gain a foothold in Salt Lake City's frozen pie market in 1957. In order to wrestle sales from three national companies that controlled the market—Continental Baking Company, Pet Milk, and Carnation—this small local company implemented a strategy of price competition. Before the big three responded, Utah Pie captured 67 percent of the market. Eventually, the national companies retaliated only to find themselves in court where it was decided that they had overstepped the bounds of fair competition.[10]

The outcome of price competition in some markets is the complete displacement of a rival. An example of this can be found in the airline industry. In 1991 when Eastern Airlines offered discount fares in its Atlanta market, Delta Airlines was at first reluctant to respond. But when it finally did, Eastern shut down within three months, giving Delta 82 percent of the business out of Atlanta's Hartsfield International Airport.[11]

Price competition may also be used to weaken a rival in preparation for a merger or acquisition. There were once two independent metropolitan newspapers serving Detroit, the *Detroit News* and the *Detroit Free Press*. Both were profitable until 1979 when a price war erupted resulting in extremely low prices and advertising charges. In November of 1989 the *News* sold for 15 cents and the *Free Press* for 20 cents compared with 25 cents or more for most U.S. dailies.[12] As a result of price competition, both companies suffered losses, which was the basis for their appeal to the U.S. attorney general to combine their business interests under the auspices of a joint operating agreement (JOA). Their appeal was approved and ultimately cleared by the U.S. Supreme Court in November 1989.

There are also cases where firms with significant power did not retaliate. Under what conditions would a firm choose not to respond to a price cut by a rival? The answer is when the profits of not responding are relatively greater. For a firm to be willing to stand by and watch its economic power erode without slashing markups, the total profits of the neutral path must exceed those of competing.

Far from being a mere theoretical curiosity, there is some evidence to suspect that this is exactly what the U.S. auto companies did when faced with price competition from abroad during the 1980s. Prices for U.S. producers apparently rose at the very time that imports increased their share of the U.S. market.[13] This was consistent with the reputation U.S. automakers had earned over the decades for being generally averse to price competition.

Another example is Alcoa, the nation's largest aluminum producer. When faced with falling prices for aluminum ingot in 1989, Alcoa steadfastly refused to follow the industry pattern of price reductions for sheet aluminum used in the production of cans. As a result, its short-run profits did not fall as much as its closest competitor, Alcan Aluminum Ltd., but it did sacrifice several percentage points of market share.[14] In this case Alcoa, the nation's largest metal producer, was so averse to price competition that it refused to cut prices even to match those of its rivals. A dozen other examples of leading firms sacrificing market share for current profits are cited by Scherer ranging from the steel industry to instant mashed potatoes.[15] In each of these cases market leaders chose to maximize short-run profits rather than respond to price competition.

Although a great number of considerations enter into the decision to engage in price competition, there are several that warrant special attention. One is capacity utilization. If firms have excess capacity they may have a greater interest in expanding future sales. Consequently, firms with substantial excess capacity may be more inclined to practice price competition.

Another important consideration in making a decision about price competition is the discount rate. When a firm uses a high discount rate it places very little value on the future, making it less willing to sacrifice current for future profits. This argument is frequently raised when American firms are contrasted with their Japanese counterparts. It has been widely noted in the U.S. business press that Japanese firms often appear more willing to sacrifice current profits because they place a far greater value on future market share than American firms. When firms apply a lower discount rate, price competition naturally becomes more desirable. The point of such a debate is usually to fault the Japanese for using too low a discount rate or Americans for using too high a rate.[16] The consequence is that the average U.S. firm appears preoccupied with short-run profits and may not compete as intensely in international markets.

A firm may also be more inclined toward price competition if it is convinced that it has some production advantage that would give it a competitive edge in an all-out battle for market share. Whatever the origin of this advantage—lower cost inputs, superior production methods, economies to scale, or some combination of the three—it must be significant enough for the firm to risk an outbreak of a price war. These advantages should be distinguished from those that originate from a superior product or better marketing strategy that can be used to gain market share without necessarily resorting to price competition.

Another spur to price competition can develop when a boundary separating two distinct markets dissolves. The fusion of two markets can take place when advances in transportation or communication reduce the barriers separating geographically disparate producers. The development of railroads and motor vehicles converted so many regional markets into national ones that there are now relatively few examples of manufactured products that are not widely traded in national markets. In more recent times, the steady progress of shipping and air freight has accomplished a similar feat in displacing national boundaries. As a result, firms that were once comfortably ensconced in their own national markets are often faced with the vicissitudes of international ones.

Market expansion directly reduces monopoly power, which is often sufficient to cause an outbreak in price competition. But the effect is even stronger when firms are abruptly exposed to unfamiliar rivals with all the uncertainties inherent in such a new environment. The threat of price competition is likely to increase at least until significant monopoly and economic power is again reestablished.

While falling transportation costs are one source of market fusion, another is the elimination of trade barriers. One of the most remarkable examples of this was the effort to create a single European market by 1992. Implementing this policy abruptly would have threatened many national producers, reducing their monopoly power and raising the specter of considerable price competition. But businesses prepared for the event by "buying out one another as if there were no tomorrow."[17] Given ample warning, firms were quick to accumulate power in order to make the transition to an integrated market with as little disruption as possible to markups and profits.

Theories of Corporate Behavior

All of the leading theories of business behavior make explicit or implicit assumptions about the reactions of other firms. In each case, individual firms form expectations that others will either respond or not respond to price competition. The simplest assumption of no response is incorporated into several popular business theories, including perfect competition, monopolistic competition, and Cournot–Nash equilibrium. In the Cournot–Nash model each firm maximizes profits taking the output of all other firms as given.[18] Because these theories assume no response by rivals, they are placed in panel A of Table 8.1.

Table 8.1

Response to Price Cuts In Popular Business Theories

No Response	Follow
A.	B.
Perfect Competition	Kinked Demand
Monopolistic Competition	Collusion
Cournot–Nash Equilibrium	

The kinked demand model explicitly assumes that other firms will follow a price cut and therefore belongs in panel B. Collusion is also placed here because if any one firm defects from a collusive agreement, it is generally assumed that other firms will follow.

The fact that each type of behavior identified in Table 8.1 can actually occur in the real economy is what makes these theories so useful. They provide plausible theoretical explanations of a wide variety of market activity, all of which can be observed somewhere or sometime in the world economy. But as a general explanation of business behavior they are inadequate. Each theory is based on its own particular assumptions and taken together they represent a patchwork of isolated ideas rather than a consistent, fully integrated theory of price competition. In none of the theories is price competition clearly defined, nor are its determinants fully delineated.

It is at this point that the model of price competition presented in this chapter is particularly useful. It is defined as the relative deviation between the actual price and the one that maximizes current profits. It is most likely to occur when entry barriers are low, long-run substitutes are strong, excess capacity exists, and no retaliation by rivals or the government is expected. Firms with low monopoly power are more likely to use it because they have less fear of government intervention or rival retaliation. Finally, price competition is more likely for firms with particularly low discount rates or production costs and where markets widen, covering broader geographic regions.

The model developed in this chapter is also useful for analyzing a variety of business practices as described in the following examples.

Dumping

A rather special case of price competition occurs when import prices are cut so severely that current profits are negative. In other words, the trader incurs short-run losses in the hopes of generating greater long-run gains. This practice is illustrated in Figure 8.5 where profits on path *A* are negative in the early period. When a domestic firm adopts this strategy it is predatory pricing, but for a foreign firm it is known as *dumping*. The goal is the same as price competition, to boost future economic power by sacrificing current profits. Milder forms of price competition may also qualify as dumping in U.S. law.[19]

Monopolistic Competition and Contestable Markets

The profit path of a monopolistically competitive firm is pictured in Figure 8.6. Because Chamberlin assumed that firms maximize their current profits, they are essentially confined to their neutral path. Profits begin at the level of economic power (E_0) and gradually recede thereafter as new firms enter and reduce demand. In the absence of barriers to entry, firms continually enter the market until profits fall to zero, at which point the market is said to be in equilibrium.

A modern version of monopolistic competition is the theory of contestable markets.[20] In a perfectly contestable market, potential entrants can produce products identical to those of the incumbents and at the same cost. It is this assumption of free entry that the theory of contestable markets shares with monopolistic competition. What distinguishes it is the assumption of free exit, that new entrants must be able to shut down and recover the full value of their investment on a moment's notice. Like a raiding party, a potential rival is poised to enter, extract the available profits, and exit. As a consequence of the raiders, the profits of the incumbent firms are eventually driven to zero, as in monopolistic competition.

By requiring free exit as well as free entry, the theory of contestable markets appears to be a special case of monopolistic competition, one that has even less relevance to the real world. While it is difficult to imagine new firms entering a market with all of the advantages of incumbents, it is even more unfathomable that the same firms can recover the full value of their investment upon departure.[21]

Figure 8.5 **Dumping *(A)* and the Neutral Path *(N)***

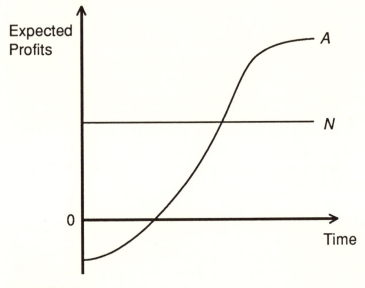

Limit Pricing

Monopolistic competition and contestable markets illustrate the important effect of entry on profits and economic power but under rather extreme conditions. In practice the ease of entry can vary widely from one market to the next. For a typical firm protected by some barriers, expected profits are more likely to approach some positive level as represented by the neutral path *(N)* in Figure 8.7. Other firms are willing to enter when profits are at the initial level but not when they fall to π_1. Barriers make it possible to deter entry before profits and economic power actually fall to zero.

Another unrealistic aspect of monopolistic competition is the assumption that all firms are constrained to maximize current profits. An alternative strategy is to reduce current prices in the hopes of slowing or even completely discouraging new entrants. This behavior is referred to as limit pricing because it is intended to limit entry into a market. By setting prices below the level that maximizes current profits, firms attempt to reduce the number of future substitutes, thus improving their future prospects.

This strategy is illustrated by path A in Figure 8.7. Profits are initially lower because prices are lower. But in order for limit pricing to

Figure 8.6. **Monopolistic Competition**

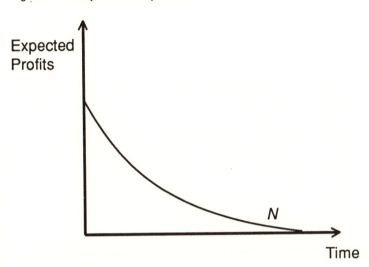

be desirable, future profits in path *A* must at some point exceed those in the neutral path. From the graph it is evident that limit pricing is a form of price competition, one specifically aimed at discouraging new entrants.

Conclusion

The focus of this chapter has been on price competition—what it is and what causes it. This goes a long way in describing the interdependent behavior of firms that is fundamental to capitalist markets. But of course not all firms are equally disposed toward price competition. Those with significant amounts of monopoly power or high capacity utilization, for example, are less likely to adopt this strategy. But these are the same characteristics that determine average economic power. This means that firms with high levels of average economic power in Figure 8.1 are also less likely to fall into the range of price competition.

   An alternative to price competition suggested in this chapter is to simply maximize short-run profits in every period. By doing this a firm with economic power can generate substantial profits without provoking other firms to retaliate. But price competition and short-run profit maximization are not the only options available to firms. They

Figure 8.7. **Limit Pricing**

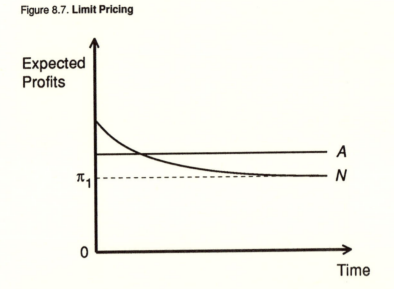

can also choose to practice nonprice competition or cooperation, two strategies that are taken up in the next chapter.

9

Nonprice Competition and Cooperation

Cooperation in price setting is extensive. Most forms of price fixing are illegal in the mainstream U.S. industries, under the antitrust laws. Yet the phenomenon is still endemic.
—William Shepherd, 1985[1]

When practiced in moderation, price competition can serve to maintain future demand, but in its more extreme form it holds the promise of greatly increasing economic power. There are also some dangers. Other firms may retaliate, the government may intervene, or future demand may be less than anticipated. Therefore for some firms, especially relatively large ones with high monopoly power, price competition may not be a desirable strategy for advancing their interests.

An alternative for the firm, suggested in the previous chapter, is to resign itself to maximizing current profits without regard to the future. At any given time, a number of firms appear to follow this strategy. But for ambitious firms that have rejected price competition, there are at least three alternative strategies. Firms can use nonprice forms of competition, they can cooperate with their rivals in setting mutually beneficial prices, or they can combine with rivals through mergers or takeovers. Each of these strategies promises higher future returns without the necessity of resorting to price competition. This chapter deals with the first two strategies, while mergers and combinations are discussed in the next one.

Theory of Nonprice Competition

Economists classify costs as variable or fixed depending on how they are associated with the level of output. In the short run, variable costs increase when output increases but fixed costs do not. Expenditures on nonprice competition represent a third type of cost. That is because the causality is reversed: output is expected to increase when these costs increase.

In nonprice competition firms aspire to increase their future market share and profitability, not by lowering prices, but by financing efforts that promise to enhance future demand, such as advertising and research and development. Of particular interest to the firm is the trade-off between the short-run costs of such expenditures and expected future profits.

The goal of nonprice competition is to differentiate the product from available substitutes and increase future demand. In order to achieve these goals it may be necessary to either change the physical nature of the product, which is the function of R&D, or alter consumer perceptions of it through advertising. Whether the approach is to introduce a new model or unleash a barrage of commercials, the economic effects are quite similar. Both entail a current cost with the prospect of strengthening future demand. R&D affects consumer demand by modifying the physical product; advertising does so by modifying the consumer.

The creation of new products by means of R&D is an important source of economic power. Any time a firm creates a unique product whose demand is high relative to production costs, it stands to increase future profitability. The patent system tends to magnify these prospective profits by granting exclusive production rights for seventeen years. It is the hope of gaining monopoly and economic power, reinforced by patents, that provides the impetus for R&D.

The emphasis in research and development is generally on development. In fact, the percentage of total R&D dedicated to product development is 90 percent, leaving 10 percent or less for basic research.[2] These distinctions are somewhat arbitrary since the purpose of all R&D is ultimately to reduce future costs or enhance future revenue. Whether the result is a new computer chip or a new variety of cola, profitability remains the ultimate goal.

The economic model of nonprice competition is very similar to that of price competition. Both entail a reduction in current profits below the maximum in order to achieve an expansion of future demand. And in both, expected profits from nonprice competition initially fall below the neutral path but eventually rise above it.[3] For this reason, the profit path of nonprice competition, illustrated by *A* in Figure 9.1, is generally indistinguishable from the path for price competition presented in Chapter 8.

Once again the strategy with the best chance of being adopted is the one that generates the highest present value of expected profits. Nonprice competition is more likely to be adopted when a relatively small expenditure today can cause a large increase in future profitability.

Competitors and Rivals

The decisive factor in determining which firms will practice nonprice competition is the anticipated effectiveness of advertising and R&D. Unless some future gain is expected, there is no reason to even consider this strategy. Therefore the firms that are most likely to practice nonprice competition are the ones where advertising and R&D are expected to have the strongest impact.

There is at least one area, producer goods, where advertising has traditionally not been very effective. Sales promoting expenditures have always played a smaller role in promoting goods and services sold to producers than to consumers. Why this occurs is uncertain. It may be because businesses are too familiar with the techniques to be swayed by them or perhaps because they use profits rather than satisfaction as the criterion for making decisions. Whatever the reason, the heaviest advertising expenditures are directed at consumers as revealed by the five largest advertising industries in 1987: automotive, food, consumer and business services, retail, and entertainment. At the low end of the list are freight and aviation equipment industries, which spend a pittance on advertising.[4]

Another area where advertising is less effective is in markets where many firms produce highly undifferentiated products. Farmers and ranchers would have a difficult time trying to promote their individual products, even if they provided them with sonorous brand names. In contrast, no such barrier seems to stand in the way of large firms producing undifferentiated products. They can solve the problem by putting the product in a unique box, or in the case of petroleum, under a unique sign.

The reason that some firms expect higher returns to R&D is partly a function of scientific potential. The prospects for innovations in recent years appear to have been greater in three areas: chemicals, electronics, and automobiles. In 1987 approximately 61 percent of all company R&D funds had gone into these industries.[5] The government

Figure 9.1. **Nonprice Competition**

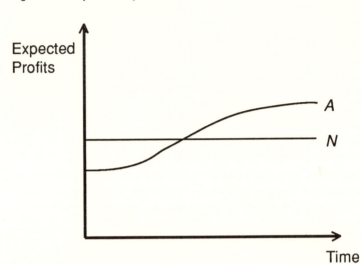

also contributes to R&D, but has a strong military emphasis with approximately half of its funds going to aircraft and missiles and an additional 27 percent to electrical equipment.

Firms that place a high value on future profitability are also more likely to practice price or nonprice competition. These firms use a low discount rate giving greater weight to future profits. In contrast, firms experiencing leveraged buyouts may have an imperative to generate immediate profits to make interest payments or retire debt. As a consequence these firms are often more likely to reject nonprice competition, and indeed, R&D appears to be one of the casualties of these deals. Commenting on the motivation of corporate raiders, the vice president for research and development at Xerox Corporation claimed, "They can make significant cuts and get cash flow. I haven't seen a takeover yet where they increased research and development activities."[6]

The response of rivals may be quite similar for price and nonprice competition. Rivals who don't respond to an advertising or R&D campaign with one of their own are apt to see profits gradually erode over time. When a firm begins advertising, the neutral curves for its rivals will drop, increasing the likelihood of retaliation. The original firm must, of course, factor in the probability of a response when it makes its original decision.

What happens when rivals respond to nonprice competition by increasing their own expenditures on advertising and R&D? Does one effort merely cancel out another—resulting in a zero-sum game? In the case of advertising or innovation, both parties stand to gain something if they can extract revenue from other markets. As mentioned earlier, salvos by Pepsi and Coca Cola in an advertising war may not alter relative market shares but could stimulate demand for both at the expense of milk and beer producers. High industry expenditures on R&D can produce a similar effect.

When one firm advertises, its demand is likely to become more inelastic and when its rival advertises, it may become even more inelastic. The cumulative effect of both campaigns is to drive a wedge between the two products in the mind of the average consumer. Again taking the soft drink producers as an example, a barrage of advertisements by Pepsi and Coca Cola could increase consumer loyalty, which means a steeper, more inelastic demand for both. The same effect is created by annual styling changes in the American automobile industry. New Fords not only look different from Cadillacs and Chryslers but they also look different from last year's Fords. The end result is that each producer enjoys a greater level of monopoly power, which translates into greater economic power and profits.

The discussion thus far has emphasized the similarities between price and nonprice competition, but there is at least one important difference. The effectiveness of nonprice competition depends on the power of advertising and R&D to influence future demand. In both cases, the effectiveness is likely to depend on scale. For example, there are likely to be certain advantages to large-scale advertising, like using network television, which can reach a large national audience.

For small regional firms there may be no reason to advertise on a national scale, and besides, the cost may be prohibitive. This means that relatively large firms, industry leaders, and firms with large national markets are likely to be the largest advertisers. This is quite different from the type of firm expected to practice price competition.[7]

There is a close correspondence among the nation's largest firms, largest advertisers, and largest spenders on research and development. Table 9.1 lists the twenty largest advertisers in 1987 beginning with Philip Morris, which spent an astounding $1,558 million. All of these are large firms, and even the smallest manufacturing firm on the list, Warner-Lambert, ranked 121st in the *Fortune* 500.

Table 9.1

The Largest Corporate Advertisers, 1987

Company	Advertising Spending, 1987 ($ millions)	Industry Rank, 1987	*Fortune* Industry	Average Net Income, 1980–87 ($ millions)
Philip Morris	1,558	12	Manufacturing	1,050
Proctor & Gamble	1,387	NA	NA	680
General Motors	1,025	1	Manufacturing	2,409
Sears	887	1	Retail	1,152
RJR Nabisco	840	19	Manufacturing	959
Pepsico	704	29	Manufacturing	366
Eastman Kodak	658	25	Manufacturing	866
McDonald's	649	21	Retail	378
Ford	640	3	Manufacturing	1,492
Anheuser-Busch	635	47	Manufacturing	374
K Mart	632	2	Retail	404
General Mills	572	77	Manufacturing	190
Chrysler	569	10	Manufacturing	674
Warner-Lambert	558	121	Manufacturing	136
AT&T	531	8	Manufacturing	3,201
Kellogg	525	114	Manufacturing	263
J.C. Penney	513	6	Retail	425
Pillsbury	474	68	Manufacturing	152
Johnson & Johnson	459	50	Manufacturing	515

Source: Data on advertising expenditures were taken from "Power Charts," *Advertising Age* (December 26, 1988), p. 11. Other company data were extracted from Compustat Database.
Note: NA = not available.

Similarly, corporate expenditures on R&D are closely related to company size and profitability. Of the twenty-five biggest R&D spenders listed in Table 9.2 none of them rank any lower than 80th in the *Fortune* 500. The sheer magnitude of expenditures on advertising and R&D suggests that nonprice competition is a dominant strategy among corporate giants. For many of the companies included in these lists, annual expenditures on advertising and R&D are comparable in magnitude to their annual average net income. At least for these companies, nonprice competition is likely to be the primary means for maintaining or augmenting economic power.

Table 9.2

The Largest Corporate Spenders on Research and Development, 1987

Company	R&D Spending, 1987 ($ million)	*Fortune* Rank (Sales), 1987	Average Net Income, 1980–87 ($ million)
General Motors	4,361	1	2,409
IBM	3,998	4	4,994
Ford	2,514	3	1,492
AT&T	2,453	8	3,201
Digital Equipment	1,307	NA	478
Du Pont	1,223	9	1,251
General Electric	1,194	6	2,129
Eastman Kodak	992	25	866
Hewlett-Packard	901	49	464
United Technologies	879	15	440
Boeing	824	20	527
Chrysler	798	10	674
Xerox	722	34	490
Dow Chemical	670	24	590
Proctor & Gamble	652	NA	680
McDonnell Douglas	648	26	259
Minnesota Mining & Manufacturing	624	37	718
Johnson & Johnson	617	50	515
Unisys	597	36	197
Merk & Co.	566	80	537
Monsanto	557	55	320
Lockheed	549	30	223
ITT	525	45	650
Motorola	524	62	218
Exxon	524	2	5,122

Source: Data extracted from Compustat Database.
Note: NA = not available.

What are the limits to advertising and R&D expenditures? Once an advertiser has crossed the threshold into national advertising, are there reasons to limit further expansion? Large expenditures may be necessary to attain an efficient scale, but attempts to exceed this level will eventually experience diminishing returns, causing the expected return on a dollar of advertising to decline. Similarly for R&D, at some point the return will no longer justify additional outlays.

Diminishing returns in advertising and R&D tend to limit the degree of nonprice competition. In contrast, price competition does not typically suffer from diminishing returns since prices can go lower and lower, imparting increasing damage to rivals. The only limit to price competition is the amount of time that a firm can endure negative profits. For many firms this makes price competition the most dangerous variant of the two.

Theory of Cooperation

Economic power represents a firm's maximum short-run profits when other firms follow similar, independent courses. If a firm decided to raise its price above the level associated with this profit, it would find lower profits today and probably even lower profits in the future. Most firms would readily reject this strategy unless there was some general understanding that other firms would follow. If rivals could be enticed to raise their own prices, it is conceivable that short-run profits for each firm would actually exceed its individual level of economic power. But in order to achieve these higher returns, firms must have confidence that their rivals will continue to cooperate.

The formal definition of price cooperation is perfectly analogous to the definition of price competition. Recall that price competition was defined in Chapter 8 as the relative difference between the optimum current price, p^*, and the actual current price, p_0:

$$(9.1) \qquad \textit{Degree of Price Competition } \frac{p^* - p_0}{p^*}$$

During price competition this index is positive because the actual price (p_0) is below the optimum price (p^*). But during cooperation, the actual price exceeds the optimum and the expression above is negative. And as the actual price increases relative to the optimum, the degree of cooperation increases. These relationships are captured in the following definition of the degree of price cooperation:

$$(9.2) \qquad \textit{Degree of Price Cooperation} = \frac{p_0 - p^*}{p^*}$$

Another way to state this definition is that the degree of price cooperation is simply equal to the negative of the degree of price competition.

The decisive question facing a firm contemplating a strategy of price cooperation is whether or not other firms will follow. The answer will determine whether the strategy has any hope of being adopted. Two possibilities are compared with a neutral path in Figure 9.2. Both paths, A and B, begin with the firm unilaterally raising its price above the level that maximizes short-run profits. As a result, its profits fall below that of the neutral curve. But in the first possibility, path A, rivals are expected to follow and profits soon recover and surpass the neutral path. In the other possibility, path B, rivals are not expected to follow and profits remain depressed. Only when the firm eventually abandons this strategy will profits return to the neutral level.

This example shows that it is essential for other firms to follow in order for cooperation to be a viable strategy. There are other factors that increase the likelihood of cooperation. For example, a group of cooperating firms is in an advantageous position when substitution between themselves and those outside the group is relatively low. A coordinated price increase among any group of firms will not amount to much if revenue flows out to ready substitutes. Prospects would be much better if price increases caused revenue to flow into the group rather than out. In order for this to happen, all of the producers of close substitutes must participate.

Another important consideration in cooperation is the likelihood of government intervention. In some cases, explicit coordination of prices is illegal and detection could lead to costly litigation and penalties, as well as damage to the firm's public image. In calculating the expected returns to cooperation firms must factor in these potential costs. The greater the expected cost of violating the law, the lower the expected profits of price cooperation.

Followers and Free-Riders

Why would a rival want to follow a price increase? The most obvious reason is to eliminate or at least reduce the possibility that the leader will rescind its higher price. Rivals can validate the lead firm's action only by increasing their own prices. If they fail to do so, there is no reason for the lead firm to continue charging high prices. Any temporary advantage achieved by noncooperating rivals will vanish as soon

Figure 9.2. **Price Cooperation**

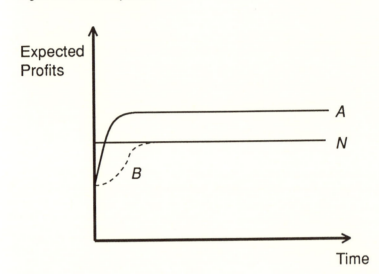

as the leader realizes the mistake and drops its price back to the original level.

When all rivals follow a price increase, their profits and those of the lead firm will exceed their individual economic power. So why then don't firms always cooperate? One reason is that cooperation makes it more difficult to alter prevailing market shares. When firms practice cooperation they give up the chance to use price competition as a means of challenging the position of market leaders. There are other ways to rearrange market shares, but price competition is one of the most powerful weapons available.

Another impediment to cooperation is the problem of free-riders. A firm becomes a free-rider when it attempts to benefit from the higher market price without contributing to it. Other firms raise their prices but the free-rider refuses to set any price other than the one that maximizes its own short-run profits. When all firms adopt this strategy, cooperation becomes impossible.

The choices confronting a rival are illustrated in Figure 9.3. If the rival cooperates and expects others to do so, it will follow path A. And if the firm expects others to cooperate but refuses to do so itself, it can anticipate even higher profits, depicted by path B. Obviously, it pays to be a free-rider if other firms continue cooperating among themselves.

Figure 9.3. **A Free-Rider**

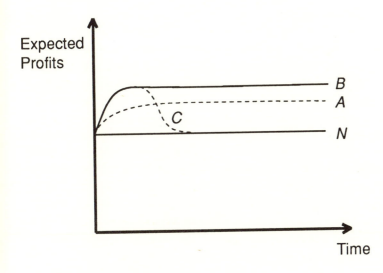

Note: N = Neutral Path
     A = Price Cooperation
     B = Free-rider (rivals cooperate)
     C = Free-rider (rivals retaliate)

However, if defection prompts others to abandon cooperation, profits may be expected to vanish as in path *C*. A free-rider strategy is unambiguously preferable only when other firms are expected to continue cooperating.

The critical question facing a firm is whether its participation is essential for others to continue cooperating. If the answer is yes, then its best option is likely to be cooperation. This is illustrated in the figure because cooperation, path *A*, would be preferable to the free-rider strategy, path *C*.[8] But if participation is not essential then a free-rider strategy would be more appealing. What determines whether a firm's participation is essential?

One consideration is the number of firms involved. If there are a multitude of small firms in the market, the participation of any one firm may not be essential. Even if one firm defects and becomes a free-rider, there is a good chance that others will still benefit from cooperation. But with many firms thinking this way, cooperation may be very difficult to sustain. Independently, each firm perceives its choice between path *A* or *B*, but in reality widespread defection will place them all on path *C*.

When there are only a few relatively large firms in the market, each is much more likely to perceive its participation as essential. Lower prices by any one firm can, in this situation, have a measurable impact on rivals. Firms are more likely to perceive their participation as essential, because in fact, it is. As a result, when there are few firms in a market, cooperation has a much better chance of succeeding.

Another reason why the number of firms in a market makes a difference has to do with the difficulty of negotiating and enforcing a cooperative agreement. When many firms are involved, it will be harder to establish an agreement that is acceptable to all parties. And when the agreement is illegal, the risk of a dissatisfied party exposing the rest can become a serious concern. Small homogeneous groups are much more likely to overcome these obstacles and reach a viable accord.

Markets with relatively few producers are also more likely to be those with high levels of monopoly and average economic power. While any group of firms can theoretically practice cooperation, the incidence and success of such a strategy is likely to increase with the level of monopoly power.

Price Leadership

In practice, there are many different ways for firms to coordinate prices and increase their collective profits. On one extreme, a process may evolve for maintaining higher prices without any formal agreement. The most familiar example of this is described as price leadership, where one firm announces a price increase that is immediately followed by similar pronouncements from rivals. It is possible that each firm voluntarily participates without any prior agreement, merely because it understands the rewards.

One does not have to look very hard to find numerous examples of price leadership in practice. The classic cases are the steel and auto industries in the 1940s, 1950s, and 1960s, when both markets had dominant industry leaders (U.S. Steel and General Motors) and relatively few rivals, making them prime candidates for cooperation. Monopoly power in each market was reinforced by the absence of significant import penetration, which did not become a major factor until the 1960s for steel and the 1970s for autos. And price competition, at least by industry leaders, was severely constrained by the threat of antitrust, leaving the door wide open for cooperation.

During the 1940s and 1950s price leadership led to higher and more stable profits.[9] U.S. Steel, with the largest market share in the industry, would typically initiate a round of price increases, invariably followed by announcements of comparable price hikes by its smaller rivals.[10] John Kenneth Galbraith pointed out in 1967 that U.S. Steel had not reported losses for a quarter of a century.[11] With a relatively small group of firms, it was clearly in the self-interest of each party to cooperate rather than compete. A similar pattern evolved in the U.S. automobile industry, where the only competition was confined to advertising and annual model changes.

The coordination of pricing decisions in the steel industry was not always so informal. In 1907, the president of U.S. Steel Corporation, Judge Gary, held a dinner where he tried to rally support against price fluctuations, a problem then afflicting his industry. The guests were particularly attentive, because together with U.S. Steel, they accounted for 90 percent of the iron and steel trade. Apparently the dinner met with some success as an advisory committee was appointed to act as arbiter of iron and steel prices.[12] Such explicit discussions were eventually superseded by more implicit arrangements such as price leadership.

Remarkably detailed accounts of how price leadership was implemented and enforced in the tobacco industry were revealed in a recent court case. Once or twice a year for an estimated 40 years or more, one of the big six tobacco companies would announce a price increase, which would be followed by similar announcements from the other five. This arrangement made it possible for the industry to steadily increase profits even during periods of falling domestic demand.

After a brief outbreak of price competition in the early 1980s originating from cheap generic cigarettes, price leadership was reestablished by the late 1980s. Price increases since then have been initiated by industry leaders, either R.J. Reynolds or Philip Morris, amounting to increases of 50 cents per carton every June and December.[13]

The structure of the tobacco industry makes it particularly well suited for cooperative behavior. The entire market is composed of only six firms and the top two control 70 percent of it. High concentration makes it relatively difficult for any one firm to violate the "community of interest" and the addictive nature of tobacco reduces the substitution between it and all other commodities. With fewer substitutes, producers have little reason to fear that a general rise in cigarette prices will cause revenue to spill out into other markets. While these cases of price leadership in steel, autos, and tobacco are probably the best documented, they are by no means the only ones. Scherer, for example, describes in more detail this type of behavior in ready-to-eat cereals, turbogenerators, and gasoline.[14]

The tobacco case also illustrates the compatibility of price cooperation and nonprice competition. Ranked by total advertising expenditures in 1987, cigarettes and tobacco placed in the top twenty industries and Philip Morris and R.J. Reynolds were among the top five firms. It is not unusual for firms to embrace price cooperation and limit any competition to advertising and R&D.

Collusion

Cooperation is not always easy, especially where market shares have not been firmly established or where prices depend on volume, transportation costs, or other product details. In such a situation it may be necessary to reinforce the will to cooperate with formal agreements detailing the obligations of each party. Particularly comprehensive contracts may even specify penalties for noncooperation, besides the obvious one of invalidating the agreement. Examples of formal agreements span the entire spectrum of business activity from motor vehicles to anesthesiologists and from electrical equipment manufacturers to realtors.[15]

Where cooperation has not been strictly prohibited by government decree, it has flourished. The complex cartel structure existing in Germany after World War I arose in response to cut-throat competition that left many firms struggling for survival.[16] One survey estimated the number of goods covered by cartels in Germany in the 1920s at more than a thousand, including such important industries as iron and steel, textile and clothing, engineering, paper, brewing and milling, chemicals, metals, and a dozen more.[17] Not all of these cartels were equally effective in enforcing cooperation, nor did they all demonstrate great resilience in the face of economic turmoil buffeting Germany between the two world wars. But the cartelization of the German economy during the 1920s illustrates the interest in cooperation where it is not explicitly prohibited.

A similar episode took place in the United States for a brief spell during the depression. The National Industrial Recovery Act, passed in 1933, permitted industries to draft "codes of conduct" that were exempt from antitrust laws. The intent was to prevent overproduction and price deflation but the effect was to foster price-fixing and production limits. Given the legal right to establish cooperative agreements, U.S. industries jumped at the chance. In a relatively short time, 557 basic codes were approved covering many important industries. The experiment was curtailed in 1935 when the Supreme Court overturned the new law as a violation of the constitution.[18]

Legal prohibitions may not have to be entirely absent before cooperative agreements begin to thrive. In some cases sufficient incentive may be created when the law is merely ambiguous. Shepherd and Wilcox concluded that U.S. policy against price-fixing "largely exempts foreign cartels, even if they have U.S. members. . . ."[19] As a consequence, the threat of antitrust action was probably never more than a minor concern for U.S. interests participating in the international uranium cartel in the 1970s. This cartel, consisting of members from Australia, Canada, Britain, France, South Africa, and the United States, met from 1972 to 1975 to establish price floors for uranium.

A similar example is the international oil cartel, which also managed to avoid antitrust sanctions despite a well-documented case of price-fixing from the 1920s to 1950s. In one of the most infamous meetings of the cartel in 1928, the presidents of Anglo-Persian Oil Company (British Petroleum), Shell, and Jersey Standard (Exxon) met at Achnacarry Castle in Scotland and, during breaks from grouse hunting, proceeded to divide up world oil markets. According to Walter C. Teagle, then president of Jersey Standard, "Sir John Cadman, head of the Anglo-Persian Oil Company [BP] and myself were guests of Sir Henri Deterding [Shell] and Lady Deterding at Achnacarry for the grouse shooting, and while the game was a primary object of the visit, the problem of the world's petroleum industry naturally came in for a great deal of discussion."[20] The discussion was formalized in the Achnacarry Agreement of 1928, specifying the need to preserve market shares and limit production.

The government's case against the oil majors alleged that they had divided up world markets and reserves, established price targets, and even specified sanctions against parties that violated the agreement. Despite compelling evidence, the case was never resolved satisfactorily due to certain politically motivated decisions.[21] However, the example does illustrate how international cooperation can circumvent national antitrust policies.

The Organization of Petroleum Exporting Countries (OPEC) provides another example of collusion in international oil markets. While OPEC set out in 1960 to restrict world oil production and raise prices, its record has been uneven. During the first thirteen years of its existence, OPEC had relatively little impact on world petroleum prices. It wasn't until the Arab-Israeli war in 1973 and the Iranian revolution in 1979 that OPEC gained the strength to impose spectacular price hikes. Since then, oil prices have been high enough to generate significant revenues for producing countries but not high enough to maintain the reputation achieved by OPEC during the 1970s.

Some analysts point to OPEC's recent infirmity as evidence that collusion cannot overcome the free-rider problem. But OPEC has been anything but a complete failure. Even the relatively "low" prices of the 1980s were far better than prices in the pre-OPEC era. More realistically, it appears that OPEC can do no better than the ambitions of its moderate members, Saudi Arabia and Kuwait. This has been a point of serious frustration for OPEC's high-price advocates, Iraq, Iran, and Libya, but it is not necessarily a signal of complete disintegration.[22] OPEC continues to influence world oil prices, albeit less decisively than in the 1970s.

In general, it seems that formal agreements are most effective when they involve firms with a strong predisposition toward cooperation. In such a situation, explicit agreements can greatly strengthen an existing tendency toward cooperation by specifying the responsibilities of each party and thereby reducing a considerable amount of uncertainty. For example, the characteristics of the market for matzo, an unleavened bread, created an ideal climate for cooperation in the 1980s. Not only were there few producers, but because of the important religious function of matzo during Jewish holidays, there were no real substitutes. According to the Justice Department's allegation, three leading manufacturers conspired to fix the price of matzo from 1981 to 1986, resulting in sharp price hikes during Jewish Passover holidays when demand typically peaks. According to details of the case, executives from three companies, Manischewitz, Streits, and Horowitz Bros. & Margareten agreed on prices while dining at Ratner's restaurant in Manhattan.[23]

Executives of General Electric and Westinghouse showed more creativity in choosing locations for their price-fixing activities. Besides meeting in luxury hotels, mountain-top retreats, and cabins in the woods, at least one rendezvous took place at "Dirty Helen's," a Milwaukee bar. The purpose of these meetings, confirmed in court proceedings in 1960, was to fix prices on transformers, switchgear, and generators.[24]

Dozens of other important cases can be cited including bathroom fixtures, domestic gasoline, folding cartons, and concrete blocks, demonstrating that cooperative behavior is more than just a theoretical possibility.[25] It describes the behavior of firms in a wide variety of industries, especially those with some monopoly power.

Prisoner's Dilemma

Many economists have been remarkably indifferent to most forms of cooperative behavior because of a belief that agreements, explicit or otherwise, cannot be sustained. The theoretical basis for this belief is often illustrated by a game referred to as *the prisoner's dilemma,* in which two prisoners are pressed for a confession, completely isolated from each other. The point of the game is to show how each of the prisoners, given the proper incentives, can be enticed to confess, thus violating the trust of the other prisoner. All of this is related to business behavior by assuming that the prisoner's incentive to confess is analogous to the incentive of a firm to cheat on a price agreement.

In a typical version of the story, two prisoners, who prior to their arrest agreed to plead innocent, are separated and asked for their confessions. Both prisoners face five years if they both plead guilty but only one year if they both plead innocent. However, if one pleads guilty and the other innocent, the former goes free and the latter receives a ten-year sentence. The possible sentences facing prisoner A are summarized in Table 9.3.

The purpose of the table is to demonstrate that prisoner A is better off confessing regardless of what B does. If B confesses, A gets five years (instead of ten years) and if B does not confess, A goes free (instead of spending a year in jail). Prisoner A obviously has a strong incentive to confess, as does B who faces the same penalties.

The broader implication of the prisoner's dilemma is that it may be worth cheating regardless of what the other parties do. Economists have used this example to illustrate why a firm may be inclined to

Table 9.3

Prisoner's Dilemma: Sentences for Prisoner A

Prisoner A		Prisoner B
	Confesses	Does Not Confess
Confesses	5 Years	Free
Does Not Confess	10 Years	1 Year

cheat on a collusive agreement. If a firm faced a similar pattern of rewards and penalties it would be just as likely to cheat as either of the two prisoners.

The key to the prisoner's dilemma, and what distances it from the business world, is that it applies to a single episode. In actual practice it is the continuous nature of agreements that make them possible. Each day that the agreement holds generates greater benefits than would otherwise be attainable. This can be illustrated by converting the traditional version of the prisoner's dilemma into one with repeated trials.

The situation is the same as before but the penalties in Table 9.3 are measured in days rather than years and the trial is repeated 365 times. The final sentence is given by summing the accumulated penalties from each trial. There is now a strong incentive to abide by the original agreement and not confess. As long as both prisoners don't confess, they each accumulate one day per trial. At any point, one of the prisoners could violate the agreement and plead guilty, thus receiving no penalty for that trial. But the danger is that the other prisoner, receiving ten days, will begin cheating as well. Once cooperation breaks down, both parties confess repeatedly, receiving five days per trial. Obviously the incentive to cooperate is much stronger in this version of the game.

The prisoner's dilemma with repeated trials has much more relevance to actual business conditions. Firms set prices every day and at any point can defect from a cooperative strategy. This may produce a small gain, but only temporarily if it causes others to stop cooperating. The advantage of cooperating only becomes apparent when the prisoner's choice is expanded from a single episode to repeated trials.

Kinked Demand Curve

A particularly important business theory that does not permit cooperation is the kinked demand theory. It assumes that rivals refuse to follow a price increase initiated by one of their peers. Although this is a reasonable response in some markets, it is certainly not universal, especially in markets with relatively few firms. The kinked demand model is equally rigid with respect to price competition. Relatively large firms are utterly discouraged from cutting prices for fear of swift retaliation by rivals. The only course left for the firm is to hold its price constant at its prevailing rate.

The kinked demand theory is analogous to the case where firms choose a strategy of short-run profit maximization over either price competition or cooperation. Therefore, this theory comes closest to describing firms that stick relatively close to their neutral paths.[26] Of course, in the real economy firms behave in more diverse and interesting ways, but these are outside the narrow assumptions of the kinked demand theory.

Conclusion

With this chapter we complete the survey of several prominent forms of business behavior. Any business must make a choice to practice competition, cooperation, or maximize short-run profits. Whether the decision is made through careful analysis as described in Chapters 8 and 9 or is based entirely on intuition, the firm's current price must place it in one of these three categories. Prices can be relatively low in an attempt to gain greater future profits, they can be relatively high requiring the cooperation of rivals, or they can be somewhere in between. There are no other alternatives.

While there are many factors that influence a firm's pricing decision, and many of them have been outlined in these two chapters, of particular importance is monopoly power. Firms with great amounts of monopoly power often favor cooperation while those without may tend to favor competition. This pattern will affect the relationship between monopoly power and actual profitability, the focus of the empirical research.

At any moment in time firms with little power are more likely to be practicing price competition, causing their actual profits to fall even further below their already low levels of economic power. On the other end of the spectrum, firms with substantial monopoly power are more likely to be cooperating, pushing their profits to ever-higher levels. There are, of course, cases where powerful firms compete and powerless ones cooperate, but these are less common. As a result the pricing decisions of firms tend to reinforce the positive correlation between monopoly power and actual profitability.

Another decision a firm must make is whether or not to practice nonprice competition. The cumulative effects of sales promotion and research and development can only serve to enhance its future economic power but is it worth the current cost? Firms that rely heavily on advertising and R&D have decided in favor of the future gain.

In addition to price and nonprice competition, firms have another option for augmenting their monopoly and economic power: mergers and combinations. By combining with rivals, a firm can increase its potential profitability. This strategy is discussed in Chapter 10.

The Process of Expansion: Mergers and Acquisitions

The most common method by which large
corporations originated was by merger.
—David Bunting, 1986[1]

One of the primary interests of businesses is to expand their capacity to generate profits. To achieve this goal, firms can choose a strategy of price competition or price cooperation, but there is an alternative—the acquisition of other independent businesses. When one firm buys another it acquires ownership and control, thus expanding its own potential profits. The market for corporate ownership and control is for this reason integrally related to the accumulation of economic and monopoly power.

One of the earliest episodes of mergers and acquisitions to receive serious attention took place at the turn of the century. Since then, tens of thousands of firms have been bought, effectively extinguished as independent enterprises. Despite the long history of this market it would probably continue largely unnoticed if not for the occasional burst of activity during which mergers and acquisitions reach a feverish pitch. The 1980s was such a period. In the peak year of 1988 there were 4,049 mergers worth a million dollars or more, for a total value of $245 billion.[2] The actual value would be even higher if corporate acquisitions valued at less than a million dollars were also included. But even this estimate is significant, representing more than half the amount U.S. businesses spent that year on plant and equipment.[3]

Merger activity, measured by the ratio of asset values acquired to gross national product, is plotted in Figure 10.1 for the years 1895 to

Figure 10.1. **Merger Intensity: 1895–1990**

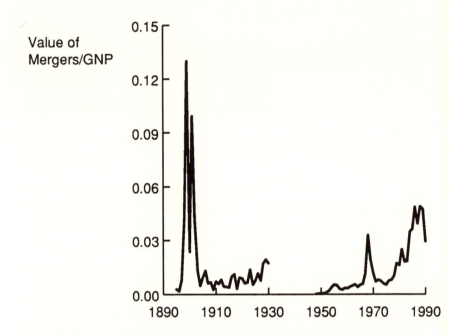

Sources: Historical Statistics of the United States: Colonial Times to 1970, Bureau of the Census; *Economic Report of the President*, 1985 and 1990, U.S. Government Printing Office; and *Mergers and Acquisitions, May–June 1991.*

1990.[4] As the figure illustrates, the 1980s was only one of several important episodes of heightened merger activity.

There are alternative measures of merger intensity but they all display the same general pattern and they all have some deficiency. A simple tally of the number of mergers, for example, is highly correlated with the pattern in Figure 10.1 but it fails to distinguish between small insignificant mergers and large, important ones. The total value of mergers is another plausible measure but it fails to account for changes in prices and overall economic activity.

The measure used in Figure 10.1, the ratio of acquired values to GNP, suffers from none of these deficiencies but has one of its own.

The total value of mergers are not available from 1931 to 1947, creating a gap in the series. Fortunately, this does not appear to be a period of significant merger activity, a belief supported by the low number of mergers.

According to Figure 10.1, a flurry of mergers and acquisitions took place in 1899 and 1901. In these two remarkable years, the amount spent by businesses to buy other firms was equivalent to more than 10 percent of GNP. But in terms of sustained merger activity, the 1980s holds the record. From 1984 through 1990 merger activity approached 5 percent and never fell below 2 percent of GNP. Other periods of heightened activity include the late 1960s and, to a lesser extent, the 1920s. In all other years, firms continued to merge but at a relatively slower rate.

Mergers and Power

There are many important issues related to mergers and acquisitions, but the focus in this chapter is their relationship to monopoly and economic power. On this topic there are three important points. First, many mergers are often transacted with the purpose of accumulating monopoly power. By combining business interests, rivals can increase their control over a market and achieve greater discretion over prices. Second, many firms that currently exercise great economic power benefited from mergers or combinations at some earlier stage in their development. And finally, once firms attain great economic power they often continue an active program of mergers and acquisitions.

Before turning to these issues it is first necessary to describe the process by which a firm decides whether to expand and if so, how? Among the most important decisions facing any firm are the ones concerning mergers and acquisitions and investments in real plant and equipment. In fact, these decisions are of such critical importance that many firms employ a battery of analysts and financial managers simply to process the available information. Among the multitude of questions involved in an investment decision, there are two of critical importance: what is the expected return and how will the required funds be raised?

The firm must weigh the expected profits and risk associated with any investment relative to the dollar expenditure. The prospect with the greatest expected return per dollar, accounting for risk, of course, is most likely to attract the firm's funds. Whether an investment is real, as in plant or equipment, or financial, as in existing enterprises, is often immaterial to the firm. What is essential is that the investment promises a return greater than that of the alternatives and greater than the anticipated cost of capital.

What is the cost of capital? These funds are primarily obtained from three sources, debt, equity, and retained earnings and depreciation. More precisely, expansion can be financed externally from the sale of stocks and bonds, or from the income of the corporation. The costs associated with each source of funds must be considered when making investment decisions. The major cost of using retained earnings and depreciation is based on the return this money could have generated elsewhere, while the cost of debt is primarily interest and for stocks, dividends.[5] Additional costs include fees for consultants, promoters, and underwriters, who share in the gains from the sale of debt or equity. It is ultimately up to the firm to decide whether the expected returns are sufficient to justify incurring these costs. This general framework provides an introduction to understanding corporate combinations.

How have mergers and acquisitions contributed to the growth of monopoly and economic power? To answer this question it is useful to look at the experience of specific firms, in particular, those that currently exercise great economic power. The task of identifying these firms is not a simple one. A precise determination would require an intimate knowledge of cost and demand curves, which are difficult to estimate even when the required data are available. An alternative is to use average profits over time as an approximation of economic power. This is not always accurate because profits will overstate economic power when firms cooperate and understate economic power when they compete. Despite these deficiencies, average profits can still serve as a useful approximation of economic power.

The top eighteen firms, ranked by average profits from 1980 to 1987, are listed in Table 10.1.[6] Because most of these firms sell in many different markets, the classification is based on the firm's primary industry. All of the top five firms, Exxon, IBM, AT&T, General Motors, and General Electric, averaged more than two billion dollars in income per year and each had the highest sales in their respective industries. The next four firms were all petroleum refiners, demonstrating the exceptional profitability of this particular industry. Of the re-

Table 10.1

The Most Profitable U.S. Corporations: Average Net Income, 1980–87

Company	Average Annual Net Income ($ millions)	Industry	Industry Rank (Sales)
Exxon	5,122	Petroleum Refining	1
IBM	4,993	Computers & Office Equipment	1
AT&T	3,200	Service	1
General Motors	2,409	Motor Vehicles & Parts	1
General Electric	2,128	Electronics	1
Amoco	1,721	Petroleum Refining	5
Mobil	1,695	Petroleum Refining	2
Chevron	1,568	Petroleum Refining	4
Shell	1,502	Petroleum Refining	6
Ford	1,492	Motor Vehicles & Parts	2
BellSouth	1,482	Utilities	1
Du Pont	1,251	Chemicals	1
Sears	1,152	Retail	1
Nynex	1,143	Utilities	5
Bell Atlantic	1,118	Utilities	3
American Information Technology	1,098	Utilities	8
Atlantic Richfield	1,093	Petroleum Refining	8
Philip Morris	1,050	Food	1

Source: Compustat Database.

maining nine firms, four were utilities in telecommunications and there was one firm each in motor vehicles, chemicals, retail, petroleum, and food.

Horizontal Mergers

Many of the firms included in Table 10.1 can trace their origin to mergers and combinations that took place many decades ago. A number of these involved firms producing substitutes, described as horizontal mergers. By reducing the number of substitutes, horizontal mergers tend to raise monopoly power. This is one of the key advantages that a firm counts on when making this type of merger.

A second advantage occurs if consolidation of production is also more efficient. The new combination can specialize production in certain plants, coordinate shipments to reduce transportation costs, and benefit generally from improved planning and coordination. Where these improvements are possible, operating costs will fall and the business becomes more profitable as a whole than the sum of its parts.[7] As a result, potential profitability and economic power rise.

There is a third advantage that can be achieved by horizontal mergers. A larger firm may benefit from being able to employ more efficient marketing methods, ranging from national advertising to deploying an army of sales personnel. As mentioned before, there are likely to be many more methods available to promote sales in a national market than in a local one. Wherever economies to marketing exist, a horizontal combination may provide strong opportunities to stimulate demand.

These three advantages from horizontal mergers—monopoly power, economies in production, and marketing—are not available to the average investor. The investor merely buys shares of a company with the expectation of strong future profits. The acquiring firm also acts on expectations, but those that are shaped by its advantages. Each advantage increases the rate of return to the acquiring firm. Whereas a particular stock acquisition may promise only an 8 percent return to an investor, the return may be 10 or 12 percent when acquired by a rival.

The case of the Standard Oil Company serves as one of the best illustrations of how monopoly and economic power can be accumulated through mergers and combinations. Starting with an initial capitalization of one million dollars in 1870, Standard was even then the nation's largest oil refiner, controlling 10 percent of the business in the country.[8] Under the direction of John D. Rockefeller, Standard proceeded to buy out twenty out of twenty-five independent refineries in Cleveland, pushing its market share to more than 20 percent. It then moved on to Philadelphia, Pittsburgh, Baltimore, and New York, continuing to absorb other producers so that by 1879 its market share had soared to approximately 90 to 95 percent.[9] Rockefeller was able to use price competition to weaken recalcitrant targets until they either failed or joined the Standard Trust. Victory was almost always assured because of the exclusive discounts Rockefeller obtained from the railroads that shipped the oil.

The pendulum seemed to swing in the opposite direction in 1911 when Standard was found to violate the Sherman Act and was split into thirty-four enterprises. While the dissolution was a setback for the Standard Trust, it hardly eliminated the monopoly power accumulated during its first forty-one years. Instead, the result of the court decision was to distribute the firm's monopoly power among a handful of large firms that continued to dominate their regional markets.

After the breakup, Standard Oil of New Jersey (Exxon) was the leader in the Mid-Atlantic states, Standard Oil Company of New York (Mobil) led in the Northeast, Standard Oil of Ohio (Sohio) in Ohio, Standard Oil Company of Indiana (Amoco) in the Midwest, Standard Oil of California (Chevron) in the West, and Continental Oil Company (Conoco) in the Mountain states. Market shares have been so stable in these regions that only eight states out of the original forty-eight had a different leader sixty-six years later. And in only two states in 1977 were the leaders not from the original Standard Oil Company.[10] As a result of the smooth transfer of monopoly power from the parent company and the stable regional market shares thereafter, many of the descendants today have substantial economic power and generate great profits. Five of the eighteen firms in Table 10.1 were once part of the original trust: Exxon, Amoco, Mobil, Chevron, and Atlantic Richfield.

Other firms included in Table 10.1 also owe their existence to horizontal mergers. General Motors was formed in 1908 with the purchase of five automobile factories. Acquisitions continued and within a few months General Motors had twenty-two subsidiaries including Buick and Cadillac. In 1918 General Motors acquired Chevrolet, and then in 1929, Adam Opel Company, producer of 45 percent of German automobiles.[11] Through these acquisitions General Motors was able to join the ranks of Ford Motor Company as the nation's other giant car maker.

E.I. Du Pont de Nemours Powder Company was formed in 1903 to hold the stocks acquired by the original powder trust. The number of plants acquired or controlled rose from forty in 1904 to sixty-four in 1907. This gave the company effective control of 64 to 100 percent of various types of explosives.[12] As in the case of Standard Oil, a court decision in 1911 convicted the company of violating antitrust laws but failed to dissipate much of its monopoly power. Despite the divestment of two smaller companies, Du Pont retained a major position in explosives and proceeded to gain even more through additional acquisitions including General Explosives Company in 1924 and the Excelsior Powder Company in 1928.[13]

General Electric was formed in 1892 with the consolidation of Edison General Electric Company and the Thompson-Houston Company. By 1903 it had acquired a total of eight plants including those of

Siemens & Halske Electric Company, Stanley Electric Manufacturing, and Sprague Electric Company. With each of these purchases, G.E. gained a greater share of the expanding electrical equipment industry.

These examples illustrate how horizontal mergers and combinations played a major role in the creation of many firms that still enjoy significant monopoly and economic power today. This does not mean, however, that horizontal mergers guarantee success. A firm may miscalculate what a target is worth and overpay the sellers or promoters, a common danger facing any investor. There is also the possibility that demand will fail to grow because of the introduction of new substitutes or changes in consumer preferences. A firm could falter from lack of foresight, bad luck, or general incompetence. Many of the early trusts fell victim to these pitfalls and did not prosper, and in some cases, did not survive.[14]

For firms that did survive and ultimately prosper, the advantage of monopoly power derived from these early mergers was often indispensable. These advantages generated a strong cash flow, facilitating even further expansion. While horizontal mergers could not ensure against failure, they could provide a valuable boost in the long climb to success.

Vertical Integration

If the first place a firm looks for potential acquisitions is within its own market, the second place is typically upstream at its suppliers or downstream at its buyers. Once again there may be some advantages to a firm making a vertical acquisition that are not available to the average investor. While there is no direct gain in monopoly power, there may be economies in production and marketing. Centralization of management functions and R&D may in some cases result in improved efficiency. And, of course, vertical integration facilitates planning by permitting the firm to match projected output with required inputs. By directly producing its own intermediate goods or selling its own output a firm may be able to avoid the costs involved in negotiating and enforcing contracts. It certainly reduces the uncertainty about what price to pay or to charge other firms. As a result of production becoming more efficient, costs may fall.

In addition, there may be some indirect gains in monopoly power. Entry by new producers may be impeded when many firms in an industry are fully integrated. A new entrant would be in the unenviable position of competing with firms that are also potential suppliers or buyers.

There are other advantages from vertical integration that may benefit certain firms. First, the fact that the market is related in some way to the firm's primary business means that management may have the rudimentary knowledge required to run the business successfully. Another advantage is the potential for tax savings when a company sells to itself. By strategically raising or lowering the prices of internal transfers, a firm can effortlessly shift its profits from one industry to another in order to take advantage of variations in effective tax rates between states or industries.[15] Even if the advantages of vertical integration do not compare with those gained from horizontal mergers, they may be sufficient to generate a return above that of the average investor.

One of the first highly integrated firms listed in Table 10.1 was Ford Motor Company. Although Ford relied much less on mergers and acquisitions to get started than most other firms, it did place a strong emphasis on integration. Ford constructed its own steel mills at the Rouge plant in Detroit and bought coal reserves of 600 million tons.[16] It also took great pride in producing most of its own parts as well as such basics as glass, artificial leather, cloth, and lumber. At the giant Rouge plant, raw materials came in one door and automobiles went out the other.

Other highly integrated companies listed in Table 10.1 are the oil companies. The same companies that originally dominated oil refining as part of the Standard Oil Trust eventually came to dominate domestic petroleum production, transportation, and retailing. These companies benefited from both horizontal and vertical integration.

Conglomerate

A firm becomes a conglomerate when it acquires another firm whose products are neither substitutes for its own nor related in the stream of production. This does not mean, however, that the products of a conglomerate are entirely unrelated. One possibility is that the acquisition will add to the assortment of products that a firm can offer a single customer. This type of merger is described as *product extension* because it adds to the firm's product line. A similar type of merger involves targets that produce very similar products but sell them in different markets. As long as the markets remain separate the merger is not horizontal but rather, *market extension*. Many multinational acquisitions are characterized by market extension.

These two types of acquisitions, product and market extension, do not directly increase monopoly power but they can offer other advantages in regard to production and marketing efficiencies. Consolidating the production and transportation of similar products may provide opportunities to reduce costs. And when a firm can consolidate its marketing activities to sell more than one product line to the same customer or sell the same product in different markets, the cost of artificially stimulating demand may fall. There is also the fact that two firms producing similar products in separate markets could someday become competitors. A merger of the two firms eliminates this possibility.

American Telephone and Telegraph Company relied on both vertical and conglomerate acquisitions to propel it into the upper strata of economic power. The original company, Bell Telephone, benefited from the monopoly power inherent in Alexander Graham Bell's valuable patent. Bell Telephone transferred its long-distance operations to the new AT&T Company in 1885 and the remainder of the company— primarily local telephone networks—in 1900. With the purchase of Western Electric Company in 1882, the company expanded vertically into the business of manufacturing its own equipment.

Despite the head start provided by Bell's patents, AT&T controlled only about half of the nation's telephones in 1907; the remainder was left in the hands of independent companies. Through a program of accelerated acquisitions, large numbers of rivals were brought under AT&T control, including Western Union and its communication network in 1910.[17] Much of this could be described as market extension since these firms were operating independent telephone systems. Three years later the supreme court forced the divestiture of Western Union and its telegraph business but left AT&T with substantial control of telephones. For the next sixty-seven years, AT&T retained approximately 85 percent of the telephone business in the United States.[18]

In 1984, AT&T was ordered by the courts to divest itself of several large regional holding companies including BellSouth, Nynex, Bell Atlantic, and American Information Technologies (Ameritech).[19] Each of these companies retained sufficient economic power after divestiture to earn a place in the 1980s, along with AT&T, among the country's most profitable corporations listed in Table 10.1.

International Business Machines is another company that benefited from mergers at an early stage of its development. The original company, Computing-Tabulating-Recording Company, was put together by the financier Charles Flint in 1911 to consolidate a number of companies producing business machines. Of the three primary divisions of the company, one produced business scales, one produced industrial time recording devices, and another produced tabulating and sorting machines.[20] This conglomerate, characterized primarily by product extension, was the ideal starting place for a young marketing wizard like Thomas Watson, whose crack sales force became the envy of the industry. The combined operations of C-R-T, later to become IBM, gave the sales department an expanded product line to offer their clients. Backed by successful marketing, IBM was able to overcome whatever foresight it lacked on the technical side to become one of the country's most powerful corporations.[21]

There is always the possibility that the business of the target firm and the acquirer will be entirely unrelated. For this class of acquisitions, described as *pure conglomerate*, there may be no real advantages over the average investor. In fact, the incentives governing these acquisitions are essentially the same for a firm as for any investment company. By diversifying, a firm attempts to reduce the risk, or variance, associated with its investments. In addition, it may have a plan to improve the profitability of the company by reducing managerial perquisites and compensation or altering the company's strategy. Or it may simply replace a long-term strategy of a company with a short-term one that emphasizes current profits. But none of these aspects of pure conglomerate mergers constitutes an advantage, suggesting that the prospects for success are typically no better than those facing other investors.

A firm must carefully screen its targets in order to avoid acquiring a loser that drains more surplus than it provides. This means that the diversified firm must devote significant effort scrutinizing stock prices and market developments. Among the many important indicators of a target's success are its market share and sales growth.[22] The first is an indicator of monopoly power, and the second, of future economic power. But these are the same indicators that would interest any investor.

Without the advantages characterizing other types of mergers, a larger number of pure conglomerates are likely to go sour. This explains why many of the diversified acquisitions made in the 1960s were resold in the 1980s. In most cases, these spin-offs were never fully integrated into the original firm, allowing them to be discarded with relative ease. In contrast, a spin-off from a horizontal merger continues to be a very rare event.

Acquiring Economic Power

Each of these examples illustrates how mergers played an important role in the origins of many large U.S. corporations with economic power.[23] Most of the these can be described as horizontal, but many involved market or product extension. While horizontal mergers advanced the firm's monopoly power directly, market and product extension served essentially the same purpose by providing opportunities to reduce production costs and stimulate demand. When marginal costs fall or demand increases, monopoly power generally rises. The outcome is typically a larger, more profitable company.

The fact that mergers increased the flow of profits at an early stage in the development of these companies was essential to their continued success. High profits improved their ability to finance further investments directly out of retained earnings. And a larger, more profitable company typically found it easier to win the confidence of investors, a necessity for financing further expansion through debt or equity. Even IBM, whose subsequent growth was primarily internal, was launched from a platform constructed from a number of much smaller companies.

As important as mergers were historically in the rise of economic power, they were not essential. Ford Motor Company enjoyed considerable success from its start in 1903, which can be attributed to its unique designs and pioneering production methods. With this advantage, mergers were not a necessity and in fact played only a minor role in Ford's phenomenal growth. But even in this case, monopoly power was an important element, obtained by being an early entrant into an expanding market. The returns from Ford's monopoly power were sufficient to finance the rapid expansion of the company, both in automobiles and vertically into parts and raw materials.

It should also be recognized that early mergers and combinations did not guarantee future success. The road to economic power is strewn with the skeletons of failed trusts, poorly managed holding companies, and unwieldy conglomerates. In some cases, promoters extracted all of the monopoly surplus, leaving little cash flow for real investment. In other cases, the organizers had more interest in selling large quantities of stock than ensuring the stability of the new combination. Mergers and acquisitions may improve a firm's chance of rising to the pinnacle of economic power, but they do not ensure immortality.

Once a business is formed and prospering, mergers and acquisitions continue to play an important role in its development. Well-planned combinations can expand the monopoly power of a firm, reduce its material costs, extend its product line, or enlarge its sales region. Mergers and acquisitions remain an alternative to real investment in plant and capacity, always competing for the investment dollar of the large corporation.

The early mergers at the turn of the century were predominantly horizontal as firms sought high returns from monopoly power.[24] They were especially promising since antitrust restrictions at this time were still untested. As mergers continued into the twenties, vertical integration became more common and by the time of the 1960s merger boom, conglomerate expansion became the predominant form of combination. Although horizontal and vertical mergers became relatively less important, they continued at a moderate rate throughout this period.

The distribution of large acquisitions by type was analyzed by the Federal Trade Commission for the period from 1948 to 1978.[25] This evidence, presented in Table 10.2, shows that conglomerate mergers were the most important, accounting for 74 percent of all merged assets. Of this 34 percent were identified as product extension, 6 percent as market extension, and 34 percent primarily pure conglomerate. Of the remainder, 17 percent were horizontal and 9 percent were vertical. There are numerous difficulties with compiling and interpreting this data but it serves the general purpose of indicating the predominance of conglomerate mergers in the immediate post–war period.

The primary benefit of being a large corporation with great economic power is the prospect of reaping great profits. In most cases these will be sufficient to compensate investors and still satisfy the investment needs of the company.

What do these firms do when they have excess funds? During the

Table 10.2

Large Acquisitions in Manufacturing and Mining, 1948–78

Type of Acquisition	Assets ($ million)	Percent
Horizontal	18,292	17
Vertical	10,094	9
Conglomerate	80,604	74
Product Extension	*36,729*	*34*
Market Extension	*6,379*	*6*
Other	*37,495*	*34*
Total	108,990	100

Source: "Statistical Report on Mergers and Acquisitions 1979," Bureau of Economics, U.S. Federal Trade Commission, July 1981.

1980s boom, firms with economic power were heavily involved in mergers and acquisitions. The largest purchases were Chevron's acquisition of Gulf Corporation for $13.3 billion in 1984 followed by Philip Morris' purchase of Kraft Incorporated for $12.6 billion in 1988. In fact all of the corporations listed in Table 10.1 made large acquisitions in the 1980s except for IBM and Sears.

Some of the acquisitions listed in Table 10.3 were horizontal, but this distinction has become less meaningful today now that most corporations are conglomerates. It is possible for a single merger to be horizontal, vertical, and conglomerate all at the same time. Nevertheless, certain mergers clearly involved substitutes: Chevron–Gulf, General Electric–RCA, Amoco–Dome, Mobil–Superior Oil, Ford–Jaguar. Even Philip Morris' absorption of two large food companies, General Foods and Kraft, could be considered horizontal. But many of the mergers listed in Table 10.3 are market extension, product extension, or pure conglomerate.

One particular industry that should not be overlooked experienced particularly rapid consolidation during the 1980s. As a result of horizontal mergers and acquisitions, concentration increased rapidly in the media industry. "In 1981, there were forty-six corporations that controlled most of the business in daily newspapers, magazines, television, books, and motion pictures. Five years later the number had shrunk to twenty-nine."[26] During this same period, the number of companies

Table 10.3

Large Acquisitions of Firms with Economic Power, 1979–90

Company	Acquired Company	Price ($ million)	Year
Exxon Corp.	Texaco Canada	4,150	1989
	Celeron Oil & Gas Co.	650	1987
	Reliance Electric Co.	1,170	1979
AT&T	NCR Corp.	7,500	1991
General Motors Corp.	Hughes Aircraft Co.	5,025	1985
General Electric	Equitable Lomas Leasing Corp.	1,200	1990
	Intel Corp. (cargo-container leasing business)	825	1990
	Borg-Warner (chemical business)	2,310	1988
	Montgomery Ward & Co. Inc.	1,000	1988
	Roper Corp.	508	1988
	RCA	6,142	1986
	Kidder, Peabody & Co. Inc. (80%)	600	1986
	Employers Reinsurance Corp.	1,075	1984
Amoco Corp.	Dome Petroleum	3,766	1988
	Tenneco Inc. (Rocky Mountain division)	900	1988
Mobil	Superior Oil Co.	5,700	1984
	Vickers Energy Corp.	715	1980
Chevron	Tenneco Inc. (Gulf of Mexico reserves)	2,600	1988
	Gulf Corp.	13,300	1984
Shell Oil Co.	Belridge Oil Co.	3,650	1979
Royal Dutch/Shell Group	Shell Oil Co. (remaining 30.5%)	5,670	1985
Ford Motor Co.	Jaguar	2,643	1990
	Associates First Capital Corp.	3,350	1989
	Meritor Credit Corp.	1,300	1989
	U.S. Leasing International Inc.	526	1987
BellSouth Corp.	Mobil Communications Corp. of America	679	1989
Du Pont	Conoco Inc.	6,820	1982
Bell Atlantic Corp. & Ameritech	Telecom	2,460	1990
Atlantic Richfield Co.	Tenneco Inc. (California reserves)	670	1988
Atlantic Richfield Co.	Britoil PLC	697	1987
Philip Morris	General Foods Corp.	5,628	1985
	Jacobs Suchard Ltd.	3,800	1990
	Kraft Inc.	12,644	1988

Source: Mergers and Acquisitions, 1979 through 1991.
Note: Includes all acquisitions valued at more than $500 million.

controlling half of all magazine circulation fell from twenty to six. By acquiring other magazine groups, Time Incorporated alone boosted its control of U.S. magazine circulation to 40 percent of the U.S. market. In much the same way, Gannett rose to the top of the newspaper market so that by the end of 1986 it owned ninety-three daily newspapers including *USA Today*. Few other industries experienced such a rapid increase in concentration during these three years.

Joseph Schumpeter described a process by which firms with monopoly power become complacent and lethargic and as such become vulnerable to challenges from smaller, more innovative companies.[27] According to this view, the "gales of creative destruction" ensure a turnover in monopoly power. But most of the firms with economic power have a history of having dominated their industries for decades. The secret is that economic power provides resources to invest in plant and capacity, research and development, and if all else fails, other firms with even better prospects. Firms with economic power are not immortal but the destructive gales may appear more like breezes when viewed from the lofty heights of corporate power.

Executives and the Merger Motive

While corporations formulate and implement investment strategies, it is important to keep in mind who ultimately makes the decisions. Most corporations are run by top management with due respect shown to particularly large shareholders. Therefore most investment decisions, including financial investments in mergers and acquisitions, can be traced to the highest levels of management.

But the question has been raised as to why corporate executives would engineer a merger that promises greater rewards for investors.[28] Why would anyone pursue profits for someone else? It is hard to imagine that the executive's reward is limited to sharing vicariously in the investor's pleasure. One would think that the acquisition of economic power must also benefit executives and the evidence suggests that it does.

In order for a company to be in a position to offer really substantial compensation for top management, it must be large and highly profitable. Mergers appeal to executives because they have the potential of increasing the size of the corporation while maintaining or increasing profitability. In this way, the benefits of a successful merger are not limited to the investor, but are shared with top management.

There are many problems in measuring each component of executive compensation, including the basic salary, benefits, bonuses, pensions, stock options, perquisites, and other nonfinancial rewards. But studies that have estimated the total value of these packages have found that they are generally correlated with two variables: profit rates and company size. One older study using a small sample but refined methods of analysis found an important role for profitability. Wilbur Lewellen and Blaine Huntsman studied top executive rewards between 1942 and 1962 for fifty companies, all within *Fortune*'s top ninety-four industrial companies.[29] Profit rates relative to assets had a strong positive effect on executive compensation per dollar of company assets. Although this effect was found to be large in 1942, it fell to nearly one-eighth of its original size by 1963.

The results of a more recent study by Kevin Murphy provided further evidence of the relationship between profits and compensation.[30] Using a sample of 1,948 executives in 1,191 corporations, Murphy found a strong positive relationship between changes in profits relative to equity and changes in executive salaries and bonuses from 1975 to 1984. This corresponds with the findings of John Abowd using data on more than 16,000 managers at 250 large corporations from 1981 to 1986.[31] Abowd found that both size and profitability were positive and highly significant determinants of executive compensation. Size was measured by assets and profitability by a variety of measures including return on assets and return on equity.

The results of these studies establish a link between size and profitability and executive compensation. Strategies that advance the firm on either account bring direct rewards to top management. This provides a goal for executives as they pass judgment on various options for mergers and acquisitions and real investment. Any strategy that advances the size of the firm and increases its profitability is bound to be given serious consideration.

When profits are converted into executive compensation they often cease being profits in the usual accounting sense. They become a regular operating cost, much like wages or material costs. In theory, some share of executive compensation can be justifiably defined as profits and another share as payment for work. But determining the actual distribution·between profits and earnings is at best a highly speculative undertaking. The most that can be said is that some fraction of executive compensation represents corporate profit.

Conclusion

Mergers and acquisitions cannot be fully understood without understanding the role of monopoly and economic power. Most large corporations with economic power got to where they are today by taking advantage of monopoly power during an early stage of their development. Many of them acquired their monopoly power by means of mergers and acquisitions, taking advantage of the legal vacuum existing prior to the first major antitrust decisions in 1911. Since then, antitrust has failed to either reverse the gains in economic power or halt its progress. In fact many businesses created from antitrust decisions are among the most profitable corporations today.

There is no reason to expect all the corporations listed in Table 10.1 to maintain the same level of economic power indefinitely. Firms with economic power may be durable but they are not immortal. Due to the recent wave of international competition, USX, once an immensely profitable steel company, did not even make it on the list. And the fortunes of number four on the list, General Motors, have deteriorated significantly. While not all the titans of American industry will survive, the ones that do will be in a position to exercise their power on a global scale well into the twenty-first century.

The Global Market

Some firms have advantages in a particular activity,
and they may find it profitable to exploit these
advantages by establishing foreign operations
—Stephen Hymer, 1976[1]

Few economic topics have received as much attention in recent years as those related to changes in the international economy. From the burgeoning growth of U.S. imports to the dismantling of trade barriers within Europe, the trend has been toward an ever-increasing degree of economic interdependence. One aspect of these changes is that firms that were once comfortably protected by national boundaries are coming into increasing contact. Larger and larger shares of national markets throughout the world are being captured by foreign firms, through either trade or foreign production.

A complete analysis of the process by which firms expand into foreign markets is obviously beyond the scope of this chapter. The more limited focus is on the relationship of these developments to monopoly and economic power. There are, in fact, four important themes. First, in a world of differentiated products, demand is just as important as cost in determining international trade. Second, foreign expansion provides an opportunity for firms to enhance their economic power. Third, firms often engage in foreign expansion only after they accumulate significant monopoly and economic power in their domestic market. And finally, markups will vary among countries as does monopoly power. Before exploring these themes it is useful to review the basic theory of trade and foreign production.

Comparative Advantage

Early trade theorists were preoccupied with the question of why some goods are produced in one country and sold in another. Obviously, the producing country has to have certain advantages in production since it faces additional costs for transportation. This observation provided the motivation for the concept of comparative advantage.

In order for trade to be profitable, relative costs must vary among countries. The one with the lowest relative cost for a particular good is said to have a comparative advantage. When each country specializes production where it has an advantage, the world's potential supply of goods increases and production becomes more efficient, providing consumers with a wider variety of commodities at lower prices. This condition can be stated by defining relative costs for countries A and B as the ratio of average costs (AC) between commodities 1 and 2. The condition for comparative advantage is,

(11.1)
$$\frac{AC_1^A}{AC_2^A} < \frac{AC_1^B}{AC_2^B}$$

In this case, country A has a comparative advantage in commodity 1 because it can produce it at relatively lower cost. One could rearrange (11.1) to show that country B has a comparative advantage in producing commodity 2. If goods were priced at average cost and transportation costs were negligible, it would be profitable for the two countries to specialize in production and trade.[2]

In order to achieve a comparative advantage, a country must be able to produce at relatively low cost. This would occur if the particular inputs required for production were especially abundant. For example, countries with relatively high education levels may have a comparative advantage in designing computers while countries with tropical climates are likely to find their advantage in producing pineapples or coffee.

Exports from many countries, especially those related to agriculture and natural resources, are often related to comparative advantage. For example, differences in relative costs explain why Guatemala produces bananas, the United States produces wheat, and Saudi Arabia produces oil. However, as a general explanation of trade, this version of comparative advantage is not entirely satisfactory for the simple reason that many traded goods are relatively unique.

In order to determine whether a good can be traded it is necessary to look at foreign demand as well as domestic production costs. A Rolls Royce may be relatively more costly to produce than a Yugo but does that prove Yugoslavia has a comparative advantage over England in producing automobiles? Obviously relative cost is only one factor influencing trade; demand is another.

General Condition for Trade

A firm will consider selling a product in a foreign market, or any market for that matter, when it is profitable. More precisely, trade becomes feasible when the marginal revenue in a foreign market exceeds marginal costs in the home market. The only peculiarity about international trade is that marginal revenue and marginal costs are registered in different currencies. Before they can be compared they must be converted to the same units. Therefore, in the following discussion, it is assumed that all values are converted to a single currency using appropriate exchange rates.

When marginal revenue exceeds marginal costs it is always more profitable for a firm to increase production. This principle is just as true for foreign markets as it is for domestic ones. Under this criterion, it could be profitable to sell Rolls Royces in Yugoslavia at the same time that it is profitable to sell Yugos in England. Neither country holds an exclusive comparative advantage in the production of automobiles.

This can be summarized as follows. It is profitable for a firm to consider exporting its product when marginal revenue in the foreign market (MR_f) exceeds marginal cost (MC). Therefore the condition for trade is simply,

$$(11.2) \qquad\qquad MR_f > MC$$

As the firm expands production for exports, marginal cost is likely to increase while marginal revenue falls. Both responses will cause marginal cost to eventually equal marginal revenue. At this point, short-run profits are maximized and marginal cost will equal marginal revenue in both domestic (MR_d) and foreign markets (MR_f). According to this condition,

(11.3) $MR_d = MR_f = MC$

Equation 11.3 not only determines the total output that maximizes short-run profits but also shows how that output is distributed between the two markets. The way this works is illustrated in Figure 11.1 where the first two panels, A and B, describe the foreign and domestic markets. Both markets have their own demand and marginal revenue curves. Since production only takes place in the domestic market, there is only one marginal cost curve and one average cost curve, depicted in panel C.

A new concept in this example is the aggregate marginal revenue curve (MR) in panel C. This curve shows the total output that can be sold in both markets given a particular value for marginal revenue. It is found by summing the output in each market for every possible level of marginal revenue.

The intersection of this curve with marginal cost in panel C determines the total output of the firm. It also sets the level of marginal cost, which is then projected into both the domestic and foreign markets. The intersection of this level of marginal cost with marginal revenue determines the optimal sales in each market. This graph is another way to represent the relationship described by (11.3).

From the information in the figure it is possible to calculate monopoly and economic power. Recall that monopoly power is defined as the markup over marginal costs that maximizes short-run profits. Profits are maximized when the firm produces q_f in the foreign market at a price p_f, and produces q_d in the domestic market at a price p_d. Since there are two prices, there will also be two values for monopoly power. In addition, the Appendix to this chapter shows that monopoly power will be equal to the inverse demand elasticity in each market (η).[3] Therefore, monopoly power (M) is defined as follows,

(11.4) $$M_d = \frac{p_d - MC}{p_d} = \frac{1}{\eta_d} \qquad M_f = \frac{p_f - MC}{p_f} = \frac{1}{\eta_f}$$

According to these equations, monopoly power will vary from one market to the next, depending on the elasticity of demand. Markets with lower elasticities will have higher levels of monopoly power.

Also illustrated in Figure 11.1 is economic power, represented by

155

Figure 11.1. Economic Power in Domestic and Foreign Markets

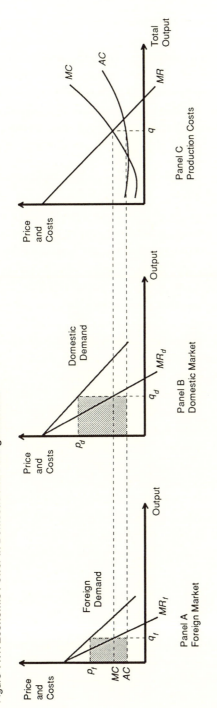

the shaded areas. Each area is equivalent to maximum short-run profits of the corresponding market and the sum of both areas is equivalent to economic power. The only difference from the original case described in Chapter 3 is that there are now two markets instead of one.

It is again useful to show how the firm's economic power is related to monopoly power in both markets. This relationship, also derived in the Appendix, shows that economic power (E) is again related to monopoly power (M), revenue (R), and a measure of capacity utilization (D).

$$(11.5) \qquad E = R_d M_d + R_f M_f + qD \quad \text{where } D = MC\text{--}AC$$

The firm has a greater potential for generating profits if monopoly power and revenue are high in either market or capacity utilization is high. It should now be evident how foreign expansion contributes to economic power. A firm benefits from the potential profits in the foreign market $(R_f M_f)$ as well as from an increase in capacity utilization (qD).

So far it has been assumed that the firm produces in just the domestic market. It is not difficult to expand these results to include foreign production. The only difference is that the additional production site creates an additional set of cost curves. Therefore, marginal costs used to define monopoly power in (11.4) must be assigned to the appropriate production location, foreign or domestic. The specification for economic power in (11.5) must also be modified for foreign production because capacity utilization may vary from one location to the next. This is accomplished by separating the capacity utilization term into two components, one for domestic production, $q_d \, (MC_d - AC_d)$ and one for foreign production, $q_f \, (MC_f - AC_f)$.[4]

These equations are not unique to firms involved in foreign production. They are also used to describe firms that sell two different products in one domestic market or sell one product in two domestic markets. In each case, economic power is derived from two essentially independent sources.

Evolution of International Activity

Foreign activity tends to unfold over time. Typically, a firm that has enjoyed a degree of success will want to extend its distributional network. If success continues, sales may spread from local to regional markets until the entire country is covered. From this position, it is reasonable to expect the firm to explore markets in other countries.

At first, the firm may rely on exports to supply the foreign market. This has the advantage of allowing it to test the market abroad without committing itself to a large increase in productive capacity. This is a cautious first step, but may be warranted where the extent of foreign demand is uncertain. All that is required to pursue such a strategy is the expectation that additional revenue from foreign sales will exceed additional production costs.

This pattern aptly describes the growth of I.M. Singer & Company, the pioneering manufacturer of sewing machines. Singer was noteworthy because it was one of the first U.S. companies to develop a comprehensive foreign distributional network, preceding the expansion of General Electric, National Cash Register, and International Harvester. After a failed venture involving the sale of its patent to a French merchant in 1855, Singer pursued direct sales of its U.S. machines through contracts with independent franchise agents. This met with great success and by 1861 the company had sales representatives in nine different countries. The widely held view that Singer produced a superior machine was the source of its expanding monopoly power at home and abroad.[5]

One of the best predictors of success in foreign markets will be success at home. A firm that has achieved monopoly and economic power at home is probably justified in being optimistic about its foreign prospects. Although the correlation between domestic and foreign success will never be perfect, consumer tastes, or at least the susceptibility of such tastes to artful persuasion, are likely to share more similarities than differences between countries.

Consequently, one would expect to see firms with high levels of domestic monopoly and economic power to be more active in foreign markets. While this is generally true for some exporters, it certainly does not describe all of them. Some exports will be associated with comparative advantage that is not confined to any particular market structure. The benefits of comparative advantage may accrue to firms with as little power as wheat farmers in the United States or as much as the state oil monopoly of Kuwait. Exporters will therefore include some firms with monopoly power and others with comparative advantages.

Once a firm has successfully entered a foreign market by means of exports it will soon face another decision: should it expand production and if so, where? Foreign production has the advantage of reducing transportation costs for the finished product but other costs will be affected as well. There are capital construction costs, labor costs, and transportation costs for raw materials, just to name a few. All that can be said in general is that the firm is likely to favor the location where average costs for production and transportation are lowest. In the case of Singer, rising foreign sales precipitated the decision to construct a small assembly operation in Scotland in 1868. Sales increased even faster as a result of foreign production, permitting Singer to surpass the sales of the market leader, Wheeler & Wilson, by the late 1870s.

There is one particular factor that affects decisions about foreign production: the cost or anticipated cost of a trade barrier. Tariffs directly increase the desirability of foreign production while quotas and other trade restrictions have a similar effect. Even where no trade barrier exists, a firm may be justified in expecting one, especially if it anticipates rapid growth in foreign sales.

There are numerous examples of trade barriers being used to entice firms to replace exports with foreign production. The first president of American Tobacco Company, James Duke, testified in 1901, "We are always selling direct from factories here [in the United States], unless there is some discriminatory duty against us that forces us to manufacture [in a foreign country]."[6] One such example is Canada, where high tariffs were once used to attract U.S. direct investments.[7]

This description of how firms gradually expand into foreign markets has become known as the *life-cycle process*. Firms begin by exporting and gradually evolve into foreign production. At some point, these foreign operations may even begin to send some portion of their production back to the home market, commonly known as platform production. While the life-cycle process describes the evolution of some firms, it does not apply to all.

It is also possible for firms to move directly into foreign production by purchasing a foreign producer. No preliminary expansion of exports is required nor any increase in productive capacity. The firm merely gains control of a foreign producer by purchasing majority ownership.

A merger or acquisition that involves a foreign firm is not particularly different from one that takes place in the domestic market. The merger may be characterized as horizontal, vertical, market extension, product extension, or pure conglomerate. Also, this type of foreign expansion may be easier to finance if the firm has relatively high levels of monopoly or economic power. General Motors was able in 1929 to purchase Adam Opel, then one of the largest producers of German automobiles, where a lesser company would have found it prohibitive. Economic power can provide the profits or attract the credit necessary to finance domestic or international expansion.

There is one important economic difference between these two methods of foreign expansion. On the one hand the firm following the life-cycle process typically begins by exporting and only then considers the possibility of foreign production. Because the firm continues to concentrate on the same basic product it can continue to exploit any advantage it enjoys in product design, manufacturing, or marketing. On the other hand, when a firm expands by means of merger or acquisition, the transferal of advantages is not always possible. The acquiring firm can modify the target's product or production method but any change is likely to be incremental, even more so in comparison to the life-cycle process, which may involve the construction of entirely new productive facilities.

In another respect the two methods of foreign expansion are not so different. Both are more likely to be undertaken by firms with monopoly or economic power. Life-cycle firms are prompted by their own success in domestic markets, a success that is typically reflected in high monopoly or economic power. And those firms in a position to make foreign acquisitions are unlikely to be powerless in their home markets. Whether firms pursue foreign markets by means of acquisitions or life-cycle expansion, they are likely to begin with high levels of monopoly or economic power in their domestic market.

Evidence

Based on the early theory of comparative advantage, one would expect countries to specialize in certain areas for export and surrender others to imports. As a consequence, specific industries should have relatively high exports or high imports but not both. The actual pattern of U.S. trade in manufacturing, however, does not conform to this simple dichotomy.

Using data for U.S. manufacturing in 1982, I calculated a simple index of trade specialization for 389 industries equal to exports divided by total trade (exports plus imports). The resulting distribution presented in Figure 11.2 shows the share of total international trade accounted for by industries with varying levels of trade specialization.

Figure 11.2. **Trade Specialization of Manufacturing Industries, 1982**

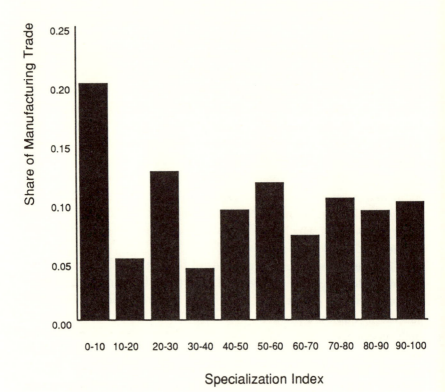

Source: U.S. Census Bureau.
Note: Specialization Index = Exports/(Exports + Imports).

Only the first (0–10 percent) and the last decile (90–100 percent), representing approximately 30 percent of all trade, correspond with the traditional notion of comparative advantage. Industries in the first group are predominantly importers, and in the second, exporters. In the remaining eight deciles, exports range from 10 percent to 90 percent of industry trade, amounting to 70 percent of all manufacturing trade. In fact, 55 percent of all manufacturing trade originates from industries where exports range from 20 percent to 80 percent of industry trade. In other words, U.S. trade is not "specialized" in the sense that some industries export while others import because most industries are involved in both.

The evidence in Figure 11.2 is much less surprising, however, when one takes into account the fact that many of the products within these detailed manufacturing industries are highly differentiated.[8] In most cases, the United States is not importing and exporting identical commodities but rather products distinguished by function, form, style, or trade name. Since each product is more or less unique it has its own demand in both U.S. and foreign markets. Production costs, which form the basis of comparative advantage, are always important, but one cannot ignore the role of unique demand curves associated with highly differentiated products.

The phenomena of intraindustry trade has been observed for Europe as well as the United States. Caves and Jones cited studies that not only found a high incidence of intraindustry trade for European countries but found no tendency for it to subside when trade barriers were removed with the inauguration of the Common Market.[9] They concluded that "Intraindustry trade has turned out to be a widespread phenomenon. . . . More intraindustry trade prevails in sectors whose products are clearly differentiated, less where substantial scale economies tend to concentrate production in a few locations."[10] Intraindustry trade is just one phenomenon that is easily explained by monopoly power.

If foreign activity were determined only by comparative advantage then we could resign ourselves to comparing relative production and transportation costs between countries. But because of differentiated products, it becomes necessary to look at characteristics of firms that engage in trade and foreign production, a topic that has received considerable attention in international economics. For the most part, the results show that U.S. firms involved in foreign activity tend to be more capital intensive and pay higher wages. These firms also enjoy significant monopoly power in their home market as indicated by elevated levels of concentration, advertising, and R&D.[11]

In a typical study on this topic, Sanjaya Lall measured the relationship between several determinants of concentration and total U.S. foreign involvement defined as exports plus foreign production in 1970.[12] Lall found that U.S. industries characterized by large establishments and high expenditures on research and development and advertising were also statistically more likely to be "involved" in foreign markets.

In each case, this involvement took the form of statistically higher exports as well as higher foreign production.[13]

It should be pointed out that between the two methods of servicing foreign markets, exports and foreign production, the latter is relatively more important for U.S. firms. In 1987, U.S. companies sold approximately $924 billion of goods and services outside the United States. Of this total only 27 percent was from exports while the remaining 73 percent was from U.S. production abroad.[14] The value of exports is not inconsequential, but is obviously overshadowed by the much larger value of goods and services produced and sold abroad by U.S. companies.

Following the precedent set by Stephen Hymer in the 1960s, many studies have found statistical relationships between various indicators of monopoly power and foreign production.[15] Neil Hood and Stephen Young cited a number of these, including works that found a significant correlation between foreign investment and home country concentration.[16] Raymond Vernon's observations that multinational firms are larger and spend more on advertising and R&D than other firms are consistent with a vast number of other statistical studies.[17] In my own study on this topic, I found that the level of concentration in U.S. markets was significantly and positively related to the extent of U.S. foreign production.[18]

In fact, it is now widely recognized that firms with high concentration, high advertising outlays, or high R&D expenditures are more likely to be involved in foreign production. This fact has been explained in the trade literature by suggesting that these measures are indicative of some sort of advantage. More precisely, monopoly power is related to foreign activity because it indicates the firm's success in gaining control of its domestic market and because it contributes funds necessary for foreign acquisitions.

All of these studies indicate a statistical relationship between measures of monopoly power and the propensity of firms to sell in foreign markets. While the relationship is sometimes weak for exports, it is generally stronger for foreign production.

Platform Production

In some cases, the output of U.S. firms abroad is not sold in those markets but instead is shipped back into the United States. The obvious reason for locating production abroad is to reduce overall costs and therefore increase economic power.

Although platform production is not insignificant, most foreign production by U.S. firms is directed toward foreign markets. This can be seen in Figure 11.3, which shows the total sales of U.S. majority-owned foreign affiliates in 1987 (black bars) and the value of sales returned to the United States as imports (gray bars). According to the figure most U.S. foreign production takes place in Europe, Canada, Latin America, and Asia (other than Japan), the same regions that account for most of the imports by U.S. affiliates. But it is also clear from the figure that platform production is small relative to affiliates' total production.

A good example of U.S. foreign production for U.S. markets can be found in the Mexican maquiladoras, primarily located in the border regions with the United States. Hundreds of U.S. companies have production facilities in this area, including General Motors, Chrysler, General Electric, RCA, United Technologies, and Johnson and Johnson. What makes the maquiladoras particularly important is the rapid growth they have experienced in recent years. Total employment in the maquiladoras rose at an annual rate of 23 percent between 1966 and 1986 when it reached 268,400. Between 1977 and 1986, employment in U.S. affiliates in Mexico increased by 19 percent compared with a 14 percent decrease in all other countries.[19] If this trend continues, Mexico could become the leading source of U.S. platform production.

Life-Cycle versus Acquisitions

Unfortunately very few studies have demonstrated whether U.S. firms entered foreign markets primarily through new construction, as they would under the life-cycle process, or by means of acquisitions. One of the few investigations into this question was conducted by Raymond Vernon who found that 55 percent of foreign manufacturing facilities were acquired as opposed to newly formed for a sample of 180 U.S. multinational firms in 1975.[20] In addition, Vernon noted that the percentage of foreign subsidiaries originating from acquisitions increased steadily from 37 percent prior to World War II to 55 percent by the 1960s. Unfortunately, more recent data is not currently available. Nevertheless, the evidence suggests that both life-cycle expansion and acquisitions have made important contributions to U.S. production capacity abroad.

Acquisitions appear to be relatively more important for Japanese

Figure 11.3. **Majority-Owned U.S. Foreign Affiliates: Total Sales and U.S. Imports, 1987**

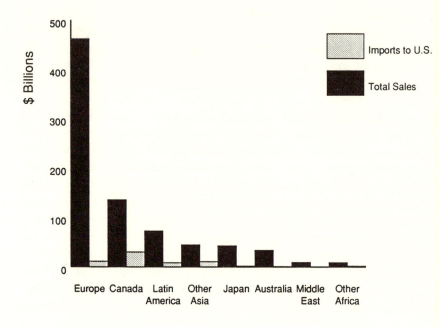

Source: Whichard (1989).

investments in the United States, a subject that does not suffer from the same data limitations. For foreign investments in the United States the ratio of acquired to newly established concerns was four to one from 1981 to 1987 and as high as twelve to one in 1988.[21]

Pricing in Foreign Markets

As a general rule, markups should tend to be higher in markets where monopoly power is higher. Exceptions occur only when firms practice price competition or cooperation. And there is reason to suspect that price competition may play a more prominent role in foreign expansion.

Recall that one of the deterrents to price competition is the fear of retaliation by rivals. A general outbreak of price cutting can thwart aspirations of growth but even more dangerous is the potential loss of market shares to rivals. The danger of this loss is significantly circumscribed when price competition is confined to foreign markets. A new entrant into a foreign market often has little to lose. It is free to launch a price war abroad while its market share at home remains secure. It is much the same advantage as fighting a war entirely on foreign soil: any destruction is at the rival's expense.

An effective deterrent to this strategy is government intervention. Such a response is most likely when imports succeed in capturing significant market share, resulting in the loss of domestic jobs. A trade barrier, or even the threat of one, may prove decisive, forcing an exporter to forgo price competition or at least moderate its ambitions in the foreign market. In other cases, firms may simply move quicker into foreign production that does not face an equivalent danger from intervention.

The evidence that exists on this topic suggests that markups do vary widely across international boundaries. For example, Caves and Jones cited a study of seventy-six U.S. exporting firms prior to World War II. Of these, ". . . forty-six of them received lower net prices on their foreign than their domestic sales, and only nine got higher prices abroad."[22]

It also appears that foreign affiliates of U.S. parent corporations charge different markups in different countries. Figure 11.4 shows how price–cost margins (PCM) of U.S. foreign affiliates compare to U.S. industries. A value of .5 means that the margins of U.S. foreign affiliates were half the size of margins in the United States for the same industries. The fact that the values for every region are less than one indicates that U.S. firms set lower margins for production abroad than at home.

One explanation for these results is that United States foreign operations have relatively lower capital costs, thus requiring a lower margin. But additional tests failed to support this hypothesis. For this sample, margins were not statistically related to capital intensity.[23]

The fact that margins are lower abroad is consistent with the general proposition that U.S. affiliates have less monopoly power or are more prone to practice price competition. This conclusion is reinforced by

Figure 11.4. **Margins of U.S. Foreign Affiliates Relative to U.S. Domestic Industries, 1982**

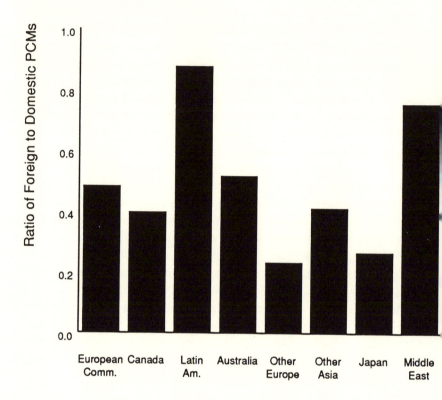

Source: Annual Survey of Manufacturers and unpublished data from the U.S. Department of Commerce.

the pattern of margins by geographical region. U.S. firms probably confront fewer rivals in Latin America and the Middle East where their margins are highest than they do in Japan, Europe, and Canada where margins are lower. Unfortunately to test whether margins are statistically related to affiliate monopoly power would require more information than is currently available. What we have at this point is a pattern of margins that is generally consistent with the likely distribution of monopoly power.

This evidence does not preclude the possibility that some U.S. firms will charge higher prices abroad. In fact, prices and markups should be higher in those particular instances where U.S. firms face few foreign competitors and have achieved a high level of monopoly power. Richard Barnet and Ronald Muller cited several examples of multinational corporations setting higher prices in Latin America. In one particular study, the prices of "global" companies in Columbia were 155 percent higher in pharmaceuticals, 40 percent higher in rubber products, and 16 to 60 percent higher in electronics.[24] Prices for "tranquilizers Valium and Librium were, respectively, 82 to 65 times higher than established international market prices."[25] In most of these cases, the multinational companies did not face any significant competition from local firms and were in a particularly strong position to exercise their monopoly power.

It should be evident that the theory of monopoly power developed in previous chapters is easily adapted to foreign trade and multinational production. In fact, because of the dominant role of large firms in the international economy, these concepts are indispensable. In today's world, giant firms with great monopoly and economic power are primarily responsible for the movement of goods and capital across national borders.

Appendix

This section defines the monopoly and economic power of a firm that produces in one place but sells in two separate markets. The subscript d is used for the domestic market and f for foreign ones. It is assumed that all foreign values are converted to the domestic currency by means of the appropriate exchange rate.

Profits (π) are equal to the sum of revenue (R) from both markets less total cost (C). The firm maximizes profits by maximizing the following:

(11.6) $$\pi = R_d + R_f - C(q) \quad \text{where } q = q_d + q_f$$

Differentiating this function with respect to domestic and foreign output gives us the general result that profits are maximized when,

(11.7) $$MR_d = MR_f = MC$$

In other words, the profit-maximizing output of the firm is determined by the point at which marginal revenue of the firm in each market is equal to marginal cost.

We can now define the firm's monopoly power in each market as the markup over marginal costs at the profit-maximizing output. This can be demonstrated for the domestic market beginning with the definition of marginal revenue.

(11.8)
$$MR_d = \frac{d(p_d q_d)}{dq_d} = p_d + \frac{q_d dp_d}{dq_d}$$
$$= p_d (1 - 1/\eta_d)$$

Setting this equal to MC (11.7) and rearranging we find the following result:

(11.9)
$$\frac{p_d - MC}{p_d} = \frac{1}{\eta_d}$$

In other words, the monopoly power of the firm in the domestic market (M_d) is determined by the elasticity of demand in the domestic market. Similarly, the firm's monopoly power in the foreign market (M_f) is determined by the elasticity of demand in that market.

(11.10)
$$\frac{p_f - MC}{p_f} = \frac{1}{\eta_f}$$

Finally, it is useful to show that the economic power of the firm in each market is also related to monopoly power and capacity utilization. By definition, the total economic power of the firm is equal to its profits at the point that maximizes short-run profits. Consequently all following values are restricted to that particular output. We begin by defining economic power as the difference between revenue and costs and then rearranging.

(11.11)
$$E = q_d (p_d - AC) + q_f (p_f - AC)$$
$$= q_d (p_d - MC + MC - AC) + q_f (p_f - MC + MC - AC)$$
$$= p_d q_d \frac{(p_d - MC)}{p_d} + q_d (MC - AC) + p_f q_f \frac{(p_f - MC)}{p_f} + q_f (MC - AC)$$
$$= R_d M_d + q_d (MC - AC) + R_f M_f + q_f (MC - AC)$$
$$= R_d M_d + R_f M_f + q (MC - AC)$$

According to this result, the total economic power of the firm is equal to the revenue weighted sum of monopoly power in each market and the capacity utilization factor.

Political Economy of Power

> *Power does not dutifully confine itself to the "economic" realm,*
> *narrowly construed. It does not passively submit to "the market." It*
> *does not submissively play according to an unalterable set of rules for*
> *survival and success. Instead, it reaches out to change the rules of the*
> *competitive game—or to dispense with them altogether—by capturing*
> *the state and perverting it to private (often antisocial) ends.*
> —Walter Adams and James Brock, 1986[1]

The preceding chapters describe a process by which firms naturally come to acquire monopoly and economic power. To the extent that some firms succeed and others fail will depend on numerous factors, only some of which are within the control of firms. It is up to them, for example, to decide whether to practice price or nonprice competition or whether to merge with a rival. Given these general strategies, they must then decide on the degree of price competition, how to allocate funds for advertising and R&D, and which firms to acquire or merge with. The decisions of some firms will turn out better than others, furthering their progress in the accumulation of power.

But the success of firms in this matter is not entirely within their control. Success will depend, for example, on the relative ease of entry. The potential to accumulate monopoly power will be much better where economies of scale and technical complexities reduce the field of possible entrants. In addition, local monopoly power will be easier to accumulate where markets are demarcated by natural boundaries. Another advantage arises where scarcity limits the number of entrants, as it does in some natural resource markets. There are only so many oil fields, coal deposits, and central city locations.

Another critical factor in the process of acquiring power is government policy. It was pointed out in earlier chapters that firms must consider the possibility of government intervention as they assess the desirability of price competition, collusion, and acquisitions. Anticipation of intervention may tip the scale in favor of a more cautious strategy, one that is less likely to rouse the interest of government regulators. But there are many other ways that government policies influence the process of accumulating and exercising power, not all of which are necessarily restrictive. In fact, while one office of the U.S. government proscribes mergers that lead to monopoly power, another grants exclusive monopoly power of limited duration. The first is the Federal Trade Commission; the second is the Patent Office.

The purpose of this chapter is to describe some of the government policies that have a direct impact on the process of accumulating power. An effort is also made to explain how these policies are justified. In some cases, these explanations may not be particularly convincing or even consistent. It is not my purpose to ascertain the wisdom of each policy, some of which have been debated for centuries. It is enough for me to describe how various government policies accelerate or retard the growth of power and occasionally modify its impact.

The fact that laws and regulations can have a strong impact on monopoly and economic power creates a related incentive for business to shape these policies. Rather than passively accept the decisions of public officials, the business sector uses political action committees, revolving doors, and honoraria in an effort to sway government decisions in their favor. These investments, like any others, must meet the criteria of contributing to the profitability of the company. The value of the gain is once again related to economic power. This topic is taken up later in the chapter.

Mercantilism

One of the first important examples of monopoly power arose almost four hundred years ago, largely as a result of government policy. In the sixteenth and seventeenth centuries mercantilist theory defended the practice of granting exclusive trading rights to specific companies with the understanding that it would stimulate trade and bring wealth to the nation. One of the greatest mercantilist companies, the English East India Company, was originally issued a charter by Queen Elizabeth in 1600, granting it a "monopoly of trade" with Asia, Africa, and America.[2] King James I expanded this already generous charter by removing the fifteen-year time limit as specified by Elizabeth, thus granting exclusive trade for an unlimited period of time. The exclusive right to sell spices from these vast productive regions launched the company on a course in which it ultimately amassed unprecedented levels of monopoly and economic power.

The monopoly charter in itself was not sufficient to put an end to all competition. The Crown was only in a position to grant the East India Company the exclusive right to sell in England, a right that was won rather cheaply compared with the much greater cost of actually acquiring the spices. For decades, the company had to fight for access to its supplies, first with the Portuguese and later with the Dutch, the French, and ultimately with the Indians themselves whose attempts to control their own resources were brutally defeated. For the most part, the Dutch successfully defended their monopoly of production in the Spice Islands while the English came to dominate the whole of India.

Another challenge to the company came in 1698 when traders linked to the Whig party prevailed upon the Parliament of William III to set up a second East India Company.[3] The reduction in monopoly power led to a swift decline in profits, prompting the government to call upon the competing companies to pool their interests, which they eventually did, forming a united East India Company in 1708. The brief experiment in competition was abandoned as confusion grew and profits declined. Other challenges came from interlopers and pirates who violated the conditions of the charter and engaged in their own version of free trade. And finally there was the problem of individual profiteering whereby employees bought and sold for their own personal gain, thus undercutting the company's success.

But all of this did little to detract from the immense profitability of the company. From its first charter in 1600 until it was stripped of its monopoly privilege and forced to pass its entire empire to the Crown in 1858, the East India Company was immensely successful. Its first two expeditions in 1601–1603 and 1604–1606 provided a return of 95 percent and its successes during the ensuing two and a half centuries were sufficient to provide an ample return to investors, private fortunes for company officials, and sufficient funds for the military conquest and administration of an entire subcontinent.[4]

The Free-Rider Problem

How could the Crown, and later Parliament, justify granting such an exclusive privilege? The answer was to stimulate trade. The East India Company could have developed this line of business without its exclusive charter but it would have faced immediate competition from new entrants. By granting monopoly privilege, the government raised the expected profits of the venture, thus increasing the amount that the company would be willing to invest. The monopoly charter was perceived as a device for encouraging an investment that would otherwise be too costly or entail too great a risk.

In modern discourse, this type of reasoning is described as a free-rider problem. Free-riders threaten to enter a market only after the lead firm has committed its capital and demonstrated the profitability of the venture. Because of free-riders, the original firm may be unable to recover the full return from its investment. As a result, investments of this kind are normally inadequate or may never take place. The free-rider argument is used to defend a number of modern government policies in much the same way as it was used centuries ago on behalf of the East India Company.[5]

In some respects the East India Company stands as a symbol of a bygone era. Within the advanced capitalist countries today, no single company can dominate the economic, political, and military activities of a nation on the same scale as the East India Company. But in other respects its legacy as a legal trade monopoly lives on in the form of modern trade policy. Since 1918 the Webb-Pomerene Act has exempted combinations of U.S. exporters from antitrust laws, thereby allowing them to engage in collective agreements governing exports.

The original purpose of this law, like the earlier monopoly charters, was to stimulate trade. It was expected that cooperation would create opportunities to capture economies of scale in transportation and marketing. Also, by allowing firms to make a collective investment in developing a foreign market, the free-rider problem is overcome. All firms participate in the initial investment and they all benefit. Whether or not this policy actually promotes U.S. exports is no more settled today than it was during the Mercantilist age.

There is some evidence that the Webb-Pomerene Act merely reinforces the natural inclination toward cooperation inherent in firms with monopoly power. A study in 1965 showed that a relatively small percentage of exporters actually took advantage of this exemption, but the ones that did were mostly in highly concentrated industries with prior histories of domestic and international cooperation.[6] While probably not as rewarding as Queen Elizabeth's monopoly charter, the Webb-Pomerene law does provide the opportunity to increase profits by avoiding competition.

Critics of the law have also pointed out the danger that cooperation in foreign markets may spill over into domestic ones. Although the law explicitly prohibits this behavior there is no guarantee that firms cooperating in export markets will turn around and compete in domestic ones.

Patents and Copyrights

Another important example where government intervention fosters monopoly power is in the area of patents and copyrights. Since its beginning, the United States has offered exclusive control of inventions and creative works. The U.S. Constitution states, "The Congress shall have power . . . to promote the progress of science and useful arts by securing for limited times to authors and inventors the exclusive right to their respective writings and discoveries."[7] U.S. law currently grants individuals monopoly control over their inventions for a period of seventeen years, assuming it meets the standards of the U.S. Patent Office. Copyright protection for creative work, however, continues until fifty years after the death of the author.[8]

Patents and copyrights are predicated on the belief that the benefits of inventive and creative processes will, in the absence of government intervention, be captured by free-riders. Once again an individual or corporation would be more reluctant to risk an investment in these endeavors where a swarm of imitators is expected. By removing this danger, the patent and copyright systems provide an incentive or reward for the inventor or writer.

A secondary motivation for this protection is to encourage individuals to use their discovery and release it to the public. The fear that an unprotected discovery might be stolen could lead to miserly and secretive conduct, thus wasting its value. By obtaining a patent or copyright, the innovator has recourse to legal channels and thus has less need to rely on secrecy.

Patents and copyrights are monopoly grants of limited duration. It is useful to think of them as assets, which, when owned by a business, contribute to monopoly and economic power. Since most employees, especially research staff, are compelled to transfer the rights to all work-related inventions to their employer, most U.S. patents are now issued to corporations.[9] The monopoly power derived from a new, patented product will be determined by the number and strength of existing substitutes. Also, the value of a patent will depend on its contribution to economic power.

It is difficult to determine the effectiveness of this system. A grant of monopoly power provides an incentive for new investment, but at the cost of creating higher levels of monopoly power. One could argue that the current patent system reflects a compromise by limiting the duration of monopoly control to seventeen years. But in industries undergoing rapid innovation, a patent may give a firm an advantage in developing additional innovations. Without effective rivals, a firm can continually update its patents, thus ensuring its monopoly power for more than seventeen years.

Some companies have been more successful than others in using patents to preserve monopoly power. Patents, in combination with strict Post Office regulations, have served Pitney Bowes for many decades. Since introducing the first postage meter in the 1920s, Pitney has managed to stay ahead of the competition and in 1991 controlled 88 percent of the U.S. market. Rivals complain that they "must either risk patent infringement suits or embark on costly attempts to 'engineer' around Pitney patents."[10]

The company's success has not gone unrecognized. An antitrust decision rendered against the company in 1959 required it to license patents to rivals. But this restriction was removed in the late 1960s. The Postal Service extracted a similar commitment from the company in 1978 which Pitney proceeded to circumvent by licensing only its older technologies, retaining exclusive control over newer innovations. Neither of these challenges has effectively prevented Pitney Bowes from using patents to protect its monopoly power.

Limiting the Accumulation of Monopoly Power

Long before it was demonstrated by economic formalism, it was widely recognized that monopoly power could alter the production and distribution of goods to the detriment of consumers and small suppliers. And while the accumulation of power is sometimes facilitated by government it also evolves naturally in unregulated markets. The recognition of these twin facts—that monopoly power develops naturally and distorts production and distribution—led to the passage of the Sherman Act of 1890. This, together with the Clayton Act (1914), the Federal Trade Commission Act (1914), the Robinson Patman Act (1936), and the Celler-Kefauver Act (1950), enabled the government to construct a strong legal basis for curbing the rise of monopoly power. These laws permitted the government to dismantle an established firm, block proposed mergers, and prevent the elimination of rivals through excessive price competition.[11] Symbolic of these powers is Section 2 of the Sherman Act, which states, "Every person who shall monopolize, or attempt to monopolize, or combine or conspire with any other person or persons to monopolize, any part of the trade or commerce among the several states, or with foreign nations, shall be deemed guilty of a misdemeanor."[12]

While inspiring in its rhetoric, the Sherman Act, like the other antitrust laws, left many questions unanswered. Over the years it has been the court's responsibility to determine when monopoly power is illegal and when it is not. Even then the verdict is not always clear because many cases end with a consent degree in which guilt is not established. Moreover, the will of the court has swung in several different directions since the passage of the Sherman Act, over one hundred years ago. All of this makes it difficult to summarize the effect of antitrust enforcement.

But at the very least, one can say that antitrust activity has not eliminated high levels of monopoly power, nor has it prevented it from increasing in many sectors of the U.S. economy. What antitrust has done is constrain the natural growth of monopoly power for market leaders by limiting their opportunities for mergers and price competition. For example, only the largest and most powerful firms, like Standard Oil at the turn of the century and AT&T in the 1970s, were ever at risk of being dismantled. Sanctions were much less likely to apply to markets with low concentration or to firms that were not market leaders. For them, antitrust regulations seldom stood in their way. And since the early 1980s, even this limited scope of antitrust regulation has been rolled back.

Antitrust is not the only government policy interfering with the growth of monopoly power. Dating back to the early days of the nation, there has been great concern about banking. Farmers and other small businesses feared that large national banks would come to dominate the entire banking industry resulting in higher interest rates on loans and lower interest rates on deposits. And there was the additional fear that a banking system comprised of a few large national banks would soak up savings from smaller cities and towns for loans in big cities. Those outside the large metropolitan areas were afraid of finding themselves in a perpetual credit crunch, unable to obtain loans at reasonable rates.

The fear of powerful banks became even more acute as a result of the experiments in national banking between 1791, when the First Bank of the United States was chartered, and 1836, when the charter of the Second Bank of the United States was allowed to expire. Opposition to national banks focused on their monopoly power—the Second Bank achieved control of one-third of all banking assets—and their affiliation with the Federalists. After the experience with the Second Bank, the federal government refrained from permitting national banks to branch in more than one state. It was not until 1922 that national banks were allowed limited branching within cities and 1933 when the right was extended to an entire state, as long as it was permitted by state policy.[13]

While government regulation limited the accumulation of monopoly power, it did not entirely prevent it. First, banks could exercise considerable monopoly power in a given city or region, especially since new banks had to be chartered and out-of-state banks were barred. Some businesses managed to evade the restrictions by creating holding companies to control banks in two different states. And finally, smaller banks often aligned themselves with larger banks, called correspondent relationships, as an alternative to direct financial control.

The public will to forestall the consolidation of large national banks appears to be waning as indicated by the fact that more and more states are relaxing the prohibition on multistate banking. By 1992, 17 states allowed the entry of other regional banks and 29 states allowed nationwide entry, often under conditions of reciprocity. The share of assets controlled by out-of-state banks ranged from 86 percent in Maine, the pioneer in national banking, to 0 percent in Hawaii, which had yet to pass a law permitting it.[14]

The reduction in barriers to interstate banking has coincided with a number of proposed mergers involving large banks. BankAmerica announced its merger with Security Pacific in 1991, which would make it the second largest bank after Citicorp. Also announced at that time was the merger of Chemical Bank with Manufacturers Hanover, making it the third largest bank. The fourth position would be claimed by the product of the proposed merger of NCNB Corporation and C&S/Sovran.[15]

The combination of interstate banking and rapid mergers may soon return the industry to its natural evolutionary path, from which it was diverted approximately two hundred years ago. An indication of where the United States may be headed is suggested by Canada, which in 1985 had 11 banks compared to the 14,451 in the United States.[16]

While banking regulation was primarily intended to prevent the rise of large national businesses, agricultural programs were designed to preserve the small, local ones. Despite the different emphasis, the result of government intervention in both cases has been to impede the natural accumulation of monopoly power.

It became clear during the hardships of the 1930s depression that the family farm was in jeopardy. During the first three years of the depression, "Farm prices fell more than 50 percent, while prices of goods and services farmers had to buy declined 32 percent."[17] Farm incomes fell by two-thirds, leading to widespread farm foreclosures. If allowed to continue, even more of the small and medium-size farms conceivably would have failed, yielding to larger commercial enterprises and agribusinesses. The advent of monopoly power would have eventually boosted profits and alleviated the wide price swings that plagued the industry.

The United States followed a different course—stabilizing the industry through government intervention. The passage of the Agricultural Adjustment Act in 1933 marked the beginning of major government intervention in farm markets. One of the goals of this landmark legislation was to support farm income, thus improving the survival rate of small family farms. Larger farms were helped as well but it was often the smaller ones that were saved from insolvency.

Current U.S. programs cover nearly every major agricultural product and many minor ones ranging from wheat, corn, and dairy to honey, mohair, and tobacco. Each commodity has its own particular set of programs, characterized by detailed formulas and esoteric terms. But despite their unique features, the basic function of nearly every program is to elevate prices and incomes and either limit production or stockpile the surplus.[18] Higher prices benefit all farmers in proportion to their size but they often keep the smaller ones in business.[19]

Agriculture, with the help of government intervention, continues to have among the lowest levels of monopoly power in the economy. But even here, the forces of monopoly power have not been dormant. Over the decades, average farm size has gradually increased and agribusiness has come to control an increasing share of the industry. "Nationally, 5 percent of farmland owners own almost half of the land: but in the Mountain and Pacific states, the share of the top 5 percent is over two-thirds."[20] The country's largest farm, Tyson Foods, Inc., generated $1.7 billion dollars in sales in 1991, primarily for chickens and pork.[21] While agricultural support programs succeeded in slowing the growth of monopoly power, they did not manage to stop it altogether.

Government regulations in other markets have had similar effects. With the passage of the Civil Aeronautics Act in 1938 the government limited the degree of both price and nonprice competition in the airline industry, contributing to stable incomes and capacity.[22] Firms that would have been unprofitable in a more competitive environment were protected from price competition through uniform rates established by the Civil Aeronautics Board. The CAB also protected the market shares of established firms by limiting the entry of aspiring rivals. New airlines had to be certified and CAB rejected the petitions of a great many willing entrants. Without these regulations, established firms would have been more likely to compete until the market naturally stabilized at a higher level of concentration.

With deregulation in 1979 the composition of the industry was no longer frozen in place by bureaucratic procedures. The thaw produced a temporary period of significant competition during which new airlines entered the industry and price competition predominated. But competition quickly took its toll forcing several leading airlines, Continental, Eastern, and Pan Am, to file for bankruptcy under Chapter 11. Unleashing the forces of competition led quickly to failures and mergers as the industry moved toward greater monopoly power and greater stability. In a relatively brief period, concentration increased from its already high levels, especially when one takes into account regional markets. By 1991, for example, Delta controlled 82 percent of the business from Hartsfield International Airport in Atlanta, giving it substantial power over airline travel in the area.[23]

Regulating Distribution of the Surplus

Once economic power is created, a critical issue is how the resulting surplus will be distributed. In the absence of other competing interests, investors and managers are prime beneficiaries. But when workers organize into unions they are in a position to compete for a fraction of the surplus. The final distribution depends on the extent of union coverage, which ranges widely both among industries and over time.

The modern U.S. labor movement can trace its origin to the early days of the depression even though union activity erupted periodically throughout the period of industrialization. Estimates placed overall unionization rates at 10.7 percent of nonagricultural employees in 1930, 22 percent in 1940, and 33 percent by 1955.[24] The reasons suggested for this rapid growth include the disillusionment caused by the depression and the hope represented by unions especially the Congress of Industrial Organization (CIO). But one important factor that should not be overlooked is the support provided by government legislation.

Prompted by growing unrest, the National Industrial Recovery Act (NIRA) was passed on June 16, 1933, giving employees "the right to organize and bargain collectively through representatives of their own choosing. . . ."[25] Although union activity was already beginning to heat up, NIRA "was the spark that rekindled the spirit of unionism within American labor."[26] The following year, 1934, was to prove a watershed for the labor movement with dozens of strikes in places across the nation including Toledo, Minneapolis, and San Francisco. Following these eruptions, the federal government reaffirmed the rights of workers to join unions with the passage of the Wagner Act on July 5, 1935.

One of the justifications offered for government support of trade unions in the 1930s was to balance the power that corporations had acquired through mergers and consolidations. It was argued that without collective bargaining, workers would always fail to gain an adequate share of national income, a problem that was widely believed to have been at the root of the Great Depression. Without adequate purchasing power, workers would be incapable of maintaining a rate of consumption necessary to avoid economic collapse. Consequently, one of the explicit purposes of pro-union legislation in the 1930s was to redistribute the economic surplus in order to provide macroeconomic stabilization.[27]

The government maintains another more direct means of redistributing economic surpluses. The corporate profit tax was first introduced in 1909 and for the next thirty-two years provided more revenue for the federal government than the individual income tax.[28] In 1960 the tax rate on profits was approximately 50 percent, generating enough revenue to finance 23 percent of all expenditures by the federal government. Profit taxes constitute a simple way to capture a share of economic surpluses.

The relative importance of the corporate profit tax has gradually eroded over time and by 1986 financed only 8 percent of federal expenditures. One reason for this decline was the gradual reduction in the statutory tax rate, which fell to 34 percent by 1988. Other reasons included an increase in tax credits and more generous depreciation methods that permitted capital to be written off at faster rates. As a result, by the 1990s, the corporate income tax has become much less important as a vehicle for redistributing monopoly surpluses than it was in the 1950s and 1960s.[29]

In addition to using monopoly charters to stimulate trade, mercantilists also endorsed policies that restricted imports, especially those that competed with domestic production. If imports could be reduced through tariffs or quotas the mercantilist believed that the drain on precious metals would be alleviated. The mercantilist preoccupation with precious metals has little standing today whereas tariffs and quotas continue as important instruments of contemporary trade policy.

In the early history of the United States, tariffs were the primary revenue source for the new revolutionary government. Tariff duties were adjusted according to the needs of the government, which at the time were relatively modest. The trend, however, was upward as the needs of government increased and as the purpose of tariffs gradually shifted from a mere revenue source to a protective shield for nascent industries. By 1824 tariffs had clearly adopted a protectionist role, insulating "U.S. manufacturers, farmers, and workers from foreign competition."[30] Duties that averaged approximately 8.5 percent under the first tariff law of 1789 climbed to over 50 percent by the 1830s.[31]

Even at this early stage in American history, tariffs were used as a device to regulate the distribution of employment and economic power between domestic and foreign producers. Again, this was not a new idea. Adam Smith had observed in 1776 that "By restraining, either by high duties, or by absolute prohibitions, the importation of such goods from foreign countries as can be produced at home, the monopoly of the home market is more or less secured to the domestic industry employed in producing them."[32] By preventing foreign producers from fully participating in domestic markets, trade barriers became an important instrument for promoting both domestic employment and economic power.

In 1824, one of the largest tariff increases applied to raw wool, an industry characterized by little domestic monopoly power and relatively easy entry. In this setting, the immediate effect of a tariff—high prices and profits—was not of great concern. Both would be corrected as new domestic firms entered the market. The same cannot be said when such protective policies are applied to oligopolized industries such as steel and automobiles.

In 1981, the Reagan administration negotiated the first voluntary export restraints with Japanese automakers under the threat of implementing actual quotas. One effect of these voluntary quotas was to expand the economic power of domestic producers. This led one industry analyst to conclude in 1988 "that protection in automobiles had heightened the oligopoly power of the industry as a whole. . . . The rise in oligopoly profits is also evident in soaring profits of domestic producers."[33] While profits were not particularly strong in the auto industry for the duration of the 1980s, the effect of voluntary restraints no doubt kept them higher than they would have been otherwise.

The situation was similar in steel. Beginning in 1978 the U.S. government assisted this oligopolized industry by introducing a trigger price mechanism (TPM), which threatened antidumping investigations if import prices fell below a specified level. The stated purpose of TPM was fair trade but its effect was to protect U.S. steel manufacturers by prompting foreign producers to voluntarily elevate import prices. Even this cautious protection contributed to monopoly power of domestic industries and paved the way for price increases above and beyond the basic inflation rate. In real terms, the price of steel increased approximately 7 percent between 1974–76 and 1978–82.[34] In both autos and steel, however, trade intervention was incapable of reversing a decline that had deeper roots.

Obviously many other factors are involved in the decision to raise or lower barriers to trade. But regardless of how laudable these may be—protecting jobs, fostering nascent industries, or responding to unfair trade practices—one possible impact is on the monopoly and economic power of domestic producers.

Separation of Business and Government

In practice, the government is neither separate nor independent of business. There is a steady flow of money and personnel from the private to the public sector, and a flow of contracts, credits, and regulations in return. From the perspective of any firm, an investment in government policy must be evaluated by the same standards as any other investment. Is the discounted present value of expected future profits greater than the proposed outlays?

In each case, the firm or industry association must determine the value of a particular government action. For example, how much is it worth to the publishing industry to change the copyright laws, to dairy farmers to protect price supports, or to large banks to allow interstate banking? The answer will be related to the expected gain in economic power. Firms will be more willing to invest in political favors when the expected profitability of a particular government decision is high, and when there is a good chance of influencing the outcome. Consequently, the magnitude of private outlays for political purposes will be related to the expected gain in economic power.

In order to cultivate favorable public policy, businesses provide both money and personnel. A large part of these contributions take the form of campaign donations from political action committees (PACs) to incumbents in the Senate and House of Representatives. Business PACs from industry associations and individual corporations, especially in banking, petroleum, chemicals, and defense, contribute millions of dollars annually to political campaigns. A few of the largest corporate PACs are listed in Table 12.1.

It is not uncommon for firms with defense contracts to make substantial campaign contributions to elected officials responsible for defense allocations. In 1985, for example, General Dynamic's PAC made a political contribution to "every single member of the House Defense Appropriations Subcommittee (the committee that actually votes the money), and to forty-one of the forty-seven members of the House Armed Services Committee."[35]

Large corporations also make contributions indirectly through honoraria for speeches or by providing free transportation to resort locations or golf tournaments. National conventions for both parties are also increasingly underwritten by corporations. The title of "Corporate Un-

Table 12.1

The Largest Corporate Political Action Committees (PACs), 1985–86

Company	PAC Rank, 1985–86	Industry Rank (Sales), 1987	*Fortune* Industry	Average Net Income, 1980–87 ($ million)
AT&T	28	8	Manufacturing	3,201
Philip Morris	40	12	Manufacturing	1,050
United Parcel Service	46	2	Transport	479
Tenneco	48	21	Manufacturing	453
Lockheed	51	30	Manufacturing	223
Rockwell International	52	27	Manufacturing	454
General Dynamics	57	39	Manufacturing	236
Textron	58	72	Manufacturing	159
Amoco	69	14	Manufacturing	1,722
Northrop	71	69	Manufacturing	95
E.F. Hutton	75	NA	Financial	NA
J.C. Penney	78	6	Retail	107
Citicorp	81	1	Banking	553
Mobil	82	5	Manufacturing	1,695
FMC	84	137	Manufacturing	146
Winn-Dixie Stores	86	NA	Retail	107
Allied Signal	90	28	Manufacturing	310
Pacific Telesis Group	91	7	Utilities	947
Union Pacific	97	7	Transport	320
Boeing	98	20	Manufacturing	527
Grumman	99	127	Manufacturing	62
Harris	100	187	Manufacturing	77

Source: Data on political action committee rank was taken from the Appendix of Stern (1988). Other data were extracted from Compustat Database.

Note: NA = not available.

derwriter" was sold for $100,000 at the 1988 Republican convention to such companies as American Express, Brown-Forman, Coca-Cola, Delta Air Lines, Pepsi Company, RJR Nabisco, Southern Company, Dresser Industries, Chevron, and American Petrofina. Atlantic Richfield demonstrated its bipartisan interest by contributing $100,000 for the Republican convention and $20,000 for a "hospitality suite" at the Democratic convention, in addition to a $75,000 donation to their party. Among the dozens of Democratic contributors, Allied Signal sponsored a brunch, GM hosted an evening reception, and Ford Motor paid for breakfast aboard a riverboat.[36]

In addition to voluntary financial support, large businesses also contribute personnel for public service, often to direct important government agencies. A precedent to the modern system developed during World War II and the Korean War, when businesses sent scores of personnel to fill high-ranking positions in government agencies. What was unique about these managers is that they maintained their corporate identity and salaries, hence the name—without compensation (WOCs). A disproportionate number of these were coming from the 100 largest manufacturing firms.[37]

The problem with this system was that it was vulnerable to charges of conflict of interest. For example, Mr. Howard Young temporarily left his position as president of American Zinc, Lead & Smelting Company to serve as deputy administrator of the Defense Materials Procurement Agency. From 1951 to 1953, Mr. Young was often the lone voice in government calling for an expansion in the nation's stockpile of zinc. Eventually, the government did purchase over a thousand tons of zinc from Mr. Young's own company, American Zinc, Lead & Smelting Company.[38]

In today's system, business executives still accept high-ranking positions in the public sector but are placed on the public payroll, often at a significant loss of personal income. After serving in public office many of these appointees return to the private sector, occasionally to the same business, industry, or law firm that they left. Perhaps the most important positions for business executives are found at the highest levels of the executive branch. A short list of the corporate affiliations of recent cabinet members is presented in Table 12.2.[39]

Like any other expenditure by a corporation, the expense of political contributions must be weighed against its anticipated return. Because public policy is so important in regulating the accumulation and exercise of power, there is much to be gained if key decisions can be swung in favor of a corporation or industry. From antitrust to farm subsidies, the value of shifting government policy in one direction or another can be substantial. An early precedent was the donation of a gold plate worth £3,000 and credits amounting to an additional £170,000 from the East India Company to Charles II in the seventeenth century. In return, the king renewed the company's precious charter.[40]

In the modern age, businesses are just as unlikely to passively acquiesce to laws and regulations that impinge on their profitability. The

Table 12.2

Business Affiliations in the Presidential Cabinet, 1980–90

Business Affiliation	Name	Cabinet Position (B = Bush, R = Reagan)
IBM	Louis Skinner	Transportation (B)
General Electric	Samuel Pierce	Housing & Urban Development (R)
ConAgra	Clayton Yeutter	Agriculture (B)
Alcoa	Richard Thornburgh	Attorney General (B & R)
Bechtel	Caspar Weinberger	Defense (R)
Pepsico	Caspar Weinberger	Defense (R)
NCR	Nicholas Brady	Treasury (B & R)
ASARCO	Malcolm Baldrige	Commerce (R)
Armco	C. William Verity	Commerce (R)
Union Carbide	Ann McLaughlin	Labor (R)
Uniroyal	Malcolm Baldrige	Commerce (R)
Georgia Pacific Corporation	Donald Hodel	Interior (R)
MITRE	Nicholas Brady	Treasury (B & R)
AMF	Malcolm Baldrige	Commerce (R)
HJ Heinz	Nicholas Brady	Treasury (B & R)
International Paper	Samuel Pierce	Housing & Urban Development (R)
Bendix	Malcolm Baldrige	Commerce (R)
Bechtel Group	George Shultz	State (R)
Bechtel Power	Caspar Weinberger	Defense (R)
Chicago-Tokyo Bank	Clayton Yeutter	Agriculture (B)
American Broadcasting Company	Ann McLaughlin	Labor (R)
Merrill Lynch	Donald Reagan	Treasury (R)
Pacific Telegraph and Telephone	William F. Smith	Attorney General (R)
Prudential Insurance	Samuel Pierce	Housing & Urban Development (R)
Mutual Life Insurance	Malcolm Baldrige	Commerce (R)
American Stock Exchange	Elizabeth Dole	Labor (B)
First National Boston	Samuel Pierce	Housing & Urban Development (R)
Diamond Shamrock	Lauro Cavozos	Energy (B)
Pacific Mutual Life Insurance	William F. Smith	Attorney General (R)
Crocker National Bank	William F. Smith	Attorney General (R)
Rohr Industries	Edwin Meese	Attorney General (R)
Indiana National Bank	Otis Bowen	Health & Human Services (R)
Indiana Bell	Otis Bowen	Health & Human Services (R)
Mosbacher Energy	Robert Mosbacher	Commerce (B)

Source: Cabinet members were listed in the *Almanac,* 1990. Corporate affiliations as either an employee or director of the company were found in *Who's Who in American Politics* and the *Federal Staff Directory.*

more likely response is to try to obtain as favorable a decision as possible, given the financial constraints. This is a normal response to any government policy that affects economic power, including the ones discussed in this chapter. Business efforts to influence public policies may not always be successful, but seldom are they entirely ineffectual.

Conclusion

Classical purists have always had a difficult time understanding the value of almost any government function. The ideal of an unregulated market, celebrated by Adam Smith, provides an intellectual basis for condemning all but a few government services. But this view failed to recognize the role of monopoly and economic power as a powerful force in the evolution of markets. Because of limited entry, advertising, research and development, and mergers and acquisitions, firms accumulate power and exercise it in ways that are not universally beneficial. In a world of monopoly power, laissez-faire loses its claim as the most efficient economic system.

The idea was introduced in this chapter that one of the central roles of government has been to regulate the conditions under which monopoly and economic power are accumulated and exercised. It should be apparent that in some cases, as in patent law or trade policy, government intervention can contribute to greater power than would otherwise exist. In contrast, other government policies, such as antitrust, tend to limit its accumulation. How can one justify encouraging and discouraging power at the same time?

The fact is that the government does not have a consistent position either for or against monopoly power, nor is it compelled to do so. Instead, each policy is defended in terms of its anticipated net benefits. For example, monopoly power awarded by patents is intended to stimulate innovation and risk. But in order to be persuasive, this argument must demonstrate that the benefits outweigh the losses associated with fostering monopoly power. The trade-off is also apparent in antitrust enforcement. Modern regulators and courts are directed to limit the growth of corporate power, at least where there are few prospects of increased efficiency.

Finally, it is important to acknowledge that laws and regulations are not objectively created in a vacuum. Businesses have an incentive to influence public policy wherever it affects their economic power. Firms voluntarily contribute money and personnel in the hope of eliciting favorable outcomes and it would be hard to imagine that such investments have gone wholly unrewarded.

The Next Economic Order

How far the public will permit the present consolidation movement to proceed under private ownership until a demand for a shift in the basis of control is made effective is impossible to state.
—Harry Laidler, 1931[1]

The theory of monopoly power provides a tool for understanding modern business and its relationship to the public sector. The final contribution of the theory described in this book is to suggest how the forces of power are changing the world we live in.

At least in the near future, few impediments appear to stand in the way of corporate expansion and the accumulation of power. Popular sentiments favoring economic growth have been rendered into support for the freedom of businesses to expand. The opportunities for this expansion are even greater today because the new market orientation of the former Soviet Union and Eastern Europe has opened up vast areas of the globe, once off-limits to multinational companies. In addition, trade barriers are tumbling and prohibitions on foreign ownership are being revoked. And in the United States, antitrust has been relaxed, trade unions are in decline, and the profit tax is shrinking. The environment for accumulating and exercising power appears to have improved significantly in only a few years.

And increasing numbers of businesses have recently been engaged in competition for markets throughout the world. Many firms that once concentrated on one or two markets are widening their range to include markets across the globe. As a result, the contest for control has accelerated in recent years. The objective is to gain sufficient shares of enough important markets to attain the status of world economic power.

The role of national governments during this period is particularly important as they are increasingly called upon to supervise the activities of multinational business. The pressure on each country is to abide by a uniform set of rules and regulations or else risk being excluded from world commerce. It is in this area that we may well expect the greatest potential for conflict as national interests collide. The growing antagonism between the United States and Japan exemplifies this friction.

Competition is often associated with overcapacity, large fluctuations in prices, depressed profits, and a high incidence of business failures or mergers. Fortunately for firms, this is seldom a permanent state because each of these developments contributes to the growth of power. When those firms currently engaged in global competition emerge with greater power they are likely to restore order by limiting capacity, stabilizing prices, and raising profits.

This chapter focuses on three general issues: the current environment for accumulating power, the role of national governments, and the aftermath of international competition.

A Changing Distribution

Several trends in the United States have shifted the distribution of economic surplus in favor of investors and executives. The first is the decline of unions. During the 1940s, 1950s, and 1960s, unions were in a position to capture a significant percentage of the surplus generated by economic power. In 1955 unions represented nearly 33 percent of the nonagricultural work force in the United States.[2] With even higher unionization rates in concentrated industries, unions were in a strong position to extract a share of economic surplus for wages and salaries.

But the union percentage began to decline after 1953 and total union employment began to decline after 1975.[3] By 1990, unions represented only about 12 percent of nonagricultural workers in the private sector. This meant that they could no longer set the standard for economywide wage increases and as a result, from 1973 on, real hourly compensation failed to increase for union and nonunion workers alike. In many sectors, unions were lucky to maintain the existing wage differential over nonunion workers.

The direct beneficiaries of this development were investors and executives who normally compete with unions for a share of the surplus. Consequently, it is not surprising to find that many firms have had a hand in speeding up this decline. Many hired outside consultants to defeat unions in certification elections while others replaced their union work force with permanent replacement workers during strikes. Business opposition has clearly been a major factor in the decline of unions.[4]

Businesses have also benefited from the gradual decline in the corporate income tax. In 1986 this tax accounted for 8 percent of federal outlays, down from 23 percent in 1960. The provision of credits, deductions, accelerated depreciation, and generally lower rates have all contributed to easing the tax burden on corporations.[5] Firms with high profits no longer contribute as much they once did in taxes. Once again, the clear beneficiaries of this development are investors and executives who are left with a larger surplus to divide.

A related development that has also boosted the share of the total surplus captured by businesses is the increasing competition of state, local, and occasionally even national governments. In what can be described as a role reversal, large firms are now in a better position to impose competition on governments. Those public officials that offer the best environment for business investment are promised thousands or even tens of thousands of jobs for their districts. Governments that fail to compete are accused of jeopardizing the economic future of their nation or locality.

In a typical scenario, government entities offer some combination of subsidies and tax breaks with the hope of enticing a firm to locate in its area. A good example of this can be seen in the bidding war that broke out in 1985 between state governments for General Motors' Saturn plant. The Saturn project was originally planned to cost $3.5 billion and employ 6,000 workers by the time it commenced production in 1988. Moreover, the new methods of production to be incorporated in the plant were billed as "America's answer to cheap cars from Japan."[6]

Substantive offers for the plant were issued by numerous state governments, generally including some combination of tax abatements, financing assistance, and cheap land. These pecuniary provisions were reinforced by more symbolic appeals including billboard campaigns, letters from school children, and even television appearances by state governors.[7] Spring Hill, Tennessee, was the eventual winner, primarily because of its proximity to transportation networks, Nashville, and electric power.[8]

Volkswagen, Nissan, Honda, and Mazda have also won generous concessions by putting the location decision for new plants up for competition. Volkswagen in particular netted $76 million in concessions from the state of Pennsylvania when it decided in 1976 to build a plant there.[9] Whether or not these bids actually influence the ultimate decision is unknown, but the fact that they improve the profitability of large firms is beyond question. A small business investment in the state of Pennsylvania can't hope to attract the same degree of attention or financial incentives. Each of these cases illustrates how the bargaining power of large firms can be used to promote government competition, thereby enhancing potential profitability.

The decline of trade unions and corporate taxes allows investors and executives to retain a larger share of their economic surplus. But another development tends to limit the gains for some firms: the increasing presence of foreign rivals. During the past few decades U.S. imports have surged to record levels. In 1991, imports accounted for 10.9 percent of gross domestic product (GDP) compared with 4.3 percent in 1960. In addition, the value of output in the United States attributed to foreign enterprise has been increasing. In 1990, foreign production in the United States was 8.4 percent as large as GDP compared with 1.3 percent in 1960.[10] In general, more and more U.S. firms are forced to confront foreign rivals because of imports or foreign production in the United States.

While international competition is generally accelerating, it is important to realize that not all firms are equally affected. First, because imports are primarily natural resources (i.e., petroleum) or manufactured goods, the service sector is less affected. Even within manufacturing, some industries have lost considerable market shares while others have not. Imports have been low for engineering and scientific equipment, plastics, fats and oils, and aircraft but captured nearly half the domestic market for motorcycles, bicycles, children's clothes, and watches.[11] Consequently, one would expect to find a much greater impact of foreign competition on U.S. producers of motorcycles than aircraft.

The increasing penetration of U.S. markets by foreign producers is only one facet of the age of international competition. U.S. exports have increased along with U.S. imports. By 1991 the United States was exporting 10.5 percent of its GDP compared with only 4.9 percent in 1960. Consequently foreign producers also face an increase in rivals, namely U.S. exporters. Altogether the number of rivals selling in markets across the globe has been expanding, giving rise to global competition.

Competitiveness and Trade Policy

In response to international competition, a concern has developed in the United States over the "competitiveness" of U.S. companies. Although competitiveness is seldom defined precisely, it connotes the ability of a company to succeed by expanding sales or market share. The question is whether U.S. firms are capable of succeeding in pitched battles with capable opponents, the outcome of which will ultimately determine who produces the world's automobiles, computers, and aircraft.

As described in this text, firms wishing to expand their operations have a choice among several general strategies. They may practice price competition, openly challenging the sales and market shares of rivals. The firm that chooses this strategy must be prepared to temporarily sacrifice short-run profits. Nonprice competition entails a similar sacrifice for the purpose of fostering growth. A very different strategy would involve maximizing short-run profits and using the funds to acquire rivals, foreign and domestic. Either strategy—competition or acquisition—can potentially produce the desired result, growth and higher market shares.

Many firms would like to be able to capture the market shares of rivals by means of lower prices and still generate high current profits. The solution is to combine both strategies: maximize current profits in one market while cutting prices in another. Firms following this course generate high profits in one market, which supports expansion in others. The most common example would be a firm that sets high prices in its home market, protected by trade barriers, but low competitive prices abroad.

As a business pursues foreign sales and world markets, its strongest ally is often its home government. What interest do national governments have in seeing the success of their native corporations? In the traditional view of comparative advantage, the question of who produces what is worked out in an efficient manner by unfettered competition. Comparative advantage is seen as an inherent characteristic of a country, essentially independent of government intervention. But in a world of monopoly power, driven by advertising and product differentiation, the outcome of competition is not inevitable and therefore not beyond the reach of government policy. The destruction of rivals by whatever means possible promises a generation of secure employment, continued growth, high wages, and profits.

Consequently, it is not uncommon for governments to provide domestic export industries with generous support. With this assistance, a company is in a better position to compete with foreign rivals in its home market as well as abroad. It can engage in more severe price competition or use its enhanced profits for strategic acquisitions. In the end, competitiveness is determined as much by the ability to obtain government protection and subsidies as by the ability to produce desirable products.

National governments often employ trade barriers to protect native companies. The profits from a protected home market may compensate the firm for the sacrifice it makes while competing in foreign ones. But countries always run the risk that any subsidy will be perceived as an unfair trade practice, thus inviting retaliation. This danger has encouraged some inventiveness in designing policies to protect native businesses. Barriers may, for example, entail lengthy licensing procedures or restrictive regulations specifying product standards. A good example of this inventiveness was cited by Bradley Schiller. It seems that at the turn of the century a German tariff applied only to "brown and dappled cows reared at a level of at least 300 meters above sea level and passing at least one month in every summer at an altitude of at least 800 meters."[12]

United States versus Japan

The competition erupting between U.S. and Japanese businesses illustrates the variety of strategies that can be employed by firms and governments in pursuit of market shares. Some U.S. businesses, especially the auto companies, have recently complained about the low prices of Japanese imports. In a partial vindication of these complaints, the U.S. Commerce Department ruled that Toyota and Mazda were "selling minivans in the U.S. below cost."[13] Nonprice competition also plays an important role in vehicle markets. For many years Toyota overhauled its mass-market models every four years in an effort to gain market share, even though it may have sacrificed immediate profits.[14] At the very least, the evidence suggests that Japanese auto producers rely heavily on price and nonprice competition in their pursuit of international markets.

The response of U.S. automakers to Japanese competition has primarily been channeled into meetings, summits, and the threat of trade barriers. U.S. automakers appear to place less of an emphasis on price competition. When given the opportunity to regain some of the lost market shares in 1988 following a significant reduction in the value of the dollar, U.S. auto manufacturers instead chose to raise prices as a way to boost current profits.[15]

There is additional evidence suggesting that many Japanese firms have relied extensively on price and nonprice competition. Japanese banks, for example, managed to gain 25 percent of the California market by setting margins far below those of their U.S. rivals. The *Wall Street Journal* cited examples of Japanese firms charging .25 percentage points over the federal funds rate while U.S. banks were charging 3 percentage points over the relatively higher prime rate.[16]

One of the repercussions of price competition is a reduction in current profits. Along these lines there is evidence that Japanese firms are less profitable than U.S. firms but stronger in sales. In *Business Week*'s 1991 listing of the largest Global 1000 corporations, the top five firms, measured by sales, were Japanese. But ranked by profits, only Toyota (seventh) and Nomura Securities (twelfth) show up in the top fifteen, the majority of which are U.S. firms. Furthermore, for the 309 Japanese companies making this list, the ratio of profits to sales was 2.4 percent, compared with 5.6 percent for the 359 U.S. companies on the same list.[17] This pattern is similar in banking where Citicorp ranks below ten Japanese banks in assets but leads in profitability.[18] It appears that Japanese companies generate greater sales while U.S. firms are more profitable. This is consistent with the hypothesis that Japanese firms are, on average, more inclined toward competition.

Why would U.S. firms be reluctant to engage in price competition? It may be based on a traditional aversion to price cutting or a strong preference for immediate returns. It is also possible that U.S. firms rely more on mergers and acquisitions for corporate expansion. And finally, it is possible that the managers running these companies are preoccupied with short-run profits because they account for a major share of their own personal income. In 1990, the average chief executive officer of a large U.S. company made approximately $2 million dollars compared with $300,000 to $400,000 for the average Japanese CEO. Additional estimates indicate that CEOs in the United States can earn "160 times more than the average employee," compared with 16 times in Japan.[19] American managers evidently rely on strong short-run profits to enhance their own personal compensation. Price competition would cut into both current profits and executive income.

U.S. producers have also complained that Japanese markets have been closed to them. These accusations, backed up with the threat of a vehicle quota, prompted Japanese producers to pledge support for boosting U.S. parts and vehicle sales in Japan.[20] A similar pledge to increase purchases of foreign-made semiconductors was recently squeezed out of the powerful Japanese electronics firms.[21] It may well be that Japanese corporations have underwritten their own foreign expansion by limiting competition from foreigners at home.

Winners and Losers

Few firms are prepared to endure stiff competition indefinitely. Low prices, excess capacity, and rapid innovation all take their toll on struggling firms. At some point, competition in many markets around the world will ebb and firms will take advantage of the market shares they have won. But at what point will they be satisfied? Will competition rage until a single firm controls an entire market? In most cases, firms will be content with something far less than 100 percent of a market. It is simply too costly to stamp out all rivals and besides, few governments would tolerate such an outcome, especially by a foreign business. In most contested markets, firms are more likely to set a target market share that allows for the existence of a few other large rivals. Toyota, for example, was understood to have a goal of capturing 10 percent of the entire world market for vehicles by the turn of the century.[22]

The end of this round of competition could be triggered by any number of events. Competition may simply ease as firms achieve their target market shares. Government intervention can also bring competition to an end. A limit on sales by foreign companies, or even the threat of such a limit, can make competition pointless. And the threat of antitrust intervention can have a similar effect. While governments are generally free to exercise these options, they are more likely to pursue them selectively to ensure that at least some of their own companies succeed.

After international competition, firms will be freer to exercise their acquired monopoly and economic power. During this period of profit taking, workers, tax collectors, managers, and investors will all have a renewed interest in claiming shares of the surplus. Will this spark a greater degree of international unionization? Will firms initiate policies of higher compensation simply to block unions? Will international agencies establish a global standard for corporate taxes? The answers to these questions will largely determine the future distribution of the fruits of economic power.

Notes

Chapter 1

1. John Moody, *The Truth About the Trusts*, p. 496.

Chapter 2

1. Joan Robinson, *The Economics of Imperfect Competition*, p. 5.
2. Adam Smith, *An Inquiry into the Nature and Causes of the Wealth of Nations*, p. 61.
3. Ibid., p. 605.
4. Ibid., p. 61.
5. Ibid., p. 144.
6. Karl Marx, *Capital: A Critique of Political Economy*, p. 837.
7. Ibid., p. 836.
8. Ibid., p. 687.
9. According to Kaldor, "What he [Chamberlin] does not seem to be aware of is the degree of unreality involved in his initial assumptions; and the extent to which his main conclusions are dependent on those assumptions" (Kaldor [1935], p. 43).
10. Kaldor's example was more complex, because he assumed that the new entrant would disproportionately reduce its own demand and those of a few firms in the market. This was attributed to spatial variations that made the products of some firms better substitutes than the products of others. These refinements are not, however, essential to the overall argument.
11. Demand elasticity indicates the responsiveness of demand to price changes and is equal to the percentage change in the quantity demanded to the percentage change in price.
12. Robinson, *The Economics of Imperfect Competition*, p. 50.
13. A. Lerner, "The Concept of Monopoly and the Measurement of Monopoly Power."
14. In order to prove this, all that is necessary is to show that $MC = AVC$ when AVC is constant. Define total cost (C) as the sum of variable cost (VC) and fixed cost (FC). Then, $C = VC + FC$, and

$$MC = \frac{dC}{dq} = \frac{d\,(VC)}{dq} + 0 = \frac{d\,(AVC\,q)}{dq} = AVC$$

15. Michal Kalecki, *The Theory of Economic Dynamics*, p. 12.

16. Michal Kalecki, "The Determinants of Distribution of National Income."

17. Lerner, "The Concept of Monopoly and the Measurement of Monopoly Power," p. 170.

18. Ibid.

19. Peter Kriesler, *Kalecki's Microanalysis: The Development of Kalecki's Analysis of Pricing and Distribution*, p. 33.

20. Ibid., p. 107.

21. Robinson, *The Economics of Imperfect Competition*, p. 21.

22. Ibid.

23. Joan Robinson, *Contributions to Modern Economics*, p. 171.

24. Kalecki, *The Theory of Economic Dynamics*, p. 12.

25. Nicholas Kaldor, "Market Imperfection and Excess Capacity," p. 339.

26. Ibid.

27. Gardiner Means, "Industrial Prices and Their Relative Inflexibility."

28. R. L. Hall and C. J. Hitch, "Price Theory and Business Behavior and Paul Sweezy, "Demand under Conditions of Oligopoly."

29. Paul Baran and Paul Sweezy, *Monopoly Capital: An Essay on the American Economic and Social Order*, p. 62.

30. Ibid., p. 63.

31. Joe S. Bain, *Barriers to New Competition: Their Character and Consequences in Manufacturing Industries*.

32. Kalecki, *Theory of Economic Dynamics*, p. 18.

33. Fuss and McFadden actually derived the result in terms of total derivatives, $-dP = Ldw$, which allowed output, price, and the quantity of other factors to vary. This is not to be mistaken for partial derivatives, which holds all these other variables constant.

34. This was first pointed out for the monopoly model by Karier (1985). The roots of this model, however, can be traced to the competitive models of J. B. Clark (1899).

Chapter 3

1. Richard B. Du Boff, *Accumulation & Power: An Economic History of the United States*, p. 64.

2. As a testament to academic inertia, it should be pointed out that a number of highly revered economic journals continue to reveal a distinct preference for theories of perfect competition and largely ignore monopoly power.

3. John Gould and E. Lazear, *Microeconomic Theory*, p. 290.

4. In order to maximize profits (π) defined as revenue (pq) less total costs (C) we proceed by differentiating profits with respect to quantity (q) and setting the result equal to zero:

$$\pi = pq - C(q)$$

$$\frac{d\pi}{dq} = q\,\frac{dp}{dq} + p - \frac{dC}{dq} = 0$$

This can be simplified because dC/dq is marginal cost (MC) and qdp/dq is equal to the negative of the price divided by demand elasticity ($-p/\eta$). Making these substitutions we find,

$$\frac{-p}{\eta} + p - MC = 0$$

or,

$$\frac{p - MC}{p} = \frac{1}{\eta}$$

5. This is in contrast to Lerner and Kalecki, who defined monopoly power as the current markup. But, as pointed out in the previous chapter, neither author was able to successfully defend this position.

6. When η is less than or equal to one, a firm can increase profits by reducing output. At lower output, costs decrease but revenue does not. An elasticity of one or less is therefore generally incompatible with short-run profit maximization.

7. Assuming p_y is constant, this can be derived as follows,

$$\eta_{yx} \frac{p_y q_y}{p_x q_x} = p_y \frac{\Delta q_y}{\Delta p_x} \frac{p_x}{q_y} \frac{q_y}{p_x q_x} = \frac{\Delta (p_y q_y)}{\Delta p_x} \frac{p_x}{p_x q_x} = SI_{yx}$$

8. Joann Lublin, "Who Has the Means and Motive to Steal in Halls of Justice?" *Wall Street Journal* (Oct. 4, 1989).

9. This can be demonstrated as follows:

$$E = \pi* = (p - AC)\, q = (p - MC + MC - AC)\, q =$$
$$\frac{(p - MC)}{p} pq + (MC - AC)\, q$$

Since pq is equal to revenue (R) and $(p-MC)/p$ at the profit-maximizing point is equal to monopoly power (M), this equation can be simplified into (3.8).

10. This derivation is based on a related proof in Gould and Lazear (1989, p. 135, fn.)

Chapter 4

1. Leonard Weiss, "The Concentration–Profit Relationship and Anti-Trust," p. 231.

2. Examples of these studies are Demsetz (1982), Brozen (1971), Liebowitz (1982), and Ornstein (1972).

3. This refers to (3.9) in the previous chapter.

4. Each of the variables, q, D, and R are calculated at the point that maximizes short-run profits.

5. We could, for example, define the distance (d) between firm x and every other firm y as the inverse of the substitution index (SI_{yx}).

6. To be precise, this type of diagram can be constructed only from the frame of reference of a single firm. If we switch to the frame of reference of y we are likely to find that SI_{yx} is not equal to SI_{xy}. However, for illustrative purposes we could assume symmetry $(SI_{yx} = SI_{xy})$, and several other technical assumptions so that the distances in Figure 4.1 are equally valid for all firms.

7. Using the same notation in the text,

$$CR = \sum_{i=1}^{4} MS_i = \frac{(1+s_1)}{\eta} + \frac{(1+s_2)}{\eta} + \frac{(1+s_3)}{\eta} + \frac{(1+s_4)}{\eta} = $$
$$\frac{4 + s_1 + s_2 + s_3 + s_4}{\eta}$$

8. Farmers have the additional disadvantage of selling their product to businesses which, as a rule, are also less easily swayed by advertising than consumers.

9. The price–cost margin is defined as, $(R–VC)/R,$ or its equivalent, $(p–AVC)/p.$

10. A (revenue) weighted average of PCMs for firms produces an industry price–cost margin.

11. Joan Robinson, *Contributions to Modern Economics*; and John Blair, *Economic Concentration: Structure, Behavior, and Public Policy*.

12. Norman Collins and Lee Preston, "Price–Cost Margins and Industry Structure," p. 274.

13. Weiss (1974) uses the conventional form, advertising-to-sales ratio, while Shirazi (1974) constructs a dummy variable based on whether the advertising to sales ratio is greater than 1 percent.

14. Weiss went on to demonstrate that the higher margins in concentrated industries persisted even when adjusted for central office employment, a cost that is not properly accounted for in the survey data. Rhoades tested the effect of firm specialization indices on margins and found that the the results depended on how the index was defined. Shirazi confirmed the concentration-margin effect for the United Kingdom, but like Kwoka, found that the high correlation between concentration and scale weakened his results. And finally, Kwoka concluded that market share for the top two firms was more critical than for the second two firms.

15. Kwoka (1979, p. 102) pointed out in a footnote that his measure of MES "produces a high correlation with market shares and concentration and requires cautious interpretation of later results."

16. In theory, barriers, along with other factors, determine both monopoly power and capacity utilization, which together determine margins. If monopoly power and capacity utilization were measured precisely, there would be no reason to include barriers in the equation.

17. Harold Demsetz, "Industry Structure, Market Rivalry, and Public Policy," p. 3.

18. Ibid.

19. Willard Mueller and Larry Hamm, "Trends in Industrial Market Concentration"; and M.A. Adelman, "The Measurement of Industrial Concentration."

20. Blair, *Economic Concentration*, pp. 102–6.

21. David Ravenscraft, " Structure–Profit Relationships at the Line of Business and Industry Level, p. 29.

Chapter 5

1. John Kenneth Galbraith, *American Capitalism: The Concept of Countervailing Power*, pp.132–33.

2. Although it is not impossible for the markup curve to be negatively related to output, it is unlikely. In order for this to happen, marginal cost must have a negative slope, which is unlikely, especially in the range that maximizes short-run profits.

3. While this describes the general tendency, there are exceptions. The elasticity could be constant or even increase with respect to output. This changes the slope of the inverse demand curve but does not necessarily alter the analysis.

4. In the situation that labor is not the only variable factor, some aspects of the analysis change and some remain the same. The effect of a wage change on employment is analyzed in Ferguson (1966).

5. More precisely, the *MRP* is equal to the product of the additional output of the worker (marginal product) and the revenue derived from additional output (marginal revenue).

6. For a more general derivation of this result involving additional variable factors see Karier (1985).

7. The relationship between product elasticity and labor elasticity was mathematically derived by Hicks (1932).

Chapter 6

1. John Kenneth Galbraith, *American Capitalism: The Concept of Countervailing Power*, p. 133.

2. Note that a damage settlement is not a variable cost but is more like a lump-sum tax or fixed cost. But the effect on economic power is comparable.

3. A similar explanation can be offered to explain how universal cost increases can moderate the loss of monopoly power. The explanation is more complicated because an increase in demand can affect both curves in the lower graph in Figure 5.3.

4. Actually, this minimum amount of economic power is typically described as a cost paid to the entrepreneur. Under this accounting scheme one could say that economic power is zero.

5. This is not an entirely novel idea. According to Kalecki, "A high ratio of profits to wages strengthens the bargaining position of trade unions in their demands for wage increases since higher wages are then compatible with 'reasonable profits' at existing price levels. If after such increases are granted prices should be raised, this would call forth new demands for wage increases. It follows that a high ratio of profits to wages cannot be maintained without creating a tendency towards rising costs. This adverse effect upon the competitive position

of the firm or an industry encourages the adoption of a policy of lower profit margins," (Kalecki [1971], p. 51).

6. Richard Freeman and James Medoff, *What Do Unions Do?*.

7. Thomas Karier, "A Proposal to Restore the Corporate Profit Tax," pp. 141–67.

Chapter 7

1. Michal Kalecki, *Selected Essays on the Dynamics of the Capitalist Economy, 1933–1970*, p. 51.

2. As in the previous studies, scale variables used to measure barriers are often strongly related to monopoly power, creating problems for statistical estimation.

3. Another way to test this is to use dummy variables to test for a unique effect of unions on concentrated and unconcentrated industries. Several of the studies used this technique.

4. We begin with all the variables that have a positive effect on monopoly power, concentration (CR), advertising (A), and R&D.

$$a_0 + a_1 CR + a_2 A + a_3 R\&D$$

The reduction in monopoly power is related to two factors, unions (UN) and imports (IM);

$$1 + c_1 UN + c_2 IM$$

Monopoly power (M) in its complete form is given by the product of these two terms:

$$M = (1 + c_1 UN + c_2 IM)(a_0 + a_1 CR + a_2 A + a_3 R\&D)$$

Multiplying this out, one would find that monopoly power includes individual terms for concentration, advertising, and R&D but also many interaction terms between these variables and unions and imports.

5. Specifically, the inclusion of many correlated variables such as the interaction terms can create problems of multicolinearity, which tend to bias estimates of the coefficients and their standard errors.

6. The former was from the Survey of Manufactures and the latter from the Internal Revenue Service. Freeman's model was a log-linear function where the dependent variable was the natural log of PCMs (Freeman [1983]).

7. Like the earlier studies, when "minimum efficient scale" was included, the high degree of multicolinearity adversely affected the significance and sign of the concentration coefficient.

8. To make Freeman's results comparable to the linear case it is necessary to multiply each of his coefficients by the mean value of PCM. Specifically, if

$PCM = b_1CR$, then $dPCM/dCR = b_1$. But if $ln(PCM) = b_0CR$, then $dPCM/dCR = b_0(PCM)$. Therefore b_0 must be multiplied by the mean PCM in order to be comparable to the linear estimate, b_1.

9. One must be cautious in interpreting the results of this study. In the equation measuring the union effects there are four variables containing the union term and five containing unemployment with considerable overlap between the two. This creates a dangerously high potential for multicolinearity, which can produce entirely unreliable results, a fact that may explain why this is the only industry study where the negative effect of unions is not confined to concentrated industries. An alternative explanation, offered by Ghosal (1989), is that the anomalous results can be attributed to the authors' failure to take into account nonlinearities.

10. High concentration is defined as a four-firm concentration ratio over 60 percent compared with 45 percent to 60 percent for moderately concentrated.

11. The union effect is overstated because it includes the deadweight loss.

12. Their data were based on averages for the years 1968, 1970, and 1972.

13. For comparability all values have been converted to 1972 dollars using the GNP price deflator.

14. See *Economic Report of the President*, Feb. 1990, Table C–89.

15. Michael Salinger, "Tobin's q, Unionization and the Concentration–Profits Relationship," p. 169.

16. The business term for this type of subsidiary is a "cash cow." Some of the steel businesses were used in this capacity during the 1970s.

17. See Phil Keisling, "The Great Train Robbery: How to Make a Billion from a Bankrupt Railroad," *Washington Monthly* (July/Aug. 1982).

18. Paul Baran and Paul Sweezy, *Monopoly Capital: An Essay on the American Economic and Social Order*, p. 77.

Chapter 8

1. Hyman Minsky, *Stabilizing an Unstable Economy*, p. 157.

2. The price, p^*, is determined only when other firms independently maximize short-run profits.

3. A useful indicator of delayed substitution is the difference between the long-run and short-run demand elasticity.

4. The appropriate discount rate for the firm is the best profit rate that it could hope to achieve by investing in some other concern.

5. In continuous time this sum is represented by the following equation;

$$*PV(\pi_t) = \int_0^\infty \int_{-\infty}^\infty \pi_t Pr(\pi_t) e^{-dt} d\pi_t dt$$

where $PR(\pi_t)$ is the probability of profits, π_t, occurring at time t. We are also assuming here that the firm is risk neutral. If it is not, then profits should be replaced by an expected utility function.

6. One criterion for predatory pricing is that prices must fall below long-run

marginal cost, inclusive of a normal return on capital (Shepherd and Wilcox [1979], p. 237).

7. William Shepherd and Clair Wilcox, *Public Policies Toward Business*, p. 241.

8. Ralph Byrns and Gerald Stone, *Microeconomics*, p. 253.

9. Stephen Adler and Alix Freedman, "Tobacco Suit Exposes Ways Cigarette Firms Keep the Profits Fat," *Wall Street Journal* (Mar. 5, 1990).

10. Shepherd and Wilcox, *Public Policies Toward Business,* p. 238.

11. Bridget O'Brian, "Higher Flier: Delta, Despite Victory in Pan Am Bid, Faces Some Big Challenges," *Wall Street Journal* (Aug. 13, 1991).

12. See Stephen Barnett, "Preserving Newspapers or Monopoly," *The Nation* (Nov. 6, 1989).

13. See, for example, John Bussey, "Did U.S. Car Makers Err by Raising Prices When the Yen Rose?" *Wall Street Journal* (Apr. 18, 1988).

14. See Thomas O'Boyle and Peter Pae, "O'Neill Recasts Alcoa With His Eyes Fixed On a Decade Ahead," *Wall Street Journal* (Apr. 9, 1990).

15. F. M. Scherer, *Industrial Market Structure and Economic Performance*, p. 240.

16. Discount rates are well known to affect savings rates as well as business behavior. The relatively high savings rate in Japan may be another indicator that the discount rate there is relatively low.

17. See "Europe's Giants are Hungrier than Ever," *Business Week* (July 17, 1989).

18. Hal Varian, *Microeconomic Analysis*, p. 73.

19. Richard Caves and Ronald Jones, *World Trade and Payments*, p. 251.

20. William Baumol, John Panzar, and Robert Willig, *Contestable Markets and the Theory of Industry Structure*.

21. For a similar criticism see Caves (1992), p. 32, note 12.

Chapter 9

1. William Shepherd, *The Economics of Industrial Organization*, p. 240.

2. John Markoff, "A Corporate Lag in Research Funds is Causing Worry," *New York Times* (Jan. 23, 1990).

3. Those expenditures on advertising and R&D that have a positive effect on current profits must be treated differently because there is no question these expenditures should always be made.

4. "Advertising Power," *Advertising Age* (Dec. 26, 1988), p. 14.

5. The specific industries are chemicals and allied products, electrical equipment, office equipment, computing and accounting machines, and motor vehicles and related equipment. See *National Patterns of Science and Technology Resources: 1987*, National Science Foundation.

6. Markoff, "A Corporate Lag."

7. There is another aspect of nonprice competition that may benefit relatively large companies more than small ones. Nonprice competition can create an impression of real competition; an image that may reassure antitrust regulators, and occasionally, even the general public.

8. Only an exceptionally high discount rate could alter this conclusion.

9. F. M. Scherer, *Industrial Market Structure and Economic Performance*, pp. 178–81.

10. Joe Bain, *Industrial Organization*, pp. 308–10.

11. John Kenneth Galbraith, *The New Industrial State*, p. 82.

12. Eliot Jones, *The Trust Problem in the United States*, pp. 225–26.

13. Stephen Adler and Alix Freedman, "Tobacco Suit Exposes Ways Cigarette Firms Keep the Profits Fat," *Wall Street Journal* (Mar. 5, 1990), p. A–1.

14. Scherer, *Industrial Market Structure and Economic Performance*, pp. 176–83.

15. See, for example, Simpson (1986); *FTC Decisions: Findings, Opinions, and Orders*, volume 110 (1988); and Shepherd and Wilcox (1979), chap. 7.

16. Rudolf Michels, *Cartels, Combines and Trusts in Post-War Germany*, p. 25.

17. Hermann Levy, *Industrial Germany: A Study of Its Monopoly Organizations and Their Control by the State*, p. 16.

18. William Shepherd and Clair Wilcox, *Public Policies Toward Business*, pp. 549–50.

19. Ibid., p. 207.

20. John Blair, *The Control of Oil*, p. 55.

21. Ibid., p. 73.

22. The Iraqi invasion of Kuwait in August 1990 was largely motivated by this frustration.

23. Michael Selz, "How Three Companies Allegedly Conspired to Fix Matzo Prices," *Wall Street Journal* (March 11, 1991), p. A-1.

24. Shepherd and Wilcox, *Public Policies Toward Business*, p. 203.

25. Ibid., chap. 7.

26. The neutral path and the kinked demand model are similar but not equivalent. One difference is that the kinked demand curve does not specify how the initial price is determined and in the neutral path it is the one that maximizes short-run profits. Another difference is that the neutral path may involve price changes, which is not possible in the kinked demand model.

Chapter 10

1. David Bunting, *The Rise of Large American Corporations: 1889–1919*, p. 29.

2. "1990 Profile," *Mergers and Acquisitions* (May/June 1991), p. 36.

3. The amount spent on plant and equipment in 1988 was $456 billion (*Economic Report of the President* [1991], p. 347).

4. The figure relies on four different sources that did not use entirely consistent methods in collecting the data. More consistent measurements would be desirable but would probably not alter the pattern in the figure.

5. This is a brief description of a topic that is covered in greater detail in any text in corporate finance.

6. Unfortunately the data are missing for some firms in some years and the data are not corrected for inflation. Neither fact is likely to have much effect on the composition of the list.

7. It is also possible that the expansion will place additional demands on management resulting in growing inefficiencies.

8. Eliot Jones, *The Trust Problem in the United States*, p. 47.

9. Ibid., p. 52.

10. Chapman (1983), p. 120. Long after the dissolution, the Rockefeller fam-

ily continued to maintain controlling interest in several of the largest descendants. See, U.S. Congress, 76th, 3rd Sess., Temporary National Economic Committee, *The Distribution of Ownership in the 200 Largest Nonfinancial Corporations, 1940*, Monograph 29, p. 127.

11. Harry Laidler, *Concentration of Control in American Industry*, pp. 176–78.

12. Ibid., pp. 30–67 and John Moody, *The Truth About the Trusts*, p. 460.

13. Laidler, *Concentration of Control in American Industry*, p. 307.

14. Bunting, *The Rise of Large American Corporations*, p. 99.

15. For many years, petroleum companies could adjust the price of crude oil they sold to themselves to ensure that they received the maximum benefit from the oil depletion allowance, a lucrative tax break limited to extractive industries.

16. Laidler, *Concentration of Control in American Industry*, p. 183.

17. According to a sales memorandum of an AT&T affiliate, "For several years it has been the common practice, where there are two competing companies, for either the independent to sell out to the Bell or vice versa. The elimination of competition and the substitution of cooperation thus naturally continue to make telephone securities increasingly attractive." Cited in Laidler (1931), p. 95.

18. Sonny Keinfield, *The Biggest Company on Earth: A Profile of AT&T*, p. 8.

19. *Moody's Industrial Manual* (1991).

20. These companies are, respectively, Computing Scale Company of America, International Time Recording Company of New York, and the Tabulating Machine Company. See *Moody's Manual of Railroads and Corporation Securities* (1916), p. 2414.

21. Thomas Watson, chairman of the board of IBM, said in 1943, "I think there is a world market for about five computers." Quoted in *Shazam, User's Reference Manual* (1990), p. 5. IBM also rejected a project proposed by Eckert & Mauchly that eventually became the precursor to the first computer (Foy [1975], p. 28.

22. According to Bluestone and Harrison, a prominent management consulting firm, Boston Consulting Group, claimed that the value of each division of a diversified company could be ascertained primarily by its market share and sales growth. (Bluestone and Harrison [1982], p. 150).

23. For an analysis of the importance of mergers in corporate growth from 1890 to 1919 see Bunting 1986, pp. 29–30.

24. Sometimes important horizontal mergers took place later in a company's life-cycle. For example, Philip Morris, originally an English company dating back to the middle of the nineteenth century, did not acquire Benson & Hedges until 1953.

25. These include only larger mergers where the acquired firm represented $10 million or more in assets. *Statistical Report on Mergers and Acquisitions*, Bureau of Economics, Federal Trade Commission 1979 (July 1981), p. 110.

26. Ben H. Bagdikian, *The Media Monopoly*, p. 21.

27. Joseph Schumpeter, *Capitalism, Socialism, and Democracy*, p. 106.

28. John Kenneth Galbraith raised this question in *The New Industrial State* (Galbraith [1967], p. 117).

29. Wilber Lewellen and Blaine Huntsman, "Managerial Pay and Corporate Performance."

30. Kevin J. Murphy, "Top Executives Are Worth Every Nickel They Get."

31. John Abowd, "Does Performance-Based Managerial Compensation Affect Corporate Performance?"

Chapter 11

1. Stephen Hymer, *International Operations of National Firms: A Study of Direct Foreign Investment*, p. 33.

2. With transportation costs the condition for trade becomes

$$(AC_1^A + t_1)/AC_2^A < AC_1^B /(AC_2^B + t_2)$$

where t_1 and t_2 are the unit transportation costs for commodities 1 and 2 respectively.

3. Transportation costs have again been ignored for convenience but could be included as an addition to marginal cost in the foreign market.

4. The derivation of this result is analogous to the one presented in the Appendix.

5. Mira Wilkins, *The Emergence of Multinational Enterprise: American Business Abroad from the Colonial Era to 1914*, p. 43.

6. Ibid., p. 91.

7. Neil Hood and Stephen Young, *The Economics of Multinational Enterprise*, p. 59.

8. Much of the intraindustry trade flows depicted in Figure 11.1 can be explained in terms of differentiated products but this is not the only explanation. The United States is so vast that it may be profitable to import a good into one region of the United States while exporting it from another. Or it is possible that imports of one industry may be semifinished goods that fall within the same detailed industry as finished goods that are ultimately exported.

9. Richard Caves and Ronald Jones, *World Trade and Payments*, p. 170. Two of these are Bela Balassa, "Tariff Reductions and Trade in Manufactures," pp. 466–73; and Herbert G. Grubel, "Intra-Industry Specialization and the Pattern of Trade," pp. 374–88.

10. Caves and Jones, *World Trade and Payments*, p. 170.

11. See for example, Dunning (1973), Caves (1971), Horst (1972), Scaperlanda and Mauer (1969), Baldwin (1979), and Lall (1980).

12. Sanjaya Lall, "Monopolistic Advantages and Foreign Involvement by U.S. Manufacturing Industry."

13. In my own research the relationship between export intensity and measures of monopoly power—concentration and R&D—was typically positive but often fell short of statistical significance (Karier [1990 and 1991a]).

14. Exports were obtained from the *Economic Report of the President*, 1990, and foreign production from Whichard (1989). The value of U.S. foreign production sold abroad was estimated by the sales of majority-owned nonbank foreign affiliates in 1987 reduced by U.S. imports shipped by affiliates and further reduced by U.S. exports to affiliates to avoid counting these exports in the value of affiliate sales.

15. Hymer's dissertation on this topic was published later, (Hymer [1976]).

16. Hood and Young, *Economics of Multinational Enterprise*, pp. 68–75.

17. Raymond Vernon, *Storm over Multinationals: The Real Issues*; Hood and Young, *Economics of Multinational Enterprise*, pp. 68–75.

18. Thomas Karier, "The Determinants of U.S. Foreign Production: Unions, Monopoly Power, and Comparative Advantage."

19. See Whichard (1982 and 1989) and *Maquiladoras: Exploiting Both Sides*, AFL-CIO, Washington, D.C., January 1988.

20. Vernon, *Storm over Multinationals: The Real Issues*.

21. See Herr (1988) and *The Economist* (Dec. 16, 1989), p. 63.

22. Caves and Jones, *World Trade and Payments*, p. 176.

23. This is based on simple regressions of PCMs on asset-to-sales ratios and dummy variables for either developed countries or specific regions. Any statistical comparison like this must be made cautiously because of differences in definitions for prices and costs, especially when international comparisons are involved.

24. Richard Barnet and Ronald Muller, *Global Reach: The Power of the Multinational Corporations*, p. 158.

25. Ibid.

Chapter 12

1. Walter Adams and James Brock, *The Bigness Complex: Industry, Labor, and Government in the American Economy*, pp. 369–70.

2. Lestock C. Reid, *Commerce and Conquest: The Story of the Honourable East India Company*, pp. 19–21.

3. Holden Farber, *John Company at Work: A Study of European Expansion in India in the Late Eighteenth Century*.

4. According to Lestock Reid, "few 'realms' have had a more profitable investment than the East India Company," (Reid [1947], p. 24).

5. A different perspective was provided by Adam Smith as he acclaimed the virtues of laissez-faire economics. According to Smith, if trade were profitable then it would certainly attract capital on its own accord without recourse to special monopoly privilege. And if such capital was not forthcoming, then this was "proof that, at that particular time, that country was not ripe for that trade. . . ." (Smith [1776], pp. 598–99).

6. A brief summary of this law is described by Scherer (1980), p. 496.

7. *Constitution of the United States*, Article 1, Section 8, cited in Bennet (1943), p. 65.

8. *The New Copyright Law: Questions Teachers & Librarians Ask*, Washington, DC: National Education Association (1977), p. 13.

9. Of all the patents granted in the United States from 1971 to 1975, 75 percent were granted to domestic or foreign corporations, (Scherer [1980], p. 440).

10. Johnnie Roberts, "Pitney Bowes Thrives From Close Relations With the Postal Service," *Wall Street Journal* (Apr. 4, 1991), p. A1.

11. William Shepherd and Clair Wilcox, *Public Policies Toward Business*, pp. 86–89.

12. Ibid., p. 82.

13. Meir Kohn, *Money, Banking, and Financial Markets*, p. 174.

14. Ibid., p. 194.

15. Charles McCoy and Ralph King, "Add Security Pacific to BankAmerica: The Result is Clout," *Wall Street Journal* (Aug. 13, 1991), p. A1. The contest to dominate the Florida banking industry is described by Paul Barrett, "Barnett Banks Agrees to Buy First Florida," *Wall Street Journal* (May 19, 1992), p. A3.

16. Kohn, *Money, Banking, and Financial Markets*, p. 172.

17. Douglas Bowers, Wayne Rasmussen, and Gladys Baker, "History of Agricultural Price-Support and Adjustment Programs, 1933–84," p. 1.

18. "Farm Commodity Programs," *National Food Review*, United States Department of Agriculture 13 (Jan.–Mar. 1990).

19. It has been estimated that one million large farms received 80 percent of this subsidy while two million smaller farms received the rest (Shepherd and Wilcox [1979], p. 577).

20. James Wessel, *Trading the Future: Farm Exports and the Concentration of Economic Power in Our Food System*, p. 51.

21. Jennifer Erickson, "Tyson Foods is Still on Top," *Successful Farming* (Apr. 1992), p. 20.

22. Adams and Brock, *The Bigness Complex: Industry, Labor, and Government in the American Economy*, pp. 219–31.

23. See Bridget O'Brian, "Delta, Despite Victory in Pan Am Bid, Faces Some Big Challenges," *Wall Street Journal* (Aug. 8, 1991).

24. Irving Bernstein, *A History of the American Worker 1933–1941: Turbulent Years*, p. 2.

25. Ibid., p. 34.

26. Ibid., p. 37.

27. This argument is based on Irving Bernstein's interpretation of Section 1 of the Wagner Act. "Industrial concentration, the declaration argued, destroyed the worker's bargaining power, leaving him with an inadequate share of the national wealth. A redistribution of income by collective bargaining would raise those at the bottom and remove inequalities within the wage structure. This would benefit society as a whole by creating mass purchasing power to fill in the troughs in the business cycle" (Bernstein [1969], p. 325).

28. Joseph Pechman, *Federal Tax Policy*, p. 123.

29. Thomas Karier, "A Proposal to Restore the Corporate Profit Tax," pp. 141–67.

30. John Dobson, *Two Centuries of Tariffs: The Background and Emergence of the U.S. International Trade Commission*, p. 8.

31. Ibid., p. 6.

32. Adam Smith, *An Inquiry into the Nature and Causes of the Wealth of Nations*, p. 420.

33. William Cline, "U.S. Trade and Industrial Policy: The Experience of Textiles, Steel, and Automobiles," p. 229.

34. Ibid., p. 226.

35. Philip Stern, *The Best Congress Money Can Buy*, p. 38.

36. Brooks Jackson, "Big Business is Back in Thick of Things at the Conventions," *Wall Street Journal* (Aug. 16, 1988), p1.

37. Walter Adams and Horace Gray, *Monopoly in America: The Government as Promoter*, p. 107.

3⁹. Ibid., pp. 204–5.

39. One company that maintained a prominent role in Ronald Reagan's cabinet was Bechtel Corporation. Both Caspar Weinberger, secretary of defense, and George Shultz, secretary of state, were affiliated with this firm, the largest engineering and construction business in the United States. Bechtel is widely renowned for its work on giant projects including the "Hoover Dam, the San Francisco Bay Bridge, the subway systems for Washington D.C. and San Francisco Bay Area, and half of America's nuclear power plants." More recently, Bechtel is playing a major role in the reconstruction of Kuwait in the aftermath of the Gulf War (Moskowitz, Katz, and Levering [1980], p. 857).

40. Lestock C. Reid, *Commerce and Conquest: The Story of the Honourable East India Company*, pp. 38–39.

Chapter 13

1. Harry Laidler, *Concentration of Control in American Industry*, p. 134.

2. Leo Troy, *Trade Union Membership, 1897–1962*, p. 2.

3. Ray Marshall and Vernon Briggs, *Labor Economics: Theory, Institutions, and Public Policy*, p. 339.

4. Richard Freeman, "The Effect of the Union Wage Differential on Management Opposition and Union Organizing Success," p. 95.

5. Thomas Karier, "A Proposal to Restore the Corporate Profit Tax."

6. "Wherever GM Puts Saturn, It's Going to Get a Sweet Deal," *Business Week* (Apr. 1, 1985), p. 36.

7. Incidently, none of the seven governors that took their appeal to the Phil Donahue show actually got the plant.

8. Less conspicuous was GM's decision at about the same time to buy 400,000 small cars annually from Japanese and Korean firms, a decision that was not put up for bid in the home market *Business Week* (Apr. 1, 1985).

9. Ibid.

10. *Economic Report of the President* 1992 and 1984.

11. Thomas Karier, "Unions and the U.S. Comparative Advantage," pp. 1–19.

12. Bradley Schiller, *The Macro Economy Today*, p. 504.

13. Eduardo Lachica, "Toyota, Mazda Found Dumping Minivans in U.S.," *Wall Street Journal* (May 20, 1992).

14. Joseph White and Clay Chandler, "Pressed by all Sides, Hard-Driving Toyota Curbs Ambitions a Bit," *Wall Street Journal* (May 19, 1992).

15. John Bussey, "Did U.S. Car Makers Err by Raising Prices When the Yen Rose?" *Wall Street Journal* (Apr. 18, 1988).

16. Rober Guenther and Michael Sesit, "U.S. Banks Are Losing Business to Japanese At Home and Abroad," *Wall Street Journal* (Oct. 12, 1989).

17. "The Global 1000: A Year of Twists and Turns," *Business Week* (July 15, 1991), pp. 52–105.

18. Guenther and Sesit, "U.S. Banks Are Losing Business to Japanese At Home and Abroad."

19. Jill Abramson and Christopher Chipello, "High Pay of CEOs Traveling With Bush Touches a Nerve in Asia," *Wall Street Journal* (Dec. 30, 1991) and "Executive Pay??" *Business Week* (Mar. 30, 1992).

20. Bradley Stertz, "Second Auto Summit Produces a Promise of Continued Talks," *Wall Street Journal* (May 19, 1992).

21. Jacob Schlesinger, "Japanese Firms Pledge to Boost Chip Imports," *Wall Street Journal* (June 5, 1992).

22. Toyota has recently claimed to have dropped this goal. See White and Chandler, "Pressed by all Sides, Hard-Driving Toyota Curbs Ambitions a Bit."

References

Abowd, John. 1990. "Does Performance-Based Managerial Compensation Affect Corporate Performance?" *Industrial and Labor Relations Review* 43 (February): 52S–73S.

Adams, Walter, and James Brock. 1986. *The Bigness Complex: Industry, Labor, and Government in the American Economy*. New York: Pantheon Books.

Adams, Walter, and Horace Gray. 1955. *Monopoly in America: The Government as Promoter*. New York: MacMillan.

Adelman, M.A. 1951. "The Measurement of Industrial Concentration." *Review of Economics and Statistics* 33 (November).

Bagdikian, Ben H. 1987. *The Media Monopoly*, Second Edition. Boston: Beacon Press.

Bain, Joe S. 1951. "Relation of Profit Rate to Industry Concentration: American Manufacturing, 1936–1940." *Quarterly Journal of Economics* 65 (August): 293–324.

———. 1959. *Industrial Organization*. New York: Wiley.

———. 1965. *Barriers to New Competition: Their Character and Consequences in Manufacturing Industries*. Cambridge: Harvard University Press.

Balassa, Bela. 1966. "Tariff Reductions and Trade in Manufactures." *American Economic Review* 56 (June): 466–73.

Baldwin, Robert. 1979. "Determinants of Trade and Foreign Investment: Further Evidence." *Review of Economics and Statistics* 61 (February): 40–48.

Baran, Paul, and Paul Sweezy. 1966. *Monopoly Capital: An Essay on the American Economic and Social Order*. New York: Monthly Review Press.

Barnet, Richard, and Ronald Muller. 1974. *Global Reach: The Power of the Multinational Corporations*. New York: Simon and Schuster.

Baumol, William, John Panzar, and Robert Willig. 1982. *Contestable Markets and The Theory of Industry Structure*. New York: Harcourt Brace Jovanovich.

Bennet, William. 1943. *The American Patent System*. Port Washington, N.Y.: Kennikat Press.

Bernstein, Irving. 1969. *A History of the American Worker 1933–1941: Turbulent Years*. Boston: Houghton Mifflin.

Blair, John. 1972. *Economic Concentration: Structure, Behavior, and Public Policy*. New York: Harcourt Brace Jovanovich.

———. 1976. *The Control of Oil*. New York: Vintage Books.

Bluestone, Barry, and Bennet Harrison. 1982. *The Deindustrialization of America*. New York: Basic Books.

Bowers, Douglas, Wayne Rasmussen, and Gladys Baker. 1984. "History of Agricultural Price-Support and Adjustment Programs, 1933–84." Washington, D.C.: U.S. Department of Agriculture, Economic Research Service.

Brozen, Yale. 1971. "The Persistence of 'High Rates of Return' in High-Stable Concentration Industries." *Journal of Law and Economics* 14 (October): 501–12.

Bunting, David. 1986. *The Rise of Large American Corporations: 1889–1919.* New York: Garland Publishing.

Byrns, Ralph, and Gerald Stone. 1989. *Microeconomics.* Glenview, IL: Scott, Foresman.

Caves, Richard. 1971. "International Corporations: The Industrial Economics of Foreign Investment." *Economica* 38 (February): 1–27.

———. 1992. *American Industry: Structure, Conduct, and Performance.* Seventh Edition. Englewood Cliffs, NJ: Prentice Hall.

Caves, Richard, and Ronald Jones. 1985. *World Trade and Payments.* Boston: Little, Brown.

Chamberlin, E.H. 1933. *The Theory of Monopolistic Competition.* Cambridge, MA: Harvard University Press.

Chapman, Duane. 1983. *Energy Resources and Energy Corporations,* Ithaca, NY: Cornell University Press.

Clark, J.B. 1899 (Recent edition, 1965). *The Distribution of Wealth: A Theory of Wages, Interest, and Profits.* New York: Sentry Press.

Clark, Kim. 1984. "Unionization and Firm Performance: The Impact of Profits, Growth and Productivity." *American Economic Review* 74 (December): 893–919.

Cline, William. 1988. "U.S. Trade and Industrial Policy: The Experience of Textiles, Steel, and Automobiles." In *Strategic Trade Policy and the New International Economics,* Paul Krugman, ed. Cambridge: MIT Press.

Collins, Norman, and Lee Preston. 1968. *Concentration and Price–Cost Margins in Manufacturing Industries.* Berkeley: University of California Press.

Collins, Norman, and Lee Preston. 1969. "Price–Cost Margins and Industry Structure." *Review of Economics and Statistics* 51 (August): 271–286.

Connolly, Robert, Barry Hirsch, and Mark Hirschey. 1986. "Union Rent Seeking, Intangible Capital, and Market Value of the Firm." *Review of Economics and Statistics* 68 (November): 567–77.

Demsetz, Harold. 1973. "Industry Structure, Market Rivalry, and Public Policy." *Journal of Law and Economics* 16 (April): 1–9.

———. 1982. "Barriers to Entry." *American Economic Review* 72 (March): 47–57.

Dobson, John, 1976. *Two Centuries of Tariffs: The Background and Emergence of the U.S. International Trade Commission.* Washington, D.C.: U.S. International Trade Commission.

Domowitz, Ian, R. Hubbard, and B. Petersen. 1986. "The Intertemporal Stability of the Concentration-Margins Relationship." *Journal of Industrial Economics* 35 (September): 13–34.

Du Boff, Richard B. 1989. *Accumulation & Power: An Economic History of the United States.* Armonk, NY: M.E. Sharpe.

Dunning, John. 1973. "The Determinants of International Production." *Oxford Economic Papers* 25 (November): 289–336.

Economic Report of the President. 1990. United States Government Printing Office, Washington, D.C. (February): Table C-89.

Eichner, Alfred. 1976. *The Megacorp and Oligopoly.* Cambridge: Cambridge University Press.

Farber, Holden. 1951. *John Company at Work: A Study of European Expansion in India in the Late Eighteenth Century.* Cambridge: Harvard University Press.

Ferguson, C.E. 1966. "Production, Prices, and the Theory of Jointly Derived Input Demand Functions." *Economica* 30 (1966): 454–61.

Foy, Nancy. 1975. *The Sun Never Sets on IBM*. New York: William Morrow.

Freeman, Richard. 1983. "Unionism, Price–Cost Margins and the Return to Capital." (Mimeograph, January.)

———.1986. "The Effect of the Union Wage Differential on Management Opposition and Union Organizing Success." *American Economic Review* 76 (May): 92–96.

Freeman, Richard, and James Medoff. 1984. *What Do Unions Do?* New York: Basic Books.

Galbraith, John Kenneth. 1952. *American Capitalism: The Concept of Countervailing Power*. Boston: Houghton Mifflin.

———.1967. *The New Industrial State*. Boston: Houghton Mifflin.

Ghosal, Vivek. 1989. "Market Structures, Price–Cost Margins, and Unionism: An Empirical Note." *Economic Letters* 29: 179–82.

Gould, John, and E. Lazear. 1989. *Microeconomic Theory*, Sixth Edition. Homewood, IL: Richard D. Irwin.

Grubel, Herbert G. 1967. "Intra-Industry Specialization and the Pattern of Trade." *Canadian Journal of Economics and Political Science* 33 (August): 374–88.

Hall, R.L. and C.J. Hitch. 1939. "Price Theory and Business Behavior." *Oxford Economic Papers* 2 (May): 12–45.

Herr, Ellen. 1988. "U.S. Business Enterprises Acquired or Established by Foreign Direct Investors in 1987." *Survey of Current Business* 68 (May): 50–58.

Hicks, J.R. 1932. *The Theory of Wages*. New York: MacMillan.

Hirsch, Barry. 1990. "Market Structure, Union Rent Seeking, and Firm Profitability." *Economic Letters* 32: 75–79.

Hirsch, Barry, and R. Connolly. 1987. "Do Unions Capture Monopoly Profits?" *Industrial and Labor Relations Review* 41 (October): 118–36.

Hood, Neil, and Stephen Young. 1979. *The Economics of Multinational Enterprise*. London: Longman Group Limited.

Horst, Thomas. 1972. "Firm and Industry Determinants of the Decision to Invest Abroad: An Empirical Study." *Review of Economics and Statistics* 54 (August): 258–66.

Hymer, Stephen. 1976. *International Operations of National Firms: A Study of Direct Foreign Investment*. Cambridge, MA: MIT Press.

Jones, Eliot. 1923. *The Trust Problem in the United States*. New York: Macmillan.

Kaldor, Nicholas. 1935. "Market Imperfection and Excess Capacity." *Economica* (February): 33–50.

Kalecki, Michal. 1938. "The Determinants of Distribution of National Income." *Econometrica* 6: 97–112.

———.1954. *The Theory of Economic Dynamics*. New York: Rhinehart. (1969 edition, New York: Augustus M. Kelley.)

———.1971. *Selected Essays on the Dynamics of The Capitalist Economy, 1933–1970*. Cambridge: Cambridge University Press.

Karier, Thomas. 1984. *The Union Impact on Profits, Productivity, and Prices*. Unpublished dissertation, University of California, Berkeley.

———. 1985. "Unions and Monopoly Profits." *Review of Economics and Statistics* 67 (February): 34–42.

———.1988. "New Evidence on the Effect of Unions and Imports on Monopoly Power." *Journal of Post Keynesian Economics* 11 (Winter): 318–23.

———.1990. "The Determinants of U.S. Foreign Production: Unions, Monopoly Power, and Comparative Advantage." Annandale, NY: Jerome Levy Economics Institute, Working Paper 34 (January).

———. 1991a. "Unions and the U.S. Comparative Advantage." *Industrial Relations* 30 (Winter): 1–19.

———. 1991b. "A Proposal to Restore the Corporate Profit Tax." *Journal of Social Economy* 49 (Summer): 141–67.

———. 1992. "Trade Deficits and Labor Unions: Myths and Realities." In *Unions and Economic Competitiveness*, Lawrence Mishel and Paula Voos, eds. Armonk NY: M.E. Sharpe.

Keinfield, Sonny. 1981. *The Biggest Company on Earth: A Profile of AT&T.* New York: Holt, Rinehart and Winston.

Kohn, Meir. 1991. *Money, Banking, and Financial Markets.* Chicago: Dryden Press.

Kriesler, Peter. 1987. *Kalecki's Microanalysis: The Development of Kalecki's Analysis of Pricing and Distribution.* Cambridge: Cambridge University Press.

Kwoka, John. 1979. "The Effect of Market Share Distribution on Industry Performance." *Review of Economics and Statistics* 61 (February): 101–9.

Laidler, Harry. 1931. *Concentration of Control in American Industry.* New York: Thomas Y. Crowell.

Lall, Sanjaya. 1980. "Monopolistic Advantages and Foreign Involvement by U.S. Manufacturing Industry." *Oxford Economic Papers* 32 (March): 102–22.

Lerner, A. 1934."The Concept of Monopoly and the Measurement of Monopoly Power." *Review of Economic Studies* 1: 157–75.

Levy, Hermann. 1966. *Industrial Germany: A Study of Its Monopoly Organizations and Their Control by the State.* New York: Augustus Kelly, Bookseller.

Lewellen, Wilber, and Blaine Huntsman. 1970. "Managerial Pay and Corporate Performance." *American Economic Review* 60 (September): 710–20.

Liebowitz, S. J. 1982. "What Do Census Price–Cost Margins Measure?" *Journal of Law and Economics* 25 (October): 231–46.

Marshall, Ray, and Vernon Briggs. 1989. *Labor Economics: Theory, Institutions, and Public Policy.* Homewood, IL: Irwin.

Marx, Karl. 1967. *Capital: A Critique of Political Economy.* Vol. I. New York: International Publishers.

McFadden, Daniel, and Melvyn Fuss. 1978. *Production Economics: A Dual Approach to Theory and Applications*, Vol. 1. Amsterdam: North-Holland.

Means, Gardner. 1935. "Industrial Prices and Their Relative Inflexibility." A report to the Secretary of Agriculture, Senate Document no. 3, January. (Reprinted in Gardner Means, 1962, *Pricing Power and the Public Interest: A Study Based on Steel*, New York: Harper Brothers, 77–96.)

Michels, Rudolf. 1928. *Cartels, Combines and Trusts in Post-War Germany.* New York: AMS Press.

Minsky, Hyman. 1986. *Stabilizing an Unstable Economy.* New Haven: Yale University Press.

Moody, John. 1904. *The Truth About the Trusts*. New York: Moody Publishing.

Moody's Industrial Manual. 1991.

Moody's Manual of Railroads and Corporation Securities. 1916.

Moskowitz, Milton, Michael Katz, and Robert Levering, eds. 1980. *Everybody's Business; An Almanac*. San Francisco: Harper and Row.

Mueller, Willard, and Larry Hamm. 1974. "Trends in Industrial Market Concentration." *Review of Economics and Statistics* 56 (November): 511–20.

Murphy, Kevin J. 1986. "Top Executives are Worth Every Nickel They Get." *Harvard Business Review* 64 (March–April): 125–32.

National Education Association. 1977. *The New Copyright Law: Questions Teachers & Librarians Ask*. Washington, D.C.

National Science Foundation. *National Patterns of Science and Technology Resources: 1987*.

Ornstein, Stanley. 1972. "Concentration and Profits." *Journal of Business* 45 (October): 519–41.

Pechman, Joseph. 1977. *Federal Tax Policy*, Third Edition. Washington, D.C.: Brookings Institution.

Ravenscraft, David. 1983. "Structure Profit Relationships at the Line of Business and Industry Level." *Review of Economics and Statistics* 65 (February): 22–31.

Reid, Lestock C. 1947. *Commerce and Conquest: The Story of the Honourable East India Company*. Port Washington, NY: Kennikat Press.

Rhoades, Stephen. 1973. "The Effect of Diversification on Industry Performance in 241 Manufacturing Industries: 1963." *Review of Economics and Statistics* 55 (May): 146–55.

Robinson, Joan. 1933. *The Economics of Imperfect Competition*. London: MacMillan.

———. 1978. *Contributions to Modern Economics*. New York: Academic Press.

Salinger, Michael. 1984. "Tobin's q, Unionization and the Concentration–Profits Relationship." *Rand Journal of Economics* 15 (Summer): 159–70.

Scaperlanda, Anthony, and Laurence Mauer. 1969. "The Determinants of U.S. Direct Investment in the E.E.C." *American Economic Review* 59 (September): 558–68.

Scherer, F.M. 1980. *Industrial Market Structure and Economic Performance*. Chicago: Rand McNally.

Schiller, Bradley. 1991. *The Macro Economy Today*, Fifth Edition. New York: McGraw-Hill.

Schumpeter, Joseph. 1950. *Capitalism, Socialism, and Democracy*, Third Edition. New York: Harper.

Shazam, User's Reference Manual, New York: McGraw Hill.

Shepherd, William. 1985. *The Economics of Industrial Organization*. Second Edition. Englewood Cliffs, N.J.: Prentice-Hall.

Shepherd, William, and Clair Wilcox. 1979. *Public Policies Toward Business*, Sixth Edition. Homewood, IL: Richard D. Irwin.

Shirazi, Javad. 1974. "Market Structure and Price-Cost Margins in United Kingdom Manufacturing Industries." *Review of Economics and Statistics* 56 (February): 67–76.

Simpson, Sally. 1986. "Cycles of Illegality: Antitrust Violations in Corporate America." *Social Forces* 65 (September): 943–63.

Smith, Adam. 1776. *An Inquiry into the Nature and Causes of the Wealth of Nations*. New York: Random House.

Stern, Philip. 1988. *The Best Congress Money Can Buy*. New York: Pantheon Books.

Sweezy, Paul. 1939. "Demand under Conditions of Oligopoly." *Journal of Political Economy* 47 (August): 568–73.

Troy, Leo. 1965. *Trade Union Membership, 1897–1962*. New York: Columbia University Press.

U.S. Congress. 76th., 3rd Sess., 1940. Temporary National Economic Committee, *The Distribution of Ownership in the 200 Largest Nonfinancial Corporations*, Monograph 29, Washington, D.C.: U.S. GPO.

U.S. Department of Agriculture. 1990. "Farm Commodity Programs." *National Food Review* 13 (January–March 1990).

U.S. Federal Trade Commission. 1979. Bureau of Economics. *Statistical Report on Mergers and Acquisitions* (July). Washington, D.C.: U.S. GPO.

U.S. Federal Trade Commision. 1988. *FTC Decisions: Findings, Opinions, and Orders*, Volume 110.

Varian, Hal. 1978. *Microeconomic Analysis*. New York: W.W. Norton.

Vernon, Raymond. 1977. *Storm over Multinationals: The Real Issues*. London: Macmillan.

Voos, Paula and Lawrence Mishel. 1986a. "The Union Impact on Profits: Evidence from Industry Price–Cost Margin Data." *Journal of Labor Economics* 4 (January): 105–33.

———. 1986b. "The Union Impact on Profits in the Supermarket Industry." *Review of Economics and Statistics* 68 (August): 513–17.

Weiss, Leonard. 1974. "The Concentration-Profit Relationship and Antitrust." In Harvey Goldschmid et al. eds, *Industrial Economics: The New Learning*. Boston: Little, Brown.

Wessel, James. 1983. *Trading the Future: Farm Exports and the Concentration of Economic Power in Our Food System*. San Fancisco: Institute for Food and Development Policy.

Whichard, Obie. 1982. "Employment and Employee Compensation of U.S. Multinational Companies in 1977." *Survey of Current Business* (February): 37–50.

———.1989. "U.S. Multinational Companies: Operations in 1987." *Survey of Current Business* 69 (June): 27–39.

Wilkins, Mira. 1970. *The Emergence of Multinational Enterprise: American Business Abroad from the Colonial Era to 1914*. Cambridge, MA: Harvard University.

Index

THOMAS KARIER is a Professor of Economics at Eastern Washington University. He received an undergraduate degree in both physics and economics from the University of Illinois in 1978 and his doctorate in economics from the University of California at Berkeley in 1985. He has written extensively about corporate power for numerous journals including *Challenge, Review of Social Economy, Journal of Post Keynesian Economics, Industrial Relations, Journal of Commerce,* and the *Review of Economics and Statistics.* In addition to his work on corporate power, Professor Karier has written a report on manufacturing trade and labor unions for the Economic Policy Institute and served as a Resident Scholar at the Jerome Levy Economics Institute from 1989 to 1991.